W9-CNE-944

THE PRACTICE OF
Group Work

THE PRACTICE OF

Group Work

WILLIAM SCHWARTZ
and
SERAPIO R. ZALBA
Editors

1971
Columbia University Press
NEW YORK AND LONDON

WILLIAM SCHWARTZ is Professor of Social Work at Columbia University School of Social Work.

SERAPIO R. ZALBA is Chairman of the Department of Social Service, Cleveland State University.

Foreword

THE PURPOSE of this collection is to present the skills of group practice at work in a wide range of social work settings. While we have included some of the traditional "social group work" situations, our major emphasis has been on the effort to light up the diversity of auspice under which social workers have turned their attention to groups. In the process we have reached for a broader conception of group work practice, encompassing not only the small, face-to-face, peer group system but other social situations in which an understanding of human mutual aid processes deepens the practice of social work. Thus, several of our accounts will describe work in which the agency's attention includes, but does not restrict itself to, the small group as a target of service.

Our interest is in the technical problems of helping people work together in specific social situations; hence, the articles are designed to show how social work is practiced, rather than to dwell on problems of philosophy, administration, or other structural concerns. While social work is, of course, supported by its values, knowledge, and objectives, it is not defined by these attributes. As with any art, social work identifies itself only as it specifies the acts and skills by which its knowing, believing, and aspiring are translated into action. These acts and skills are the subject of this book. Each author has sought to throw some light on the subject by revealing and discussing his own work within his own setting.

The opportunity to put together such a group of papers emerged from the program planning processes of the Annual Forum of the National Conference on Social Welfare. Under the then chairmanship of William Schwartz, the Group Work Section arranged for a series of presentations that would describe work with groups in a variety of agencies, including many that were known primarily as "casework" settings. Each author was asked to write to a specified format: he would begin with a brief statement of the practice problems in his particular setting; he would review the literature on these problems; and he would describe the setting itself. Then, with the aid of excerpts from the process records of his own practice, he would identify and discuss the skills he was called upon to use in his work. And finally, he would try to identify some questions for study.

Most of these papers were prepared in response to this invitation. Farris, Murillo, and Hale described the work that grew out of the efforts of a settlement in the Southwest to find a modern function in a low-income neighborhood; the result was the development of a "mediating" conception and a strategy that sought out the skills required to help families negotiate the complex systems in which their lives are enmeshed. Joan Shapiro read a paper on her practice in single-room occupancies in New York City, describing a new area of service into which she had moved to develop the mutual aid possibilities in a population long considered too depressed and overwhelmed to lend itself to such efforts. Hyman Weiner documented the important and as yet underdeveloped connections between the self-help tradition of the trade union movement and the skills brought by social workers into the trade union setting. David Birnbach wrote of his work in a children's residential treatment center, where he demonstrated the practice of child care by a social worker trained in group work, and defined the skills he was called upon to use in the process. From the hospital field, Lipton and Malter discussed the tasks of ward work in a service for paraplegic war veterans, illustrating the movements of the practitioner as he helps patients and staff make their much-needed connections with each other. And, from a neglected area of service, Forthun and Nuehring revealed some of the unique techniques and patterns of group work practice in a maximum-security prison.

Several other papers produced in this effort have since found other outlets. Two of those included here—by Shapiro and Weiner—were published in the volume of practice papers produced by the Conference. They have been reprinted here with the permission of the National Conference on Social Welfare and the Columbia University Press and are the only papers in this collection to have been printed elsewhere.

To this first group of papers we have added several more, to broaden the scope of the book. The theoretical paper by Schwartz, first presented to the field instructors and faculty of the Columbia University School of Social Work, is offered as a general frame of reference for the study of social work with groups; it serves to identify some of the major themes that appear in the practice papers that follow. The article by David Heymann, defining a function for social workers in the antipoverty context, was prepared for this book from experiences by the author in that setting. The Garfield and Irizarry piece on the recording of group practice was also specially prepared, distilled from the work of the authors with a number of settlements serving preadolescents and their families as part of a delinquency project conducted in New York City. Alex Gitterman's paper on group work in the public schools was adapted from an address to a meeting of the United Neighborhood Houses Committee on Social Work in the Neighborhood. Jean Peterson and Calvin Sturgies wrote for us about their practice with adolescents in foster care at the Bureau of Child Welfare of New York's Department of Social Services. And we were again indebted to the stimulus of the Annual Forum of the National Conference on Social Welfare for

Lawrence Shulman's paper on group programming, read in 1968 in San Francisco.

There is considerable consensus in these papers on certain basic concepts—the mediating function, the significance of "contract," the role of systems work, the stress on the here-and-now, and other central notions; several of them do, in fact, reflect Schwartz's consultative work with a number of agencies over a period of years. But there are also some theoretical variations, and several of the papers develop somewhat different versions of what group work is about. At this stage of practice development, it is less important to "prove" theories than to examine the work processes in detail and learn to identify with some precision what we do to help people in groups. Although we could not include all the settings in which we were interested, there are enough here to reveal something of what is happening at the frontiers of group service and to make a contribution to the scanty literature of practice in these areas.

This, then, is a book about group practice, showing social workers in action as they respond to the needs of people in a variety of group situations. Our writers are young, talented, and deeply interested in the nature of the helping process. Their impact is only partly in the quality of their practice—although this is of a high order; mostly, it is in their willingness to reveal what they do, to stimulate discussion of practice problems, and to encourage others to write about their own work. Far from being ashamed of their interest in technique, they are among the many who see it as a true measure of their importance in the social scene. Their work is part of a larger effort to convert abstractions and rhetoric, dreams and aspirations, into the specific skills needed to help real people struggle with real problems in actual situations.

THE EDITORS

Contents

THE PRACTICE OF
Group Work

He who would do good to another must do it in
    Minute Particulars:
General Good is the plea of the scoundrel,
    hypocrite & flatterer,
For Art & Science cannot exist but in minutely
    organized Particulars.

WILLIAM BLAKE

On the Use of Groups
in Social Work Practice

WILLIAM SCHWARTZ

IN THE INTRODUCTION to his book on social behavior, George
Homans describes his subject as a "familiar chaos." By this
he means that we "have been at home with the evidence since
childhood," but our knowledge remains unsystematic and
poorly organized, and generalizations consist mainly of prov-
erbs, maxims, and other half-truths (2, p. 1).*

Many social workers think of their small group experiences
in just this way; they have been in groups all their lives and
they have developed maxims to express their understanding
of those experiences. But they feel vaguely inexpert when
asked to consider this area of work from a professional's point
of view. Nevertheless, it is important to remember that the
familiarity is as vital as the chaos. Any theorizing about the
group experience should have a familiar ring as one measures
the ideas against his own sensations and recollections. This
requirement has important implications for both professionals
and their clients.

SOME BACKGROUND ISSUES

It is helpful to recall some of the institutional and professional events that have led up to the present situation in which

* The parenthesized numbers refer to the bibliographical references
listed alphabetically at the end of each paper.

workers trained in the traditional settings of "social group work" talk to audiences composed largely of "social caseworkers" for whom the subject of groups is fast becoming highly relevant to their professional tasks and to the service of their agencies.

We should understand, for example, that this is not a new tradition but a tradition reclaimed. Group work historians are now fond of quoting Mary Richmond on the importance of groups; and she did, in fact, comment "with great pleasure" in 1920 on "the new tendency to view our clients from the angle of what might be termed *small group psychology*" (emphasis in original) (4, p. 256). But the paths of individual and small group preoccupation soon diverged and went their separate ways—to the point where Eduard Lindeman complained, in 1939, that "I cannot see why . . . groups and group experiences do not stand at the very center of social work's concern" (3, p. 344). Now, more than 40 years after Mary Richmond's observation, the group experience has indeed begun to move closer to the center of social work's concern, and caseworkers are again coming to view their clients from the vantage point of small group psychology. What is it about today's world that has compelled social workers to look again to the forces of mutual aid and peer group association—not only in the group work and community organization settings where you might expect it, but in the family agency, the hospital, the school, the child welfare setting, and others that have from the outset identified themselves as the "casework agencies"?

The rebirth of interest seems due more to the necessity in clinical settings for professionals to utilize techniques that help meet the needs of their clients than to any particular influence exerted by the traditional group workers; the latter have indeed complained of the paucity of classical group work references—the Coyles, Treckers, Wilsons, *et al.*—in the developing literature of group services in the casework and clinical settings. One might, in fact, say that the lines of influence have been reversed; as the small group has become a more general instrument of social work practice, group workers in the traditional leisure-time agencies have had to re-examine some of their historic confusions and ambiguities. The portion of their work that is related to creating people in their own image—good Americans, good Christians, group-identified Jews, middle-class prototypes—seems less and less useful, and the part that is connected with the traditional social work function of helping people negotiate difficult environments assumes new significance. So, as we move into this new era of group work, we must think not of an old service teaching a new but of both services striving together to redefine and clarify the function of the social work profession. And this presents another theoretical problem undergirding the problems of group service—namely, how to define social work function in a way that will explain the operations of all social workers.

When professionals grow tired of a difficult problem it is a familiar gambit to sneer at the problem itself. So it is with the current fashion to belittle efforts at defining social work function in generic terms. But no amount of indifference or disdain will change the fact that the various parts of social work have been drawn together from the most diverse sources of experience, and that there is a strong need to examine their relationships to each other to find out what they have in common. It is no accident that we are developing into a single, unified profession, integrating the widest differences in practice, philosophy, and social origins—no accident, but something of a mystery. Over the years we have made many efforts to probe the mystery, but from rather safe ground. We have said, for example, that we are held together by a common body of knowledge, common values, common aspirations; but we have hesitated to explore what it is we *do* that identifies us as social workers, and by what professional *skills* we want to be recognized. It is this formulation of a common methodology—a commonly characterized way of working—that provides the context in which any contemporary definition of group practice must be embedded.

In actual fact, the requirements of practice are forcing most workers into the role of expert in the generic enterprise. The work itself is beginning to persuade us that the idea of a common method is neither utopian nor premature. On the contrary, practitioners will inevitably fashion their group skills out of those they learned in their work with individuals; and they will learn, in the process, the integral connections between the two. Casework students comment repeatedly that the group work courses help them understand their casework more deeply; and I have no doubt that a good casework course is similarly significant for group work students. And so it is that as we build our understanding of social work in groups, we are both drawing from and adding to a general theory of social work practice.

It would be possible, in a longer exposition, to describe in detail how the face-to-face group is a special case of the encounter between the one and the many—between the individual and his social surroundings. What are the ways in which people try to negotiate the various systems of demands and relationships with which they must come to terms in their daily lives? And what are the ways in which collectives—people working together—integrate their individuals into a working whole, producing things, dividing the work, and making decisions? How we view this encounter between a human being and his society will fashion our view of work, our conception of function, and our theories about how to have an impact on this children's club, that patients' group, this group of mothers on welfare, and others.

Finally, there are issues related to the problem of coming to terms with the tremendous upsurge of knowledge and hypotheses emerging from the small group research of recent years.

How does one develop work strategies incorporating this over-whelming accumulation of new knowledge about group behavior?

Having thus outlined all the themes that *could* be developed, let me now try to move into the middle of my subject by citing a few connected propositions about the nature of group experience, the settings in which groups are embedded, and the operational skills of group work practice. I would also like to make a few points about the problems faced by agencies moving anew into the area of group services.

THE "CLIENT" DESCRIBED

In considering the nature of the client group, what we have before us is *a collection of people who need each other in order to work on certain common tasks, in an agency that is hospitable to those tasks.* This simple definition carries within it all of the necessary ingredients for a strategy of practice. The following are some of the propositions it yields.

Need. The group members' need for each other constitutes the basic rationale for their being together. If people do not need to use each other, there is no reason for them to be together—which may seem like a truism until we recall all the experiences in which the mutual need was not apparent and the members struggled to understand what brought them together and why someone thought they had to interact with each other.

Tasks. This need for each other is specifically embodied in certain common tasks to be pursued. Defining "tasks" as *a set of needs converted into work,* we may say that these common tasks will constitute the purpose of the group and the frame of reference from which the members will choose their responses. It follows, then, that unless there is some fair degree of consensus about what these underlying tasks are, the members will find it difficult to find responses, judge the appropriateness of their responses, and plan their impact on the culture of their group. The number and complexity of these common tasks will, of course, vary with the nature of the group—ranging, in a broad spectrum, from the multipurpose adolescent gang, to the six-session group of foster parents discussing child-rearing problems, to the single-meeting group of prospective adoptive parents, and others.

Agency. The group purpose is further clarified and bounded by the agency service in which it is embedded. In society's division of labor the agency has been designated to apply itself to some human problems and not to others. Thus, the agency has a stake in the proceedings; it is not simply a meeting place, or a place of refuge. Its own social tasks are involved and become an integral part of the group experience.

Contract. The convergence of these two sets of tasks—those of the clients and those of the agency—creates the terms of the *contract* that is made between the client group and the agency. This contract, openly reflecting both stakes, provides the frame of reference for the work that follows, and for understanding when the work is in process, when it is being evaded, and when it is finished.

Work. The moving dynamic in the group experience is *work*. Let me define the term "work" as I am using it: (a) each member is trying to harness the others to his own sense of need; (b) the interaction beween members thus reflects both the centripetal force of the common tasks and the centrifugal force of those tasks that are unique to each member; and (c) there is a flow of affect among the members—negative and positive in varying degrees—generated by their investment in each other, their sense of common cause, and the demands of the *quid pro quo*. This emphasis on the importance of work, on an output of energy directed to certain specific tasks, is also a comment on the common fallacy that the group process, in itself and in some mysterious way, solves problems. This naive belief that the sheer interaction of people with problems is somehow productive is often reflected in the records of workers who describe the group process in great detail yet all but obliterate their own movements. Indeed, the function of the worker emerges from the fact that the group process is not a panacea: the members must work for everything they get; they must invest heart and mind in the process; and they need all the help they can get in doing so.

Self-Consciousness. At any given moment the group members may be working on their *contract,* or they may be occupied with their *ways of working.* As in any problem-centered enterprise—casework, research, education, psychotherapy—obstacles to the pursuit of the group's basic work will require diverting energy to the task of finding ways through and around them. When a group is frustrated by such obstacles it will need to work collaboratively on them; and when the obstacles are, for the moment, cleared away, the members are then free to put their strengths together to work on what they came together for. The important point here is that group self-consciousness—attention to its own processes—is not an end in itself, however attractive this might be to the worker; it is a way of wrestling with the obstacles that impede the group's work.

*Authority and Intimacy.** In the culture of the group two main themes come to characterize the members' ways of working together: one, quite familiar to the caseworker, is the theme of *authority,* in which the members are occupied with their relationship to the helping person and the ways in which this relationship is instrumental to their purpose; the other, more strange and threatening to the caseworker, is the theme of *intimacy,* in which the members are concerned with their internal relationships and the problems of mutual aid. It is the interplay of these factors—external authority and mutual interdependence—that provides much of the driving force of the group experience.

---

* For further inquiry into the group themes of *authority* and *intimacy,* see Bennis and Shepard's discussion of the T-group experience (1).

THE TASKS OF THE WORKER

Having described some of the essential features of the client group system, let us turn now to the job of placing the worker inside it. What is his part in the internal division of labor? What is his function within the system? I have written elsewhere about the movements of the worker in the group (5) and will not repeat the details of the scheme here. For present purposes, let me simply present some general propositions about the worker's major tasks.

Parallel Processes. Most important is the fact that the tasks of the worker and those of the clients are different and must be clearly distinguished from each other. Where one takes over the tasks of the other—as workers are often asked to do by supervisors who demand that they state their "goals for the client"—the result is a typical confusion. The worker, trying hard to understand the nature of his helping acts and their impact on the client's process of taking help, is, in effect, asked to obliterate the differences between the two sets of movements rather than to sharpen and clarify them. I have tried to clarify the differences by positing the principle of the *parallel processes,* by which I mean that the worker has his tasks and the client has his, that these processes are interdependent but different, and that any violation of this division of labor renders the work dysfunctional and the encounter itself manipulative, sentimental, and generally frustrating for both parties.

Mediation. The worker's central function is to mediate the engagement of client need and agency service. For a long time we have been ruled by two major fallacies about how needs are met in social welfare: one is that we meet a need when we have learned to identify it; the other is that needs are met when we have established the appropriate structure of service. Granted that both of these achievements are necessary, the sad fact is that the landscape is littered with identified but unmet needs within elaborate but impotent agency structures. The encounter between client and agency is not in itself productive; it can, and too often does, misfire. What is needed is a catalytic agent to activate both client and service. That catalyst is the skill of the worker, which helps the client reach out actively for what he needs and helps the agency reach out for the clients whom it seeks to serve.

Demand for Work. In general terms, the worker carries out the mediating function by clarifying and calling for adherence to the terms of the contract that keeps client and agency together. This means that the worker, of all the participants in the system, must see most clearly into the symbiotic relationship between the client and the agency—must see the specific ways in which they need each other to carry out their own purpose. Furthermore, the worker also represents what might be called the *demand for work,* in which role he tries to enforce not only the substantive aspects of the contract—what we are here for—but the conditions of work as well. This demand is, in fact, the only one the worker makes—not for certain preconceived results, or approved attitudes, or learned behaviors, but for the work itself. That is, he is continually challenging the client to address himself resolutely and with energy to what he came to do; and he is also, at the same time, trying to mobilize his agency to clarify what it has to offer and to offer it wholeheartedly.

Authority. In the group, as in the interview, the authority theme remains; there is the familiar struggle to resolve the relationship with a nurturing and demanding figure who is both a personal symbol and a representative of a powerful institution. But the theme is modified by the addition of numerical reinforcements to the dependent member of the relationship. The caseworker first experiences this as "there are so many of them and only one of me." From both sides of the relationship interesting things begin to happen: the worker moves—a little reluctantly at first—to share his authority and

to learn to live with a "diluted" control over the events of
the helping process; and the client's battle with authority is
markedly affected as he learns that his feelings about dependency and strength are part of the human condition and
not necessarily a unique and personal flaw. The "all-in-the-same-
boat" dynamic has a strong impact on the nature of the trans-
ference phenomena.

Intimacy. Complementing the work with the authority
theme, the social worker in the group helps his clients exploit
the theme of intimacy, mobilizing the healing powers of human association and mutual aid. The group members' investment in each other constitutes the new dimension to which
professional skill must be addressed. Not only must the worker
be able to help people talk but he must help them talk to each
other; the talk must be purposeful, related to the contract
that holds them together; it must have feeling in it, for without affect there is no investment; and it must be about real
things, not a charade, or a false consensus, or a game designed
to produce the illusion of work without risking anything in
the process. We might say that much of the client's "internal
dialogue" should be out in the open, with the internalized
parts represented by real people, and the worker's movements
directed more clearly and openly to the actions and reactions
among them.

The Power of Specific Purpose. Finally, it should be pointed
out that just as the member's role is limited by time and
purpose, so is the worker's. This is a limitation that adds to
the power of the worker because it directs his energies to
what he and his clients are working on *together,* what they are
doing together, rather than what the clients *are,* how he can
make them different, or how he can change their characters,
their personalities, their morals, their manners, or their habits.
As a practitioner I am strengthened by the idea that I do not
have to change anybody's basic state of being; but there is
work to be done and my skills can help the work. And, in
order for the professional to accept this idea, he must accept

another—namely, that the life processes into which he enters and makes his limited impact have been going on for a long time before he arrived and will continue for a long time after he is gone. The process by which the client reconstructs his experience is not one that the worker creates; he simply enters, and leaves. Another way of saying this is that he is an incident in the lives of his clients. Thus the worker should ask himself: What kind of an incident will I represent? What kind of impact will I make? More specifically, how do I enter the process, do what I have to do, and then leave?

THE PHASES OF WORK

The above questions serve to introduce another dimension that may be helpful in describing this way of analyzing work with groups—the dimension of time. I believe the tasks of the worker can be understood more precisely if we watch him move through four separate phases of work in sequence. The first is a preparatory *"tuning-in"* phase, in which the worker readies himself to enter the process, to move into the group experience as a professional helping person. The second phase is that in which the worker helps the group make its *beginnings* together. The next is the period of *work*, encompassing the essential business of the enterprise. And the final period of *transitions and endings* concerns itself with the problems of leaving, of separation and termination.

As I discuss each of these phases, I am suggesting that they apply not only to the total group experience but to each of the separate meetings that comprise it. Each encounter has its own tuning-in, beginning, middle, and end-transitions; the same logic and the same necessities of work make the terms of the analysis equally applicable, although considerable work remains to be done in testing out the details of this conception in action.

The process of preparation, described here as the "tuning-in" period, is one in which the worker readies himself to receive cues that are minimal, subtle, devious, and hard to detect except by a very sensitive and discerning instrument. It is important to note that the tuning-in idea is different from certain current conceptions about the preparation of workers, where the main emphasis is on the formulation of "goals" and the construction of "diagnostic" pictures—that is, on developing a structural and cross-sectional version of what the client *is* (and what he ought to be) rather than of what he might *do* in a given situation. If you say that a person tends to do what he is, and is what he does, that proposition needs more detailed examination. The fact is that we have not been very successful in predicting behavior from personality assessment; people tend to do different things in different situations, and they may thus be said to "be" different under different conditions. In any event, the tuning-in process tries to use prior knowledge to anticipate clues that will be thrown away so quickly, and in such disguised forms, that the worker will miss them unless he is somehow "tuned" to the client's frequency. We may, if we like, call this a kind of "preliminary empathy," as the worker prepares to enter the life-process of his clients. A young person properly attuned to a group of aged clients may instantly perceive and address himself to the possibility that the comment "What a nice young man!" may be a suspicious rather than an approving judgment—that is, "What could you know about our troubles?" In this phase the worker tries to unearth both the themes that may emerge in the worker-group engagement and the ways in which these themes may be expressed. For example, a group of adoptive parents in the supervision period may be expected to express in various ways the themes of the "bad seed," the problem of whether, how, and when to tell the child that he is adopted, the tyranny of the agency, and the ambivalence toward the supervising social worker. Thus, the tuning-in phase is devoted to making oneself receptive to veiled communications, making use of our knowledge about the issues that tend to be of concern to any particular type of client—to the aging, the adoptive parents, adolescents under stress, and others—and our knowledge about these clients in particular. It is an attempt to relate knowledge to action as the worker prepares himself for this action.

The second phase is that in which the worker tries to help the group make its beginnings under clear conditions of work. He asks them to understand the terms of the "contract" under which they have established themselves within the agency context. In effect, he is asking the members to understand the connection between their needs as they feel them and the agency's reasons for offering help and hospitality; the contract embodies the stake of each party. This beginning phase is particularly important; if its tasks are not properly and directly addressed at the outset, they will plague both group and worker for a long time—in the prolonged testing, in the endless repetition of the what-are-we-doing-here theme, and in the fits and starts with which the group approaches its business. Record analysis discloses many ways in which group members can raise and re-raise the questions of who the worker is, what he is supposed to do, what the group is for, what the agency *really* expects, what the hidden rewards and punishments are, how much latitude they *really* have, and what the talking is supposed to be about.

Simply put, the worker's tasks in this phase are: (a) to make a clear and uncomplicated (unjargonized) statement of why he thinks they are there, of their stake in coming together and the agency's stake in serving them; (b) to describe his own part in the proceedings as clearly and simply as he can; (c) to reach for feedback, for their reactions to his formulation and how his formulation squares with theirs; and (d) to help them do whatever work is needed to develop together a working consensus on the terms of the contract and their frame of reference for being together.

It is not assumed that this settles everything; nor is it true that contract work is limited to the opening stage of the group experience. Negotiation and renegotiation take place periodically, as they do in any relationship. But this does not negate the need to develop an initial working agreement, a frame of reference from which to choose one's first responses. The only alternative is ambiguity of purpose, which results in a prolonged period of subtle dickering about the terms of the engagement.

The third phase is related to the main body of the work together and is directed to the primary tasks of the helping process. Assuming that the worker has sensitized himself, that he has helped establish a fairly clear sense of purpose, and that the members have begun to address themselves to the job ahead, the worker's skills can now be employed freely in carrying out his part in the process. His central questions now become: Are we working? What are we working on? At this point there is a high premium on the worker's ability to make accurate judgments in identifying when work is going on, what it is about, when it is being avoided, where it runs into obstacles, and when the group is remobilizing itself.

I have written elsewhere about what I believe to be the five major tasks to which the worker addresses himself in the group situation (5). I have suggested that these consist of: (a) finding, through negotiation, the common ground between the requirements of the group members and those of the systems they need to negotiate; (b) detecting and challenging the obstacles to work as these obstacles arise; (c) contributing ideas, facts, and values from his own perspective when he thinks that such data may be useful to the members in dealing with the problems under consideration; (d) lending his own vision and projecting his own feelings about the struggles in which they are engaged; and (e) defining the requirements and limits of the situation in which the client-worker system is set. For present purposes let me simply identify some of the skills required to carry out these tasks. I have mentioned the ability to perceive when work is going on and when it is being avoided; further, there is the ability to reach for opposites, for ambiguities, for what is happening under the good feelings or the bad; there is the skill of reinforcing the different ways in which people help each other; of partializing large problems into smaller, more manageable pieces; of generalizing and finding connections between small segments of experience; of calling not only for talk but talk that is purposeful and invested with feeling; of being able to handle not only the first offerings but the second and third stages of elaboration; and, throughout, of being able constantly to make the demand for work inherent in the worker's helping function.

Most of these skills are familiar to those working with individual clients; what is less familiar is the set of adaptations required in the small-group situation where, as I have said, "there are so many of them and only one of me." What is crucial here is that there is a *multiplicity of helping relationships* rather than just one, and this is disconcerting to many who have not realized how much professional control they are accustomed to using in the one-to-one interview. The role of the authority factor comes home with renewed force to the caseworker who begins to work in the spontaneous, interactive, mutually-reinforcing, rather unpredictable climate of the small group. Workers begin to question how much control they have really been using and how comfortable it has been to be able to regulate the flow of the interview, to turn themes off and on, and to take a new tack when the present one is too confusing to them.

However, the disease is not incurable; when such an evaluation takes place it often has significant effects on the worker's practice—not only in the learning of group skills but in deepening the casework skills as well. The group process has the power to move the worker as well as the members.

In the final phase of work—that which I have called "transitions and endings"—the worker's skills are needed to help the members use him and each other to deal with the problem of moving from one experience to another. For the worker it means moving *off* the track of the members' experience and life-process, as he has, in the beginning, moved *onto* it. There is a great deal to be said about how people join and separate, what beginnings and endings mean to them, and the kinds of help they need in the process. For example, one of the most interesting of the separation phenomena is what has come to be called "doorknob therapy." Within the life of any particular group we have found that the last few minutes of every meeting yields us the most significant material; that is, people will raise their most deeply-felt concerns as a "by-the-way," almost with a hand on the doorknob. We find, further, that these themes do not lend themselves to easy reintroduction at the beginning of the next meeting. The intention to "start with that at our next meeting" is more often subverted, and the theme re-enters only at the next doorknob period. The point is that beginnings and endings are hard for people to manage; they often call out deep feeling in both worker and members; and much skill is needed to help people help each other through these times.

THE MOVE TO GROUP SERVICES

What happens when the "casework" agency begins to serve some of its clients in groups? The first point that needs to be made is that those involved should not be trapped into making invidious comparisons between the one-to-one situation and the small group as contexts of treatment. There is a kind of tempting chauvinism in this "battle of methods," but it is a useless enterprise that blocks the development of agency service. The fact is that the authority theme creates certain kinds of demands for professional skill, and the intimacy theme calls for others, with different possibilities and limitations. There are things clients can do in a group that they will find more difficult to do in an interview; and there are things they feel free to share with a worker alone that they will not part with in the peer group. We need to learn more about what these differences are, and we are learning all the time. But we are learning from the work itself, not from the arguments of those who, by a strange historic arrangement, first learned to specialize by numbers.

The workers in one agency, evaluating their first group experiences to determine which phenomena seemed to offer the most interesting new dimensions for service, described the following factors (6). A worker reported on the "amazing rapidity" with which her group members moved into intensive consideration of their problems. She felt there was something about the small group climate that stimulated an early sharing of important ideas and feelings. Another worker talked about the ways in which her members found "echoes" in each other of wishes and feelings that were hard to express; this seemed to create an atmosphere in which there was "less emphasis on denial." One commented on the release of anxiety that seemed to accrue from "the knowledge that such feelings are shared by all."

There was emerging awareness among the workers that the group created a considerable degree of peer pressure to face reality and work on it. A dramatic example was given of a father who produced heart symptoms while the group was on a difficult subject; he was reminded forcefully by the members that this was his familiar reaction to tough problems, and he promptly returned to what he was struggling with. This was offered as an illustration of how the members regulated and supported each other in their reactions to pain and shock. In several connections the point was made that the group seemed to make more demands for tolerating negatives than the professionals themselves dared to make, and that it supplied, in addition, both the support and the incentives for the members to reach for difficult themes, explore self-doubts, endure painful feelings, and search into tabooed areas.

The group process seemed to lend itself particularly well to the way problems need to be broken down and elaborated

in order to work on them. The members called for more information, swapped examples, asked for details on this or that
aspect, contributed ideas, and shared their interpretations from
different perspectives.

These points are all related, of course. The thread that ties
them together is the theme of *mutual aid,* and the helping
process is tangibly affected by the ways in which people
challenge and support each other in the common work. I have
already mentioned some of the effects upon the worker—the
problem of giving up some controls, the need to adjust to a
situation in which there are not one but a multiplicity of
helping relationships, the feeling of "so many of them and
only one of me." In addition, there is at the outset a considerable uneasiness about what is experienced by caseworkers as
a "lack of privacy" in the group situation. Reared in the rig-
orous and respected tradition of confidentiality, many workers
have begun by promising their group members that material
emerging in the group would not be shared with other workers
and stipulating that they should observe the same rules of
confidentiality. To their surprise, they have subsequently
found that their clients wanted more communication between
their different professionals rather than less. A worker with a
group of adolescent boys in foster care found himself repeatedly charged with messages to take back to the caseworkers, to be sure they understood what had happened in
the group. Another found it impossible to prevent communication between her girls and their parents about what was happening in both the daughter and the parent groups. Furthermore, the sharing of information, far from creating the problems she expected, actually seemed to contribute greatly to
the process in both groups. She concluded that in this context "confidentiality is a myth." It takes time for the caseworker
to learn that the group has its own regulatory powers, and that
people will make their own decisions as to what they will and
will not share with workers, with peers, and with those outside the system.

However, the practice similarities far outweigh the differences; it has become a familiar event to hear caseworkers exclaim, as they discover a group work principle, that this is just what they have always done in the one-to-one relationship. It is true. The group work problems of developing a clearcut contract, helping the members talk to each other with feeling, breaking big problems into smaller, more manageable parts, putting small clues together into generalized learnings, setting the tone of tolerance for ambiguity and struggle, helping the group deal with the various parts of its environment, and helping the members use the resources of this and other agencies are familiar to the caseworker and are part of his stock-in-trade.

What is most important is that, in moving into work with groups, the object of the enterprise should not be to develop a new esoteric terminology to take its place alongside the old; the language of group dynamics can be as seductive and as mystical as that of psychoanalysis. Workers should be prepared not to write articles about the group process but to learn how to *move* in the group situation, how to develop the skills and perform the operations needed to help people in groups. And I do not believe it is possible to teach these skills to social workers by placing them in groups as observers, or even by making them co-leaders with members of other disciplines. I am not saying that these may not be interesting experiences, or that workers cannot learn from them. What I do question is whether they can learn what needs to be taught—namely, the skills of practice. I believe that what we know of pedagogy will bear out the idea that the student can learn how to do something only by taking the responsibility for doing what he is trying to learn to do.

There is a related problem here about which I would like to state another bias; it concerns the question of who should supervise the work with groups—whether this function should go to specialized personnel in group work "departments" or to existing casework staff making itself expert in the new form of service. I believe the latter is the only feasible alternative if the new service is to be securely incorporated as a basic requirement, and if the conditions created are to be the most effective for education of social workers. The unnecessary specializing and the dual supervision that often accompanies it (the group practice supervised by group workers and the casework by caseworkers) create both administrative and technical confusion without any sound professional reasons to justify the arrangement. My position implies that casework supervisors will need to work with groups of their own, at least in the first stages of the enterprise. They can then begin to teach from their own practice, from first-hand experience with the problems their workers are being called upon to face.

It is most important—returning to the note on which I began—that the subject of groups be kept close to the professional experience, uncluttered by any new mystique. To the professional, good practice in any context should have the same moving quality and the same ring of simplicity. Here is a caseworker in one of her first group assignments:

My opening was brief—after a warm greeting I mentioned that this was the first foster parents group meeting we have held in the community. . . . I continued by stating that we are coming to them, as we recognize that travel can be difficult for them. Several mothers shook their heads vigorously in agreement. I added that being a foster mother is a tough job; but they have it even rougher because the area in which they live lacks so many essential services. We want to know their concerns; and what they think and feel will enable us to learn from and help each other.

I then asked if someone would like to start off. . . .

Later in the meeting:

From this point, the discussion, which revolved around a foster child's search for identity, became more and more animated. For example, a member felt that it is too painful for a foster child to learn the truth as to why he is different. After a long discussion as to a child's uncomfortable feelings around using a name that is different from that of his foster parent, I asked if we could always protect a child from learning parts of the truth in the outside world. Mrs. W. felt that even though she had told her youngster about his natural mother, the child thinks of her as his "real" mother. This statement brought forth many contributions by the group that were in a similar vein. I added that they seemed to be saying that in many senses of the word they are the real mothers. A group member said this was really so; but she thought that a child should be helped to understand that he also had a different biological mother. I said that perhaps if they thought they were the true mothers it might be hard for them to talk to their youngsters about their biological mothers. . . .

Mr. F., a foster father, then spoke. He announced that he guessed he was the first man to speak this morning, and I gave him brief and good humored recognition for this. Mr. F.'s voice was calm and very earnest when he started; but as he finished his comment, his voice broke with emotion. He told the group that he was a stepchild, but that he was never told the truth. He regarded his stepmother as his real mother until he was thirteen years of age, when a distant relative informed him of his true identity. His real mother was not only living, but residing in the community. He described the pain of this sudden discovery, and said he would never want this to happen to his foster children.

There was a hushed silence in the room; but the expressions on the faces of the foster mothers showed that Mr. F. had their sympathetic understanding. I supported Mr. F. by telling him that his sharing of his childhood experience with us certainly helped us understand a great deal.

And here is a group worker talking to an individual member of her group:

At Coney Island Judy and I were standing alone while the others were on a ride. Judy asked if we were going to the beach, and I said I thought so if they all wanted to go. Judy said she couldn't understand why some people wanted to get tans. She looked up at me pointing to her skin. "You know, most colored people would like to take their color away," and she laughed as if it were the funniest joke. I didn't laugh or say anything, and she added, "It really isn't so pretty." I replied, "On you it looks good, Judy." "No," she answered, "black don't look good on nobody." She didn't move away as I had expected but just stood beside me, now with a perfectly serious face. She seemed to have expressed so directly and with such feeling the essence of this whole issue and struggle. I felt very moved by her words and said, "I guess it is easy for me to say that, just standing here looking at you. But the hard part is to know what you are really feeling like inside your skin." We were interrupted by everyone rushing back, screaming from the ride, and with them I began gathering up things to move to another place. As we started walking along, Judy slipped her arm through mine.

REFERENCES

1. Warren G. Bennis and Herbert A. Shepard, "A Theory of Group Development," in Warren G. Bennis, Kenneth D. Benne, and Robert Chin (eds.), *The Planning of Change* (New York: Holt, Rinehart & Winston, 1962), pp. 321–40.
2. George Caspar Homans, *Social Behavior: Its Elementary Forms* (New York: Harcourt, Brace & World, 1961).
3. Eduard C. Lindeman, "Group Work and Education for Democracy," *Proceedings of the National Conference of Social Work* (New York: Columbia University Press, 1939), pp. 342–47.
4. Mary Richmond, "Some Next Steps in Social Treatment," *Proceedings of the National Conference of Social Work* (Chicago: University of Chicago Press, 1920), pp. 254–58.
5. William Schwartz, "The Social Worker in the Group," *The Social Welfare Forum, 1961* (New York: Columbia University Press, 1961), pp. 146–77.
6. William Schwartz, "Discussion" (of three papers on the use of the group in providing child welfare services), *Child Welfare*, Vol. 45, No. 10 (December 1966), pp. 571–75.

Group Work with Urban Rejects

in a Slum Hotel

JOAN SHAPIRO

FIRST EXPERIENCES are unique. We approach them anxiously, curiously, yet may come away with a sense of sudden, intense awareness and a fresh synthesis of observations. We have had such an experience in our hospital.

Our project reflects one facet of the work of the Community Psychiatry Division of St. Luke's Hospital Center in New York City that seeks to affect, in ways other than by direct psychiatric service, the mental health of the community. Besides offering consultation and training to service agencies and institutions in the community, the division attempts to locate underserviced populations, to develop methods of reaching and serving them, and to focus public and professional concern so that appropriate social planning may be achieved.

In New York City hundreds of slum hotels known as single-room occupancy buildings (SROs) provide one-room housing for single, destitute, and sick people. The more dilapidated of them constitute the only shelter available to many of the city's rejects: the alcoholics, addicts, aged, crippled, the chronically ill, the mentally ill, and jobless migrants from rural areas—all people who have difficulty caring for themselves in urban society. Most are not sufficiently sick or socially disturbed to

Reprinted from *Social Work Practice*, 1967 (New York: Columbia University Press, 1967), pp. 148–164. Slightly edited.

be in hospitals, nursing homes, or prison, nor well enough to use traditional services effectively.

While many SROs are well-managed and blend into their immediate neighborhoods, other show marked physical deterioration and are conspicuous for the antisocial behavior of their tenants. In the recent past such buildings have caused neighborhood blight, which resulted in community action to close them. The tenants were then scattered to other SROs, and an endless, costly, and heartbreaking pattern emerged in which each neighborhood successively tried to sweep away its undesirables.

In 1963 an SRO interagency demonstration project, in which we were part of a team, revealed a shocking picture of chronic physical and mental illness, loneliness, and deprivation (4). (Major co-sponsors were the Department of Welfare, the Neighborhood Conservation Bureau, and St. Luke's Hospital. These agencies as well as Roosevelt Hospital and the Community Service Society are currently sponsoring similar projects.) Tenants in the demonstration buildings seldom sought the help of hospitals, the police, or other resources. The only agency that was consistently and widely used by them was the Department of Welfare. In 1964 we began a second SRO project, using only one staff worker. As that worker, I was of necessity forced to use whatever help I could find among the tenants themselves. This situation brought a new and unexpected perception into focus: the tenants were not, by and large, transient, reclusive, or rootless. On the contrary, socially the building resembled more a closely knit, isolated, poverty-stricken village than a rotting six-story building in metropolitan New York. Within the tenant group itself existed substantial resources that could be mobilized, provided the worker's efforts were in harmony with adaptive and healthy aspects of the complex social structure already present in the building (9).

Since that time, four additional projects in SROs have been

undertaken by social workers from St. Luke's Hospital, several of them group work students, each working 2 days a week alone in a single building. They worked with groups and individuals, with welfare workers, with referral agencies, and with people living in the neighboring community. The five buildings varied in size, population composition, and management policy. Although the workers, all women, differed in personality and used different styles of intervention, their experiences have been strikingly similar. The basic framework for intervention rests upon the decision not to work primarily with the individual tenant as such but with the residents of each building as a total community. The short-range results were surprising and, we think, especially promising.

Many streams of knowledge and experience have influenced our approach to the SRO as a self-help community. Among them is applied anthropology (7), with its combined goals of preserving the ethos of a particular people and helping to alter those patterns that endanger survival in a rapidly changing world. A second stream is the sociology of the American class structure (2, 3), which helped to clarify the values and norms of the SRO clients and workers respectively. A third is milieu therapy (6), in which the patient becomes part of the therapeutic team on behalf of his own and others' treatment. Its more specific extension in group work practiced in the psychiatric hospital applies group work skills to a mentally ill population by working primarily to improve their ego strength in dealing with reality problems (8). The fourth and most closely analogous model is the socialization of the street gang by the "detached" group worker (1, 10). The New York City Youth Board pioneered in this field (5). The worker, alone and detached physically from his agency, offers only himself: his personality, integrity, and skill. Problems of initial contact, of establishing rapport, of value conflicts, of structuring his role, and, finally, of using his relationship with the gang to change socially destructive and self-destructive

behavior have many parallels to work in the SROs. The
worker's task is the same: to influence the behavior of an already formed group on the group's—not the worker's—home
territory.

Structurally the SROs are tenements with a central core ele-
vator shaft and corridors extending out on each floor. Off each
corridor are from six to eight rooms with a community kitchen
and shared bathroom. The halls and stairs are dark and often
smell of garbage and urine. Roaches overrun the walls, doors,
and ceilings. The managers furnish each small room with a
bed, bureau, and chair. Weekly rentals average 15 dollars.

The policies of the managers are crucial in determining
physical conditions in the SROs; they are also pivotal in
determining social conditions. Some managers extend protection to tenants by means of a front-door lock and a night
watchman; some protect tenants by extending loans, reading
and explaining their mail to them, helping with their personal
crises, and mediating with the police, hospitals, and the Department of Welfare. And some exploit them financially and emotionally.

In "wide-open" buildings no prospective tenant is refused,
and internal order in the building is unenforced. In these
buildings, mutual cooperation may evolve between manager
and tenants in carrying on illegal activities, such as selling
wine to alcoholics at a high price, conducting two-for-one
credit operations, pushing narcotics, allowing "shooting gal-
leries" for addicts, and permitting prostitution. Indeed, the
tenants depend on the manager to help to keep these activities
from being flagrantly visible to the outside world. The five
SROs in which projects are taking place are moderately "wide-
open" buildings.

The populations of the five buildings are similar: most
tenants are forty years of age and older; the men outnumber
the women two to one; there is a mixture of Whites, Blacks
and Puerto Ricans. A small number are Blacks from the rural

South. At least three-quarters of the tenants have major chronic diseases or disabilities, such as tuberculosis, heart conditions, diabetes, cirrhosis of the liver, and blindness. Superimposed social and mental problems are conspicuous. In some buildings well over half the tenants are alcoholics. The majority are welfare recipients, and most of the others are only sporadically employed. The most frequent sources of referral into these buildings are hospitals, mental institutions, prisons, and the Department of Welfare. There is often no alternative housing. The tenants are not conspicuously transient, and those who do leave usually move within the neighborhood from one SRO to another or go to hospitals or prisons.

The residents tend to stay within a two-block radius of their buildings, many spending days on end, some even years, without going any farther. Some do not know how to use the bus or subway system and feel incapable of traveling alone to distant parts of the city. A trip to a clinic might be a major, anxiety-provoking event. These people are well aware of the strongly negative attitude of the surrounding neighborhood toward their building. They also perceive depersonalizing or hostile attitudes on the part of institutions of all kinds. Their response tends to be one of passive watchfulness, masking anger and fear. Most SRO tenants do not vote, nor do they belong to voluntary groups, such as churches and clubs. Ties to a primary family tend to be absent or tenuous. These limited social experiences reinforce their tendencies toward self-isolation.

However, the lives of all but a few of the tenants are actively intertwined, a finding that sharply contradicts the stereotype of the single, unattached individual as reclusive. A recurrent pattern of relationships is the well-defined matriarchal quasi-family. The dominant women tend to feed, protect, punish, and set norms for "family" members. These families sometimes share meals, and the room of the mothering person is the hub of continuous social activity.

This produces an informal system of mutual help. For example, one older woman, a welfare recipient, considers it her task to care for certain bedridden residents in her SRO. She cleans, cooks for, and feeds them on a fairly regular basis, for which she receives no compensation other than status. A young man who has a substantial supply of tranquilizers does not use these drugs himself; instead, he dispenses them, one by one, to people in trouble who come to talk to him. A strong former boxer is called upon to stop dangerous fights. A woman who looks after seven alcoholic men keeps a jar of cigarette butts, collected for anyone who needs them.

Passivity, enforced by debilitating disease, malnutrition, and severely limited life choices, creates a vacuum in which sporadic arguments, binges, and violence are sources of external excitement. The passage of time is rhythmically marked in 2-week cycles by "check days." When a person's welfare check arrives, the manager cashes it, withholds the rent and money owed to him, and gives the balance to the tenant. Check day means binges for some, a meal for others, preying, extorting, or "rolling" for the petty racketeers. Over the remaining 13 days tenants eke out an existence with an average of 19 dollars for food for one person. Things are at a low ebb on the last day, when most are broke and hungry.

Thus, the SRO is a ghetto with a scarcity economy. Into it the group workers brought events, excitement, satisfaction, and stress; they also brought demands for cooperative behavior, as well as for conformity to changing group norms.

TENANT-WORKER INTERACTION

The emotional journey of each worker into her building and into the lives of its tenants proceeded from distance to intimacy, and from focus on the self to focus on the tenants and the task. This journey had two phases. The first was that of the initial encounter, a 2- to 6-week period, which ended when the worker and key leaders in the SRO had developed sufficient trust to work together in planning a program fitted to the tenants' needs. In the second phase the existing system of mutual aid was shifted and expanded to include recreation, control of antisocial behavior, and a reaching for medical and social services. Some common problems for all five workers in this phase were ambivalence about dependence and self-reliance of tenants, control and leadership, and value conflicts.

Initial Encounters. The moment of entry into the SRO system was a professional and personal identity crisis for the workers. Each was aware that these people, over many years, have been given up as patients and clients because of their "lack of motivation," irresponsibility, and erratic behavior. Also bedeviling each worker was a fear of violence (which had some basis in reality), specifically, the fear of being the victim of sexual attack. Entirely alone in a setting in which professional values, traditions, and customary role performances had no apparent ready application, the worker felt that even methods and goals of intervention were vague. Formidable questions about her role and task confronted her. Could such isolated individuals relate sufficiently to create a viable group? How much, if any, casework should be attempted with individuals? Was the manager or the Department of Welfare a client? Should the primary target of her efforts be the community groups who wanted the building closed? Was she to be a group worker, a community organizer, an educator, a generic mental health worker, a sociologist, a foster mother, a consultant? Each worker responded in her unique way to the stress and ambiguity.

Overoptimism, denial, and intellectualization were means of overcoming unmanageable anxiety. Each was used as a delaying action to help the workers master fears and move closer to their clients. One student worker postponed going to the building, then arranged to be accompanied; when there, she spoke only to the landlord, and left. It took several weeks of this kind of skirmish before she was able to notice the tenants in the lobby and to individualize them. Then, at the first large tenant gathering arranged by the worker and several tenants, the following occurred:

He [a gentle and philosophical ex-addict] took care of me for the rest of the evening, making sure I met people, correcting my way of reacting, pointing out my fears, and reassuring me that they were groundless. After his few comments, I felt much more at ease even with one of the alcoholics who was high. I attempted to speak to as many people as possible, usually sticking to the topic of establishing a recreation room. I began to feel at ease enough to make a few jokes with them. I was walked out of the maze of corridors down the dark stairs to the bus by another tenant.

My own fear was reflected in vacillation about whether or not to take my purse on the first visit. I decided to take it, a gesture carefully rationalized as being respectful of the tenants and of myself. I later learned that the fact that I brought it was widely and carefully noted by the tenants I met that day. Reviewing the incident, I now feel that my decision was partly counterphobic, an exaggerated personal statement of optimism and trust that I did not wholeheartedly feel, but which, had I but known it, was justified.

In one project, the worker found herself profoundly impressed by the initial welcome that the tenants extended to her in her first two visits. Her "noble savage" image of them—"they expressed their affection so freely"—was only later balanced by a perception of the amount of pathology, pain, hunger, and fear visible in the building.

Mutual Support and Teaching. As the workers became aware of the vitality of a social system that they had not expected to find, they were required to fit their initial expectations and goals in with the expectations and goals of the tenant group. Tenant leaders seemed to teach workers to do this and to protect them as they learned, a process that became mutual as the workers became more comfortable. Usually the worker developed a close relationship to one or more tenant leaders.

This alliance was achieved early, as the leaders usually sought out the worker. The leader was invariably sensitive to the worker's anxiety and dilemma, and made it possible for her to begin to delineate a helpful role:

It was my first visit to an SRO. I kept mouthing all the comforting phrases I had heard at the office: They're just people . . . the murders, face slashings, have all been calmed down. Et cetera. I had never seen an addict in my life; would he know what I was thinking? I politely entered the room and extended my hand to everyone who came up to me. One man, large and disfigured, squeezed my hand hard; he would not let go. I guess my face showed a flash of panic, and I tried to jerk my hand away. Another tenant, seeing my need, came over and whispered to me, "You just gently ease your hand away and talk to him." It worked.

And again, in another building:

I was talking to Robert (a leader) when Johnny staggered into the gathering, very drunk. He headed for the couch, flung his arms around one of the tenants. She slipped away, and he remained where he was, too drunk to get up. I was afraid, never having talked to anyone so intoxicated. However, I thought I had better talk to him. He was leaning over toward me as though he was going to fall over or maybe kiss me. He began to talk about how no one in this world was left, how his parents had died young, how he was raised by a woman as white as I, who called him "Son." Then he began to cry. He started to apologize. I said it was all right, sometimes one just had to cry. Robert came over with a napkin and wiped his eyes. I had the feeling that Robert was watching to see that everything was going all right for me. I brought Johnny something to eat, and he seemed to feel better. I began to relax too, and Robert brought my plate as I kept sitting with Johnny.

In another instance, a tenant leader told me angrily once, "Don't go by the social workers' book with us!" Her sensitivity to emotional dishonesty and mechanical interventions encouraged me to develop a style of helping that could be trusted by the group. This style included touching, hugging, physical nearness, mutual sharing of cigarettes, the giving and accepting of food, and visible, direct, immediate emotional responsiveness—attention, delight, annoyance, boredom, anxiety, admiration, and affection. In fact, what often appeared to be a sexual approach by male tenants was bravado, a thinly disguised hunger for closeness and dependency.

The leaders also taught the workers to understand the inner life of the building:

About eight people and I were sitting and talking in Sugar's room. Everyone chimed in about the addict who had died. They had all known him; he came around for food when he was hungry. They didn't have much, but if someone was hungry, they shared. I said I'd learned this about them and was impressed with their ways of helping each other. The talk about the man dying continued, and I said it was frightening to think about someone dying and not being discovered; that there must be the worry that it might happen to them. Betty said that this was exactly it; she hadn't been able to sleep all night after she heard. This is why they look in on each other so much.

The worker came to know the tenants and understand their most pressing life needs, which were in appallingly short supply. Food, alcohol, money, cigarettes, a "fix," physical care and protection, and the relationships that helped provide these, were highly valued and especially meaningful. Those innovations in the projects that dovetailed with these life needs were quite successfully utilized by the tenants; those that had no relevance to their needs were simply ignored.

Food, therefore, became a key vehicle for group organization. Through meetings to plan and cook and serve dinners for the entire building, to hold parties, or have *Kaffeeklatsches,* new friendships were formed, and responsibilities spread to many tenants. For example:

Mama had to carry a lot of the work of cooking, and I asked who was going to help clean up. She hadn't thought this far. Champ volunteered, and Mama thought she would find some others.

I said that I wished she wouldn't have to do so much next time. Mama was "pooped" and agreed. Together, we picked out some likely people who might be able to try a small part of the next cooking job.

From this, it was generally a smooth step to discussions of complex issues, such as the uses of emergency funds, or systematic help by tenants to help each other carry out medical and other referrals for treatment and rehabilitation. Meetings were held weekly for all tenants who would come, and their regularity also came to provide some sense of predictability, security, and identity for the group.

DEPENDENCE AND SELF-RELIANCE

The workers sought to find that delicate balance point between protecting and enabling, between focusing on the pathology and on the strengths, between expecting or encouraging too little or too much behavioral change. The majority of tenants in each project became deeply involved with their worker. The tenants were curious about her as a person, were highly observant about her values, strengths, and anxieties, and became alternately jealous, competitive, seductive, helpless, and manipulative, and above all, eager to please her. To accept and work with this emotional attachment was a continuous and difficult process. There was a tendency on the workers' part to deny its existence at first. When one worker went away at Christmas time, there was simultaneously an outbreak of drinking and fighting; the connection between the two events was not recognized by the worker until tenants pointed it out.

We carried forward bravely the notion that our task was to leave behind a functioning, self-reliant group, and that the group could realistically judge the limits of its own activity. The romanticism and even absurdity of these expectations were at times forcefully demonstrated. The key to the group's initial capacity to carry out unfamiliar responsibilities was the strength of their relationship to the worker. Only later could they function in more formal groups and activities when she was absent. For instance, in the planning of one dinner party where the worker's avowed intention was non-involvement, those who volunteered to take on responsibilities, almost to a man, went on a binge. A group shopping trip downtown for clothes, too, proved to be a disaster, much to another worker's dismay. Much of the money went into bottles, and some tenants did not turn up until the next day.

On the other hand, overprotection was also a common error. For example, I thought that an initial dinner, planned, cooked, and served by tenants for the entire building, might demand more capacity for organization than could be expected of the group at that time. However, I said nothing, and the tenants went ahead with it. While tempers and confusion ran high, the dinner materialized, with my support but without the necessity for my active participation. In another situation, I had unspoken qualms about a spiked-punch party. Their awareness of my ambivalence was neatly summarized during the meeting with the remark, "Don't worry! We can manage it." And they did. These parties were held, as a rule, with great enjoyment and appropriate restraint.

The workers struggled both to give of themselves consistently and generously to an orally deprived, profoundly dependent population, and to seek out and support impulses of individuals to take up again the interrupted process of growth toward independence and autonomous achievement. Early signs of initiative, task persistence and completion, work satisfaction, and the healthy expression of anger were encouraged by the workers. Active mastery and exercise of choice, even if it were merely to resist an impulse to flee a forbidding intake clerk, or to press one's welfare investigator about the needed winter coat, were warmly praised and supported—at first by workers, then by the group. Gradually, such efforts of individuals became recognized as a new social norm. Clinic visits, neatness, or volunteering for a heavier responsibility were announced and acclaimed in meetings.

CONTROL AND LEADERSHIP

The worker's expectation of reasonable behavior in the group seemed to help limit individuals who might get out of control, whether these were "high" alcoholics or severely disturbed people. Early in the development of formal group meetings individuals would impose controls on one another in an effort to make a more favorable impression on the worker. Later, the group itself was genuinely irritated by disruptive behavior, and gradually norms of propriety were adopted and enforced throughout the building. The most obvious indicator of change in the project buildings was a decrease in visible drunkenness, midnight brawls, bottles thrown out of windows, and police visits; this attests to the tenants' susceptibility to influence, containment, and order. The norm of "good" behavior was accepted to such a degree in one building that, although the tenants openly discussed the need of the addicts to snatch purses, they formally requested them to do this at least ten blocks away, so as not to give the building a bad name.

Since workers wanted to increase participation and extend responsibility, they had to help the leaders relinquish some of their customary control, which was usually absolute and undisputed, and simultaneously develop new and larger areas of involvement with them. For example, as tenants decided to have the lounge open longer, one leader resisted by refusing to give the key to anyone. As the worker and leader discussed the issue, the leader began to share the worker's goals, and the key was cheerfully relinquished. Both worker and leader were proud of a senile woman's first visit to the lounge, and of the willingness of a frightened, isolated girl to shop for flowers for Christmas dinner decorations. The leader began to see her role as enabling others to grow. She then moved on to represent the building in the larger community, dealing with a block association and even with the hospital.

In another project building, the worker reported the following conversation with a leader, after the group had voted that decisions about the use of an emergency carfare fund should be based upon the opinions of more tenants than just the leader alone. Here the worker was attempting to deal with the leader's anger, while supporting a new role for her:

I said that I felt she'd been sore at me because I was pleased at the group's decision to handle carfare in a new way. She said she was just as glad because she didn't have to worry about all the problems; she could just say she didn't have anything to do with it. I wondered if she couldn't help them learn how to do this better, rather than washing her hands of it. She looked at me, then nodded slowly. I said that at the same time she would be able to try new things, like the clinic committee we had talked about. With a shy smile she said she had already gotten some people together for this and she hoped I didn't mind.

In the following example, the worker helped the whole group move from apathy to reasonable action:

At a weekly meeting, several months in operation, the tenant chairman said matter-of-factly that the manager was angry with tenants for drinking in the lobby and was going to close the recreation room. This was met with complete silence. Then someone said quietly, "I knew it couldn't last." Another said, "He always has it in for us, anyway." A discouraged and defeated discussion ensued. The worker asked just what had happened. It then became clear that it was a threat made by the manager in a moment of anger to one tenant. The worker then helped the tenants to recognize their apathetic and unquestioning attitude. Anger toward the manager and possessiveness about the room then rose to the surface, and after this had drained off, discussions with the manager were decided upon.

VALUE CONFLICTS

Learning about minor illegalities, understanding their function for the tenants, and dealing with the ethical and professional issues they raised was a troublesome experience for the workers. There was the residents' ever-present need for alcohol, heroin, or bootlegged psychiatric drugs. The workers were forced to examine their own attitudes about this, as well as about illegitimacy, prostitution, and fickle sexual liaisons.

One worker was carefully tested about her attitude toward drinking. At first, bottles were invisible. Then tenants would hide the bottles, but would confess to having been drinking. The worker, disguising her ambivalence, reported as follows:

October. Sugar said she wanted a drink before she went, asking me could she have one. I said, "Of course," but as she poured, Mug said angrily, "You should have a little respect!"

November. George said he was going to spike the punch for the dinner. Sugar said he had to ask me. I said they could keep asking me, but I'd answer by asking them what did *they* think. They said they were over twenty-one and wanted it spiked.

February. George, Sugar, Phil, Lenny, and Mug were drinking wine, and Phil asked if I wanted some. (First time they'd offered!) I said, "Just a little, I don't want to fall asleep on you." Phil poured me a huge glass, and I said, "Well, thank you, but we'll have to see if I finish it." Lenny said, "You know, you're really a nice person," but Mug said he didn't want to see me drinking this stuff. I said, "You saw me drink at parties. Why is this different?" He said he didn't mind if I drank gin or vodka or even good wine, but this stuff was no good; they drank it because they had to. I said that I certainly didn't want to offend him, and if it bothered him, I wouldn't do it again, but I did want them to know that I felt their sharing of wine was a close and warm time and I didn't look down on it.

The workers found that middle-class concepts, such as postponement of immediate satisfaction for long-range goals, control of physical aggression, rationality in decision-making, planning and time use, and respect for property and privacy were unfamiliar to tenants and in total opposition to their life experience. Acceptance of some of these values accompanied successful group experience and identification with the workers. The core group of leaders seemed to show the greatest change in adopting these values as their own.

Because of the newness of the programs, only some generalizations can be made about the more obvious short-term effects of these interventions. The amount of noise and nuisance perceived by the neighboring community was drastically reduced in every instance. Arrest rates and police calls became infrequent but did not disappear. The morale of many tenants seemed higher, as was evidenced by improved personal appearance, better care of rooms, extended social relationships, greater protectiveness toward one another. Check day, a customary time for acting out, became indistinguishable from other days.

Rehabilitation aspects of the programs involved many tenants in satisfactory social, psychiatric, and medical referrals. In several buildings nearly half the population became patients or clients successfully in new referrals. While medical referrals accounted for a large majority, psychiatric referrals became common. However, no tenant was able to accept referral to Alcoholics Anonymous, and no alcoholic went on the wagon.

Much of the planning, encouraging, and handholding needed for clinic visits was provided by other tenants on a regular basis; some of them became highly adept at steering their "patients" through the intricacies of obtaining full service from a large hospital. A simplified routing to the hospital for detoxification was established for addicts and was often used.

Although each building developed its own formal leadership, thus far no building has been able to conduct its own program entirely without some intermittent help from the worker. In two buildings where students were placed, program activities ceased when their field placements were over; however, there was no conspicuous relapse to notoriety in these SROs. Thus, it would appear that such buildings need some form of permanent generic social work services, if only on an *ad hoc* basis.

Some indigenous leaders became highly skilled in group management, were comfortable in dealing with the larger community, and served as a source of helpful referral for the wider tenant group. As this shift took place, they became busy and important people, and their own symptomatology decreased. Those who were alcoholics tended to drink less; two of the addicts stayed free of drugs for many months.

Three of these leaders are now paid staff workers in new project buildings. Imitation of the former worker's style and strategies is apparent in their work: they reproduced the problems of the social worker, such as exaggerated fear of contact in the initial phase and competition with indigenous leaders. They have also been able to stimulate similar programs and effects.

The data suggest that the SRO population constitutes a delinquent subculture with a self-assigned identity, and with mores and predictable norms unique to it; the style of living forms a recognizable pattern in one SRO after another. The profound alienation from the majority culture produces a ghetto in which sporadic violence makes visible the pain and rage of an otherwise forgotten population.

To understand the nature of antisocial behavior in or near SROs one must distinguish two types. The first has an economic function, designed to maintain income or a habit of alcohol or drugs. The violence takes the form of mugging, purse-snatching, and theft, with its victims usually the middle-class population, and only occasionally another SRO dweller. The second type of antisocial behavior seems to be an expression of pent-up emotions, dammed behind a wall of loneliness, boredom, hunger, and frustration. This is enacted within the buildings in the form of fist fights, knife slashings, brawls, throwing bottles out windows, binges, and retreats into psychotic episodes.

The rhythm of life is no different for this group than for any other idle lower-class group where a flat psychosocial landscape is punctuated by seeking or creating excitement and thrills. A few individuals in the SRO population, those whose impulse control is the poorest, become conspicuous in the community and give the whole building a reputation for disturbance. The remaining majority experience the uproar vicariously. These two forms of violence, having different causes and involving different personality types, call for different solutions. The violence, however important to the community, must be viewed only as a symptom of intense suffering. The surrounding community, in its reaction to this disruption, isolates the building and further polarizes the negative identity of the tenant group.

The presence of a subculture does not imply the presence of a highly organized group. The SRO social structure can be more accurately described as a "near group," with a flexible, floating membership and many unrelated marginals. The projects attempt a structural shift from a series of interlocking near groups toward a task- and pleasure-oriented formal group. The goal is to move the population toward the adoption of behavior that increases their potential for survival. Thus, the intervention directly attacks the roots of the alienation by generating hope, gratifying urgent needs, increasing physical security, reducing hunger, and creating a sense of group relatedness. For many tenants the goal is a strengthening of ingroup ties. For some the goal may be detachment from the group, a loosening of the pathological bonds that prevent the individual from joining fully into the larger society. For others the goal may be temporary or permanent separation from the group in the form of hospitalization or institutionalization.

However, I hope it is clear that the work attempted in these buildings is, at best, a band-aid on a massive sore. The ultimate treatment must be directed toward the causes of social disequilibrium in the city that produce abandoned, sick, and frightened people with regularity and in great number. The human suffering and neglect that are encapsulated within these buildings are so gross as to be incredible, overwhelming, and painful to accept as a social reality in the United States in 1967. The SRO population is very nearly invisible to a large segment of the helping professions. It is a family portrait of our major failures in understanding and skill as helpers, healers, and social engineers. A vivid picture emerges of inadequate medical and psychiatric care and knowledge, antiquated housing regulations, punitive welfare legislation, and depersonalization and rejection by our society of its least adequate members.

SROs can also be viewed positively, as laboratories where we renew our faith and optimism about the related, loving, and helping qualities inherent in deprived and damaged human beings.

There are many myths attached to this population; it is said to be unreachable, untreatable, and unresearchable. In our initial encounters we have found this not to be so. The population appears to be a cluster of alienated and sick individuals bound into a subculture that has the latent capacity to move toward socialization through group process. Social workers, using themselves generically to work with the total building as a system, seem to have been effective in producing a therapeutic change within it.

We need now to ask: What, in the specific relationship to the worker or in the program content, stimulated this change? What additional skills, personnel, or content would enable greater movement? What application does this generic on-site method have to other isolated groups?

REFERENCES

1. J. P. Feldstiner, *Detached Work* (Toronto: University of Toronto Press, 1965).
2. August B. Hollingshead and Frederick C. Redlich, *Social Class and Mental Illness* (New York: Wiley, 1958).
3. Genevieve Knupfer, "Portrait of the Underdog," in Reinhard Bendix and Seymour Martin Lipset (eds.), *Class, Status and Power* (Glencoe, Ill.: The Free Press, 1953), pp. 255–63.
4. New York City Housing and Redevelopment Board, "World of 207" (New York: The Board, 1966), mimeographed.
5. New York City Youth Board, *Reaching the Fighting Gang* (New York: The Board, 1960).
6. Robert Rapoport, *Community as Doctor* (London: Tavistock Publications, 1959).
7. Robert Redfield, *A Village That Chose Progress* (Chicago: University of Chicago Press, 1950).
8. Saul Scheidlinger, "Social Group Work and Group Psychotherapy," *Social Work*, Vol. 1, No. 3 (July 1956), pp. 36–42.
9. Joan Shapiro, "SRO: Community of the Alone," *Social Work*, Vol. 11, No. 4 (October 1966), pp. 23–33.
10. Lewis Yablonsky, *The Violent Gang* (New York: Macmillan 1962).

Group Work in the Public Schools

ALEX GITTERMAN

MANY BLACK AND PUERTO RICAN children living in the ghetto areas of New York City have been struggling with increasingly serious problems in their efforts to use the schools. For many, the educational experience has had debilitating effects on their subsequent social and psychological development. At the same time, teachers and other school personnel also encounter serious obstacles and frustrations in trying to do their jobs. Despairing in their own efforts, they often abandon hope and withdraw, or turn to punitiveness.

Community groups trying to deal with these problems frequently polarize the issues. They divide themselves into opposite camps, attributing the burden of failure either to the children and their families or to the educational system. The issues then emerge as large dualisms—decentralization versus centralization, a deprived culture versus an insensitive system, community control versus professional control, freedom versus structure, "ego-building" grades versus the maintenance of standards. Such polarizations produce a growing distrust, misunderstanding, and hostility while the real problems involved in teaching and learning remain obscure.

The teachers and the children face many obstacles that make it extremely difficult for them to find their common interests and tasks. The children's background of poverty constitutes a major stress, limiting their ability to function at full capacity. A significant number of these children come from large families characterized by disorganization and transience. Approximately 20 to 40 percent of black children do not have their fathers present in the home (11, p. 36). Evidence suggests that these children, especially the males from fatherless homes, have greater than average learning problems in the schools (4, p. 103). Specifically, the negative effects of family disorganization upon the children's ability to grasp causal relationships, and the children's use of trial-and-error learning, have been identified (20, p. 32). Puerto Rican children have similar difficulties (8, 18, 21).

The teachers, by and large, are white, with middle-class value orientations. They have been socialized into a certain life style, being taught from grade school through college by teachers with similar experiences. They have developed curricula with certain established methods of learning and teaching. They have also come to fear and develop stereotypes of cultures that feel alien to them. Numerous studies of black children attest to the impact of race and class upon learning (13, pp. 401–402; 1, p. 135). Similarly, Vinter and Sarri spell out the effect of teachers' perceptions and school conditions upon learning (19, pp. 9, 10), and Landes identifies the resulting breakdown in communication that leads to "indifference and hostility" (7, p. 91). In essence, the different value and attitude orientations of predominantly white middle-class teachers and administrative personnel and a curriculum that is typically discontinuous with lower-class life and culture represent serious sources of strain.

At the same time, students and teachers have a basic need to work together in the educational process. Black and Puerto Rican children have been found to fall within the normal range of innate capability and most possess adequate motivation (20, p. 8). Similarly, teachers are generally motivated to fulfill their professional duties. This is particularly evident in the published experiences of Kozol (6) and Kohl (5).

SOCIAL WORK IN THE PUBLIC SCHOOLS

Although social work has had a long history in the public school setting, its function was not always clearly delineated from that of teaching. In fact, the worker has had a somewhat composite role and was generally referred to as the "visiting teacher" (2). In more recent times a clearer division of labor emerged; social casework became the method of service offered to children with school learning and adjustment problems, and the primary emphasis was on helping the child to adjust to the school situation. Social work offered an "adjustment service" and emphasized the professional relationship to help the child to "find and to test out his own positive wanting of and capacity for growth and development" (17, p. 26).

However, a number of social workers grew dissatisfied with the purely psychological emphasis and tried to broaden their perspective of a child's problem to include the school system within which he worked. Some social workers dealt with the relationship between the child and the school in general terms. For example, Poole recognized the primacy of the child-teacher relationship and warned against potential social work interference (14, p. 48). Coleman stressed that "the interest of disturbed children in school might be further advanced if the social worker could more consistently and sympathetically appreciate the real difficulties of the teacher" (3, p. 162). Others searched more specifically for an operational statement of function that would encompass the child's need and the system-situation, suggesting that the worker needs skills beyond those of working with children—"equally important are his skills in relating to teachers" (9, p. 303).

Nesbit conceptualizes the helping process as a triangular interaction between the child, the teacher, and the social worker. She identifies the common purpose and interdependence: "I am requested to help him (the child) and to help them (parents-teacher) with him in the area of specific situation(s) or problems. It is working together to this specific purpose which creates the unique tie" (10, p. 65). She perceives the professional role as one of keeping the lines of communication untangled and assuming the responsibility for being an acting member and organizer of the interrelationship (10, p. 66).

More recently, Vinter and Sarri have identified the social work function in the school, focusing on their area of specialization—group work. In reporting on a study of five schools in Michigan they state that the school problems of children must be viewed in the perspective of the particular child's characteristics and the school's conditions. They assert that educational malperformance must be considered in terms of the interaction between the school and pupil (19, p. 4). They place the problem in the social context of the school experience and perceive the social worker as the helping agent in the ongoing engagement process, focusing on both the child and the school. They stress the position that "the social worker retains dual perspectives, and attempts to resolve problem situations or process: both pupil and school conditions should be targets of interventive activities" (19, p. 13).

FUNCTION—A FRAME OF REFERENCE

Schwartz, while not dealing specifically with school social work, offers a model that would bring together the need of the child to use the school and the need of the school to serve the child. His conception has been referred to as a "reciprocal model" (12). He views the encounter and relationship between man and society as a "symbiotic" one—an interdependent relationship between people and their systems. With the increasing complexity of modern institutions, the mutual interest between man and society becomes diffuse, and Schwartz describes the social work function as one of helping these two parts (man and the social system) to find their common ground (15). He further identifies the enormous potential of *mutual aid* (16, p. 273), as people help each other negotiate the various systems with which they must come to terms.

This frame of reference thus calls attention to the common ground between the child and the school. At times this mutual need becomes diffuse; the social work function then is to help the child and the school system to rediscover their stake in each other.

THE SETTING

This chapter will describe the process by which a service was offered to a local intermediate junior high school and its children by an outside agency, the Social and Community Service Department of the New York City Housing Authority. The agency and the Columbia University School of Social Work received a National Institute of Mental Health grant to explore the role of social work in public housing. To this end, a satellite branch of the Social and Community Services was established in a vast, low-income housing project. The development consists of approximately thirty buildings, housing about eighteen thousand tenants. The agency office was located in a project apartment, staffed by six graduate social work students, a full-time professional social worker, and the writer, who served as Field Instructor. The agency helps clients with a wide range of problems, using individual, family, and group encounters where they can be of most assistance. These services are offered to clients who have personal problems, marital difficulties, child rearing concerns, and difficulties in negotiating institutions impinging on their lives. The agency also establishes and serves tenant groups composed of clients facing common concerns—relationships with public welfare agencies, retarded children, school difficulties, housing problems, and others.

The school serves youngsters from the sixth through eighth grades. It has been in existence approximately 1½ years, with a history marked by racial tensions, open disharmony between

local and central school boards, and a high turnover rate of
faculty and administrative personnel.

The agency felt it could offer a service beneficial to both
the children and the school system. In discussions with school
personnel, the target population was defined to include those
youngsters living in public housing, those entering the sixth
grade for their first year in this particular school, and those
having had learning and emotional problems in the elementary schools they previously attended. The specific service offered to several groups was to help the children and the school
system make their beginning negotiations together and work
on their common interests and needs.

The group described in this paper consisted of ten boys,
eleven to thirteen years old; four were black, five Puerto
Rican, and one white. The youngsters had lived through a
great deal of family disorganization and violence. Most had
been identified in their former schools as "troublemakers,"
"extremely withdrawn," or "poorly adjusted." Specifically, the
school records described one very nervous youngster who stut-
tered, another who was extremely angry and bitter, a day-
dreamer unable to concentrate, several acting-out youngsters,
and others identified as passive and shy. The worker was a
second-year graduate student of group work.*

FIRST PHASE: THE "TUNING-IN"

In our work with these clients, we accepted Schwartz's assumption that the operation of the helping process can be
profitably divided into four distinct phases.** In the first, the
"tuning-in" phase, the worker prepared himself to move into
the processes of school and group life. By placing ourselves

----

* We are indebted to Eugene Richard Wulf, Sandra Jackson, and
Gretchen Borrero for the record material cited in this chapter. Some
excerpts have been put together in composite form to clarify an aspect
of the helping process.
** See Chapter 1 of this book.

in the shoes of the students and the social systems representatives we developed a kind of "anticipatory empathy," which allowed us to sensitize ourselves to their potential concerns and obstacles. This helped us to respond more appropriately to their difficulties in making use of our services.

In preparing the worker to reach out to the school, for example, we were quite concerned as to how the school personnel might react to our offer of a collaborative service. Through an extensive use of role-play, we put ourselves into the roles of the school administrators; this anticipatory empathy was extremely useful in helping us identify potential obstacles. And it enabled us to develop appropriate practice strategies.

We became attuned to the school's potential doubts about an outside agency working with their children. Consequently, our practice strategy focused on involving the school personnel in an exploration process, rather than simply offering them a predefined service. Our sensitivity to the school's potential resistance enabled the worker, over the period of several contacts, to deal with a variety of concerns and to identify areas of common interest.

In preparing ourselves to reach out to the children we once again found role-play an extremely helpful tool. The worker developed a "feel" for the youngsters' previous school experiences—the despair, the anger, the distrust, the fear, and the hope. He identified the children's struggle for dignity and their behavioral responses, represented by truancy, aggression, and passivity, with their repeated failures. At the same time, we felt the children still cared, and that they possessed the essential strength to involve themselves more fully in the educational process.

We attempted to anticipate the children's reactions to our offer of help. For example, we realized that they might be confused and frightened in being called out of their classrooms, so we were prepared to reassure them quickly that they were not in any difficulty: "Listen, I know you're nervous, but you didn't do anything wrong, you're not in trouble, and there is nothing to be afraid of." We also realized that the youngsters' suspicions might make it difficult for them to trust our statements of intent about the service, and we prepared ourselves to be very honest and specific in our statements of what we were doing there. We anticipated their mistrust of the worker—"Who is this white guy; what's his angle?" And, finally, we concentrated upon anticipated specific reactions to the terms of the service. For example, for the children who might have concerns over modes of receiving parental approval, we rehearsed the suggestion, "Don't feel I have to come to your home, I can contact your parents in whatever way you decide."

SECOND PHASE: THE CONTRACT

In the second phase, that of "contracting," the worker tried to establish an understanding of the service among the school system, the children, and himself. In essence, he attempted to help the group and school system make their beginnings together. The main focus was to establish a common purpose and frame of reference. By clearly intermeshing the group's needs and the proposed agency service, the worker tried to avoid ambiguity and provide the essential guidelines for what would be relevant in the work. His task was to state the agency's service clearly and concisely to the children and school system, to elicit their feedback, and to partialize their common tasks.

In developing our contract with the school we placed major emphasis upon the system's involvement in identifying its own service needs. In the initial contacts with guidance personnel we described our agency's services and expressed our interest in potential collaborative work. We called attention to areas in which they had feelings of ambivalence toward the service and helped them relate their feelings to very specific concerns. The acting Principal was involved in our discussions and helped us address ourselves to the guidance counselors' uneasiness about proceeding without greater assurance of administrative support. In the fourth exploratory session we suggested the involvement of the New York City Bureau of Child Guidance, and this proved to be an extremely important step as it provided the counselors with internal support and professional consultation.

We devoted further conferences to defining specifically the terms of our collaborative relationship. The group met after school hours twice weekly at the agency office; the guidance counselor assumed the administrative responsibility for in-school coordination; the agency provided practice supervision; and both would meet regularly to assure the continuance of this essential communication. Our agency's conception of service was carefully interpreted to include the difficulties of both the children and the school system. We felt it to be extremely important for the guidance staff to have a clear understanding of our service, as they would be responsible for its interpretation to the administration, to the teaching faculty, and to the children. We selected twenty-five children as potential participants on the basis of their school records. The guidance counselor and our agency worker jointly introduced the service to these children, and ten of them expressed interest in further exploration.

In developing our contract with the children we were particularly concerned about our ability to explain the service clearly and to elicit their feedback responses. We realized that in our statements about the service we needed to clarify what the participating children had in common, what their potential working tasks were, and the stake the agency had in the service. We anticipated that the youngsters would have difficulty in grasping our statement of purpose, and we developed a practice strategy to engage them in the service. The worker's record shows the contracting process:

Charles asked, "What are we going to do?" I said, "This is probably the main question on all your minds." They all agreed that this was what they wanted answered right now. I mentioned that maybe we could start over. I asked, "Do you remember anything about what Mr. Jones (the guidance person who introduced the service) told you last week?" There was a long hesitation. Then Bill said, "He told us that we were all from the project, and we had problems in school." I said, "This is what the school is concerned about, that you get more out of school than you did last year, and that is why they asked me to see if I can help you."

At this point we can see the youngsters beginning to develop a conception of what they have in common; but their tasks, and the school's stake, seem somewhat vague. They continue:

Charles said, "You mean we're not going to play basketball?" I answered, "This group will not be like a community center club, because the community center is there for that." I continued, "The school wants you to have a chance to talk about some of the things that are bothering you about school." Their facial expressions spoke loudly. Bill and George and some of the others wanted this kind of chance to talk about school problems. Charles and a couple of the others wanted fun doing recreational type of things. I asked, "You're afraid that talking about what is on your minds about school won't be fun?" They acknowledged that they didn't think it would be fun. I said that we had hoped that this kind of thing would make school more fun for them. This sounded possible to them and George said, "Well, what will we do?" I replied, "Let's see if I can explain. We can get together and talk about the troubles you're having in school, and things that are on your minds, and while we do it, we might find reasons for some of those problems." Bill asked, "Do you mean we tell you our problems and you tell us what to do about them?" I answered that that wasn't it, but he was close. I said, "I'm here to help you say what you're thinking, to help you think about what you can do. You have to do the thinking 'cause you know what the problems are like."

The worker must be careful not to polarize the "talking" and the "having fun," recognizing that the children may have fun through talking and may deal with their common concerns through playing:

Bill said, "Oh, I get it. This will help us pass school." I said, "I hope so. Sounds like you're all afraid that you won't pass the sixth grade." Remarks came fast. "Boy, are we!" "We're lucky to get this far." I said, "It's a scary thing to think about failing." Charles said, "Yeah, my folks. . . ." Charles and John both made statements that their folks would kill them if they didn't pass. I said, "This would be one of the reasons for the club—to help you pass." After a long silence, Eddie said, "You can make us pass?" in a hopeful tone. I said, "Wait a minute, I can't do miracles. I can't change you into A students—you have problems getting in your way. They're your problems and only you can try to solve them. You can give each other ideas, and I can give you some, too, but you have to do the work on trying them out." There were comments that sounded like: "Let's give it a try." "Sounds good."

The worker begins to listen more carefully and elicits the youngsters' concern about not passing. He stresses the children's problems, but without attending to the system's limitations. However, the children respond to his concern and become involved in developing a contract. At this point the worker senses their need to deal with specifics:

I asked if they wanted to see what it would be like. They all anxiously said they would. I asked if anyone right now could think of anything that was bothering him in school. They all thought it was too difficult for them. I asked if they wanted me to give an example. All said, "Yes." "Okay," I said, "Suppose I was in your school and had something on my mind. Maybe I had a fight with my brother. Even if I wanted to think about my studies, I can't because I can't stop thinking about how I would like to get even with my brother." Bill broke in and said, "You can't do the writing." I continued, "Okay, I can't think about the writing. And the teacher comes along and I get into trouble. I get mad because she doesn't understand that I have something that bothers me." Every ear was involved, and it seemed real to them. Their remarks came fast. "Those teachers are mean sometimes." "Yeah, that Mr. Johnson, he's mean."

The worker's offering of a specific example (prepared through his tuning-in) helps the group experience what they have been trying to define. The youngsters proceed to test out the contract in subsequent meetings, and the worker frequently has to renegotiate. For example, during the initial four meetings they could not agree on whether they should elect members to leadership positions. Finally the children decide that this issue was an obstacle to their tasks:

Eddie said, "Are we going to settle this officer stuff?" Bill and Charles reacted, "We don't want to do that. We're here to deal with school problems. This just gets us mad." The others backed them up.

THIRD PHASE: THE WORK

In the third phase the worker helps the group and the school system focus on the tasks at hand. He helps individual members use one another within the group, and he helps the group deal with the school and other immediately relevant systems. The worker also needs to help the school interact with individual students, and with the group itself. In order to do this the worker has to address various tasks: he needs to help the various actors find their common ground; he needs to help the group and the school identify and challenge the obstacles that obstruct their view of these commonalities; he needs to have a genuinely open attitude and to contribute his own ideas, feelings, and facts when they are useful in helping group and system work on their tasks; he needs to convey a stake and faith in the process of work itself; and he needs to guard the *focus of work* at all times.

The worker thus perceives his mediating tasks as both internal and external. In the former he helps the youngsters to use each other, while in the latter he helps the group and the school to reach out and engage each other.

The process of internal mediation may be seen in the work with José. This youngster had many problems in using the group, and the group, in turn, had difficulty in understanding him. As early as the first meeting José's restlessness disrupts the group:

The youngsters became angry with José. We were talking at the moment about how they could help each other with problems. They wanted José to move away from sitting near me because they thought that was the trouble. I then said to José after he had moved, "José, you have a lot of trouble keeping your mind on what is going on, don't you?" Everyone was listening as José admitted more seriously that he usually does have trouble and that is why he was goofing off. He said that he couldn't keep his mind on one topic for so long. I asked "if this was what happens in school, too?" He looked a little surprised and smiled and said, "Yeah."

The worker's focus on José's "trouble," rather than on the problem he creates, is the first step in engaging José and the group. At a later meeting José tries to meet group expectations by offering that he also had a school problem. However, when the youngsters try to help him, he withdraws in embarrassment and reverts to disruptive behavior. The boys become upset and consider José's expulsion from the group:

Bill repeated his question. "I mean, if this is really our group, then can we kick somebody out?" I asked whom he wanted to kick out. He said, "José" and pointed to him. A few others agreed. I asked, "Why?" They answered that he goofed around too much. Bill asked again if I had anything to say about who was kicked out. I told the group that I guessed they could kick out someone, but that I would want to let them know how I felt about it. They said that would be okay. I said, "You see, you all came here because you have problems and I would hate to see anyone kicked out because he has a problem, because that's why you're all here." Bill said, "But José goofs around all the time." I said, "Yeah, José has trouble listening to everybody." I looked at José. He wanted to say something very badly, but was having trouble. I said to him, "Even though it's tough, can you say what you want to tell the group?" He started off (his English is poor and he speaks care-

fully), "It's not that I don't want to hear everybody's problems, I
do—very much—I have this problem in school." The group started
saying that they don't want to kick him out. They were talking to
José and someone actually said, "We want to help you." I asked
José if he could tell the group why it was so hard to listen.

He said he wanted to tell them but he couldn't. After struggling
a while, José finally stated, "I want to hear, but I bounce my ball
so that I can think and forget." I said that it was really hard to
listen to other people's troubles, because sometimes it was sad and
sometimes it may remind you of your own problems. José said that
this is kind of why he bounces his ball. I said that I could understand as it is hard to think about your own problems.

Here the worker helps to identify the group's purpose and
offers José the opportunity to deal with the others' reactions.
The focus on José's difficulty rather than on his symptomatic
behavior enables the group to reach out to him.

In time José begins to work on his school problems. In the
midst of one meeting he blurts out that he hates school terribly. His excitement and poor language skills make it difficult for the youngsters to understand, but they try to be of
help:

Bill said that he understood José, and repeated that José said that
the other kids in school make fun of him. José came in at this point
and said much more clearly, "They—they—make fun of me—especially when I read like this—'the—boy—went home.'" (He was
emphasizing that he reads slowly and the kids laugh at him.) The
whole group was seriously thinking and there was a silence. I
said, "That must make you feel badly, no wonder you don't like
school, José." José said that it was miserable. Then Bill said slowly
and thoughtfully, "José, I think they're laughing at you because you
read so slowly." José said, "Yeah, I think so, too." After a brief
pause, Edward came in, "I think they make fun of you because
you can't talk so well. I mean you have trouble." José said, "I
think that's right too." After a short pause, Charles came in and
said, "I think they make fun of you because you clown around and
wander around and make jokes." Greg said, "Yeah, like you walk

around here." The group didn't know where to go from there and needed a little direction from me. So I said, looking at José, but talking to the whole group, "Can you think of anything to make things less miserable?" The group thought and Bill said to José, "You can practice at home with your mother." There was no response. It was my feeling that the group got the message—that his mother could not read English. Edward said excitedly, breaking into the discussion, "You should go to the special reading class that meets after school, and they could help you read better." Charles got excited as did everyone else including José and said, "Yeh, if you learned to read better your speaking will improve." I asked José if he would like some help with that class. The others said, "You should, man, they can help you and the others won't make fun of you so much." Soon José said, "OK, how can I get in?" The group offered suggestions. I then said, "Would you like me to find out the information?" He said that he would, and the others supported this.

In summary, the worker's conception of function enables him to help José and the group work on their common tasks. He carefully avoids taking sides in conflict situations, focusing instead on using his skills to help the members work things out together. This is in recognition of the fact that the worker has his job to do, and the group members have theirs—what emerges are two parallel and interdependent processes.

In doing his job the worker reflects many professional skills. Besides displaying general concern and interest in his group, the worker shows more sophisticated skills. He demands that his clients work on what they are there for—"I think José wants to know if you will make more fun of him." He observes both overt and covert cues—". . . is this what happens in school, too?" He focuses on their commonalities— "You all came here because you have problems. . . ." He helps to break down material into smaller pieces—". . . can you think of anything to make things less miserable?" And with smaller pieces he forms more meaningful connections— "It was really hard to listen to other people's troubles . . . be-

cause sometimes they may remind you of your own problems."
He related to the youngsters' feelings—"You guys feel bad
about what happened"—and also to the more complex ambivalent emotions—"You're really not sure. . . ." One can see the
worker facilitate the *mutual aid* process through the use of
skills and techniques defined by his conception of his professional function.

In his *external mediation* the worker has a dual focus—helping the children to work on their external concerns, and
simultaneously helping the school system to deal with those
concerns. Specifically, the major difficulties arise in the chil-
drens' communication with people in authority positions—
school monitors, administrative personnel, and teachers.

The process of external mediation may be seen here in work
with children and teachers. Obstacles to effective student-
teacher communication were a constant source of tension and
frustration. Children repeatedly verbalized feeling perse-
cuted and "not loved"; teachers described the children as "not
caring" and "unwilling to learn."

In an early meeting Bill describes a situation in which he
stood up for a friend "falsely accused" by their teacher, and
as a result had been quickly dispatched to the principal's
office:

I said, "You sound pretty mad at the teacher and probably worried that you will be in trouble." Bill commented, "I am mad, but
what I want to know is will I get a charge for standing up for a
friend?" All paid attention to this question but no one commented.
I asked if anyone could help Bill with this and what they thought.
Charles said, "No, you won't get a charge if your friend sticks up
for you." Greg confirmed this. Bill's face showed that this did not
help with what bothered him. Eddie said, "It depends on how
you stand up to the teacher." The point hit home, and there was a
reflective silence and confusion as to how to react to this remark
and carry discussion further. I asked if they thought it would help
if they acted it out and saw how Bill stood up for his friend. They
liked the idea and all wanted to be in it.

The worker helps the group to focus on Bill's problem. At the point where the discussion reaches an impasse, he involves the group in role-playing the situation. By recreating the experience, he brings the group and himself closer to what actually happened.

In another instance Charles discusses a fight he has had in class. He is furious at the teacher for not taking his side in the argument and storms out of the classroom. He requests help from the group:

Eddie said, "You should not have hit him. You wouldn't have gotten into trouble." I said, "Well, Charles was so mad that he had to say how mad he was in some way." Charles told how mad he really was. There was a silence, which I let go for a while, because it was obvious that they were all thinking and looking for solutions. All of a sudden Ronald, a big husky kid who just looks like he gets into lots of fights, said to Charles, "You shouldn't have hit him, you just get into trouble. Instead, you go up and tell the teacher and she'll get him into trouble . . . then beat him up after school." The response was that this made a lot of sense to the group. Greg said, "No, not after school, you could still get into trouble. Beat him up on Saturday." Charles said he liked that solution for now. . . .

"Charles, do you want to know what to do to make the teacher not pick on you and like you?" He said he did. Somebody said that he shouldn't have run out of class. It didn't help. They still had a rough time. I had to take a more active role after they showed me some signs of frustration. I said, "You know this is similar to what happened here with Bill's gripe earlier. Bill thought I was playing favorites and was picking on him. And then he did something that solved his problem. Do you remember what he did?" José said, "He came in and said that he quit. He got mad." I said, "That is all true, but he didn't get any good results until he told me what was bothering him, what he was mad about, and what I did that makes him mad." Bill's face lit up and he said in a long drawn-out way, "Yea—ah—a!" The others then caught on because they could see that Bill really believed *that* was what helped him. Then they started telling Charles what he could do. The group recommendation turned out to be to go to the teacher after class and tell him that he was mad because he always picks on him. Then Charles said to me, "But he's not like you." Others said, "Yeah, you understand." I said, "I'm different, but lots of times I understand because you tell me what's bothering you. He doesn't know what's bothering you, he can't understand. He probably doesn't know that you think that he is picking on you." The others said to Charles, "You can give it a try." They were through with this one and I said, "You can give it a try, and if it doesn't work, you can bring it back here, and we'll try to see what else we can do."

In these sessions much of the worker's effort is devoted to the task of helping the youngsters deal more effectively and directly with the school system, and most particularly with the teachers. It soon became apparent that the worker would have to throw his own strength into the work with the teachers. Thus, when he offers to talk to one of them, the boys eagerly prepare him for the proposed encounter:

Bill started in with what he thought I should say. He said, "Well, first I think you should tell him who you are." The other boys picked this up and mentioned that I could be anybody and if I didn't tell him who I was, he might get mad and say it was none of my business. I said, "I thought that was a good thing to remember." Then Charles said, "I think you should tell him about how you happen to know me, that you work with us and stuff." José added that I should tell him about the group and that we talk about our problems. I asked the others if they thought it was okay to tell him that about the group. They said, "Yeah." Bill said that he thought "it might be a good idea to ask him why he failed us all, and get his side of the story." I said, "I thought that might be good because then he would feel that we were working together on it and I wasn't there to tell him off." I asked them if they thought that was fair. They said, "Yeah, it was right to let him tell his side anyway."

The worker states his desire to work with the teacher rather than to "tell him off." The youngsters accept this, as the contract for the worker to operate in this way had been clearly established earlier. In reaching out to the teacher the worker is interested in the teacher's perceptions and in identifying the common obstacles in the learning-teaching endeavor:

We went into the teachers' room to talk. I took the opportunity to tell him where I was from and the group's purpose. He said that he had taken a course in the summer about teaching in this kind of school and neighborhood. He knew that there were such things as "ego-building" grades and tests to make the kids feel good, but he didn't believe in it. I asked him about the letters he sent home. He said, "Oh, yes, several of them continually create a disturbance . . . always talking and turning around. I finally got fed up and when I get fed up, I send a letter home. Not that it does any good." I stated that most of the children were quite upset. He seemed surprised at this. He said, "I still don't understand why they didn't do their homework." I said that I knew that several of them were in the middle of a real family crisis and that their lives were quite confused. He said, "You mean, they can't find a quiet place for their homework for an hour?" I said that I knew for several children it was very difficult. He said that you had to learn to concentrate and that there was an afternoon study center. I added, "And an afternoon play center—I guess I'm saying that you're asking for more self-discipline than I think a lot of kids have." I began to feel that I was pushing too hard and stated, "I guess you're probably tired of hearing what problems these kids have at home and that you should be more understanding—it doesn't make your job any easier." I could see him relax as he nodded. He responded that he supposed he'd have to give the kids a lot of credit for coming to school at all, with all they had to contend with at home. He suggested that we discuss each child individually.

Initially the worker reacts to the teacher's defensiveness. He intensifies the barrier by immediately focusing upon the letters and the children's problems. It was his sensitivity that enabled him to recognize that "I was pushing too hard." Subsequently he moves to the teacher's problems and the tone and direction of the interview change dramatically. As the conference continues, the worker identifies a major obstacle, namely, the youngsters' feeling that the teacher thinks them to be incapable of doing the work—consequently they devote less energy to their school work and fulfill this inferred prophecy:

I said, "You know, I'm not sure what you say to them, but they hear it wrong. Something you've said to them has given them the idea that you think they are the stupidest class and that they are all dumb." He thought for a moment, and then said, "No, they're right, I had said that. I've gotten so angry with them that I have said that. And I can see how they've taken it." I said that I could see that they make his job rough for him. He said that initially he said these things because they didn't finish their work. Then he said that he definitely thought that he shouldn't have said those things. I said, "Because you're telling them that they are stupid, they get mad and are going to get back at you some way—probably by acting bad and giving you a lot of trouble." He said that he thought that this made some sense.

A little later he asked if I had any ideas as to how he might reverse things, or better help them to finish their work. I said that since they had the idea that he thinks that they are too stupid to do the work, maybe he could try saying to them things like, "I think you guys can finish your work and learn, if you can try a little harder." And when he gets mad, maybe he could tell them that he was getting mad at them because he is trying to teach them and they aren't trying—and that he thinks they can learn. We discussed other types of actions. Then he thanked me in a very sincere way for the help I had given him and I thanked him for the information he had given me. We set up a future meeting.

As the meeting progresses, the teacher senses the worker's acceptance and is able to work on the problem. However, at the point that the teacher requests help the worker too quickly offers an oversimplified solution, which has the effect of closing further exploration. On the other hand, when the worker engages the teacher in dealing with their common concerns, the groundwork for future work is established.

In subsequent conversations the worker helped the teacher move beyond his initial defensiveness and become actively engaged in providing more effective teaching services to his children. The worker identified a serious obstacle in the children's and teacher's relationships—namely, *their* feeling that he did not care, and *his* feeling that they did not want to learn. Subsequently the teacher became increasingly involved and identified with the children. In fact, several weeks later when Bill was involved in a minor fight and, because of his previous school record, the principal was considering his expulsion, it was the teacher who prevented it:

We all (the principal, guidance counselor, and myself) went up to talk with Mr. Smith. The principal requested a report on Bill's class behavior. Mr. Smith said that over the past couple of weeks Bill was not bad at all, he didn't start fights and was rather cooperative in class. He said that Bill had been doing his homework lately and seemed to be really trying. The principal asked why Bill ran out of class and got himself into a fight. Mr. Smith explained that a friend had taken his pencil, began teasing him, and Bill ran out before he could intervene. I added that this occasionally happened in the club; when Bill was hurt, he had trouble expressing his anger. Mr. Smith informed the principal of our work and how Bill had been responding to his extra efforts. The principal called Bill into the classroom, praised him on his improvement and warned him never to be seen out of his classroom again.

The problems were not, of course, limited to teacher-student relationships. Another major school difficulty was the unclear division of labor among various staff members—the Dean of Boys, the guidance counselors, and the Assistant Principal in charge of guidance. Often they duplicated their efforts or left service gaps. The worker defined this as an area of service activity and tried to help them coordinate their efforts to serve the group members. To this end he organized several case conferences and found that the staff was trying earnestly to help the youngsters, but they were continually frustrated by the unclear conception of their job functions. At his suggestion a general staff meeting was held, where they discussed the problem of the division of labor.

In summary, the worker brought to bear a wide variety of skills. In working with the youngsters he helped them to identify their concerns—"You sound pretty mad at the teacher and are probably worried that you will be in trouble." He helped them to break down and examine complicated problems through the use of role-play and re-enactment of situations. He encouraged them to share their concerns with teachers— "He doesn't know what's bothering you, he can't understand." At the same time, he used his skills to help the teachers deal with their concerns. He engaged one teacher by relating to the difficulties of his job—"I guess you're probably tired of hearing what problems the kids have at home. . . . It doesn't make your job any easier." The teacher was not perceived as an enemy, but rather as someone who also needed help—"I could see that they make his job rough for him." He identified an obstacle to the teacher and helped him to look at it— "Something you've said to them has given them the idea that you think they are the stupidest class and that they are all dumb." He offered relevant information—"Bill is the same way in the group." In this way, he helped the children and teacher find their common interests and needs. At the same time, the worker addressed himself to the total school system that created obstacles for both teachers and students.

FOURTH PHASE: THE TERMINATION

For the worker the final phase is one of preparing himself to leave the situation and helping the group members deal with the separation. By preparing himself he becomes attuned to the meaning of the experience to the children, and to their potential reactions. For example, he anticipates that the intensity of the experience will create resistance to ending it; that the more sudden the ending, the more difficult it will be to handle the sorrow and anger at his leaving; and that he, the worker, will also be subject to some of the same feelings. Based upon this understanding the worker develops a practice strategy: to call attention to the expected ending at an early date; to listen carefully for expressed and implied feelings in this area; to demand that the group address itself to this difficult experience; and to involve himself in the process by sharing his own feelings.

The worker expects that each youngster will handle the experience differently, but that there will also be certain common reactions. He is prepared for group members to be upset and to resist dealing with their feelings. The experience would also be a difficult one for the worker, involving his sense of loss and unwillingness to "give them up."

He begins by calling their attention to the impending ending several months prior to the final group meeting. These early attempts, however, are marked by mutual avoidance and resistance in dealing with the separation. As the time passes the youngsters and worker become increasingly despondent:

The boys were subdued today. Again they moved slowly, conveying a general sense of disinterest. I offered them some candy, but they all said they didn't want any. After many attempts their resistance broke down and each one took a piece. However, their responses continued to be monosyllabic. In general, there was a lot of listlessness, and I realize it was on my part also as I didn't want to think about our last meetings either.

At this point, the worker is unable to move beyond his own depression. Later, in one of the last few meetings, the worker brings himself into the process and helps the youngsters deal with their intense and ambivalent feelings:

They wanted to know if they could have a party on our last meeting. I responded that I wondered whether they really would feel like having one. They said, "Yes." Then Eddie got hold of the masking tape and one by one they put the tape over each member's mouth. They began making humming kinds of noises. They also began moving around the room, gesturing madly and trying to communicate their thoughts to each other and me. Every so often Bill and Charles would come up and shake their fist at me. They all seemed extremely angry. Their expressions of anger and frustration came through. I said, "We have been a talking group all year long and gotten to be very close. I am very sad now that you can't talk to me." Soon they took the tape off, and immediately began to run around the room. They were shouting and wrestling. They were trying so hard to express their anger and trying to make me angry. I was quite upset and shared this with them. They continued to run around, when finally Bill yelled, "Okay, cut it out, this isn't any fun." There was an immediate silence. I stated, "You must be really mad to have to act like this." Charles said, "Yeah, you're right; we're really angry and we're mad too, because you're leaving us." José said, "Yeah, it's not fair for you to do this—to go away and leave us alone." I replied that I knew it would be hard because we had gotten so close to each other. They talked about my going into the service, and moving far away.

I looked at them and said slowly, "It seems like you feel that I am going to forget all about you after I leave, and will not care about you anymore." Bill blurted out, "Yes—you will forget us." I said, "That would never happen. I know you so well and I like you so much." We talked some more and it was very sad. Charles asked whom he would turn to if he had trouble in school or at home? The other boys raised similar concerns. They began to consider having a different worker next year, but quickly closed off this topic. After the meeting, they walked me to the subway. Ronald said that he wanted to tell me something. "I think I know why we acted so bad today." I asked, "Why?" He continued, "Well, you remember how we were bad all the time—it was because we had all these problems and we couldn't talk about them. And today we were bad—like in the beginning—I think it was because we had a big problem—your leaving us." All I could do was hug him as I left for my train.

At this meeting the worker does not remove himself, but rather focuses and demands that the children deal with what is bothering them. He relates to the feelings underlying their behavior—"You must be really mad to have to act like this." He enables them to more openly express their reactions by connecting their anger to the hurt they feel in losing him. He further identifies their feelings of being abandoned and forgotten, and in turn articulates his own deep feeling for them. This continues in the final meeting, where the group and worker struggle with their feelings as they spend their last session together:

I stated that I guessed it was so quiet because this was our last meeting together. José said that it was a sad day. After several minutes they began to act out their sadness, anger, and frustration—they began jumping on the tables. I suggested that I didn't think that this was going to help. Eddie got angry and demanded that I stop reminding them that this is their last meeting. "I want to be happy," he said, calling the others to join him in a game of tag. I stated that I didn't think that this would really help them with their sadness and that I wished they'd join me at the table. Charles went over to the shade and began to play with it. I said that it had been a long time since he had to resort to the window shade. He didn't respond and turned out the lights. The room descended into a gloomy darkness conveying quite accurately our feelings. Finally, I told them that I was very unhappy also and that we were all having a terrible time saying some awfully important things to each other.

They continued, but suddenly clustered in the far corner. I asked them to tell me what they were buzzing so intently about, but they moved their backs to me. Then Charles came over and said, "We are sorry for how we acted today. We like you very much." I felt speechless and the room was in total silence. I noticed a tear forming in José's eyes. After a while, I said, "I know how hard this day is for all of us, we have come to like each other very much since that first group meeting. And now it seems like all our closeness is coming to an end. Thank you very much for what you said—I know how hard it is to say that I mean very much to you and that you like me. I was also worrying how I was going to tell

you that I like you very much and am going to miss you. I want
you to know that even though I'll be far away, I will worry about
you and how you are." They didn't respond, several turned away
to hide their struggle for composure. I remained silent. Finally,
José came over and just leaned close to me. I put my arm around
his shoulders. We went over for some ice cream sundaes and then
to the subway station to have our pictures taken. We continued to
drag it out as long as we could and finally exchanged sad goodbyes.

The worker helps the youngsters move beyond their anger
and share their closeness together. He identifies the mood—
"I know how hard this day is for all of us, we have come to
like each other very much. . . ." He shares his own feelings
—"I like you very much and am going to miss you." The
worker helps the group to experience its own feelings of anger,
mourning, intimacy, and the separation itself.

In terminating with the school the worker coordinated several important evaluation meetings with guidance and administrative staff. They reviewed the experience, identified various
obstacles, and made specific plans for the subsequent year.
They felt, for example, that the worker's separateness from the
school system limited his contacts and impact, and they
decided to plan for school office hours for the next worker.

Within the urban community today there are serious obstacles that hinder black and Puerto Rican children in their
effective use of the schools. Likewise, the schools have great
difficulty in engaging these children and providing them with
sound educational experiences. Real concerns about teaching
and learning become obscured as people take polarized positions regarding the causes and solutions of the many difficult
problems involved. Yet the child continues to need the school,
and the school continues to need the child, and this is a key
commonality and the ground upon which a more fruitful
future might be built. It is precisely on this common ground
that the social worker can find his most useful function—

mediating in one of the most important settings of the encounter between people and the social environment in which they live and work.

REFERENCES

1. Robert T. Amos, "The Accuracy of Negro and White Children's Predictions of Teachers' Attitudes Toward Negro Students," *The Journal of Negro Education*, Vol. 21, No. 2 (Spring 1952), pp. 125–33.
2. Bertram Beck, "School Social Work: An Instrument of Education," *Social Work*, Vol. 4, No. 4 (October 1959), pp. 87–91.
3. Coleman, Jules, M.D., "Meeting the Mental Health Needs of Children in School Today: Psychiatric Implications for the Practice of School Social Work," in *Helping the Troubled School Child* (New York: National Association of Social Workers, 1959), pp. 158–67.
4. Martin Deutsch, "Minority Group and Class Status as Related to Social and Personality Factors in Scholastic Achievement," in Martin Deutsch, *et al.*, *The Disadvantaged Child* (New York: Basic Books, 1967), pp. 89–131.
5. Herbert Kohl, *36 Children* (New York: The New Amer. Lib., 1967).
6. Jonathan Kozol, *Death at an Early Age* (New York: Houghton Mifflin, 1967).
7. Ruth Landes, "Minority Groups and School Social Work," *Social Work*, Vol. 4, No. 3 (July 1959), pp. 91–103.
8. Oscar Lewis, *La Vida* (New York: Random House, 1965).
9. John Nebo, "Interpretation of School Social Welfare Services to Educators and Other Professionals Who Serve the Schools," in *Helping the Troubled School Child* (New York: National Association of Social Workers, 1959), pp. 302–309.
10. Elsie Nesbit, "The Triangle—The Parent, The Teacher, The Visiting Teacher," in *Helping the Troubled School Child* (New York: National Association of Social Workers, 1959), pp. 65–69.

11. Office of Policy Planning and Research, *The Negro Family* (Washington, D.C.: Department of Labor, 1965).

12. Catherine P. Papell and Beulah Rothman, "Social Group Work Models: Possession and Heritage," *Journal of Education for Social Work*, Vol. 2, No. 2 (Fall 1966), pp. 66–77.

13. Benjamin Pasamanick and Hilda Kroblock, "Early Language Behavior in Negro Children and the Testing of Intelligence," *Journal of Abnormal and Social Psychology*, Vol. 50, No. 3 (May 1955), pp. 401–403.

14. Florence Poole, "An Analysis of the Characteristics of School Social Work," in *Helping the Troubled School Child* (New York: National Association of Social Workers, 1959), pp. 46–51.

15. William Schwartz, "Group Work and the Social Scene," in Alfred J. Kahn (ed.), *Issues in American Social Work* (New York: Columbia University Press, 1959), pp. 110–37.

16. William Schwartz, "Toward a Strategy of Group Work Practice," *Social Service Review*, Vol. 36, No. 3 (September 1962), pp. 268–79.

17. Ruth Smalley, "Philosophy and Objectives of Adjustment Services as Expressed in Practice," in *Helping the Troubled School Child* (New York: National Association of Social Workers, 1959), pp. 21–31.

18. Piri Thomas, *Down These Mean Streets* (New York: Knopf, 1967).

19. Robert D. Vinter and Rosemary C. Sarri, "Malperformance in the Public School: A Group Work Approach," *Social Work*, Vol. 10, No. 1 (January 1965), pp. 3–13.

20. Jeannette Vosk, "Study of Negro Children with Learning Difficulties at the Outset of Their School Careers," *American Journal of Orthopsychiatry*, Vol. 36, No. 1 (January 1966), pp. 32–40.

21. Dan Wakefield, *Island in the City: Puerto Ricans in New York* (New York: Corinth Books, 1959).

The Settlement House: Mediator for the Poor

BUFORD E. FARRIS, GILBERT MURILLO,
and WILLIAM M. HALE

THE SETTLEMENT MOVEMENT emerged around the turn of the century as a response to the rapid influx of rural European immigrants into the major urban centers of this country. The main concept of the early settlements was that of *neighborhood*, with stress on its organization and integration. If the neighborhood could become more democratic, unified, and representative, the individual's relationship with the larger society would grow stronger and more secure. The early settlement workers saw the neighborhood both as a unit of study and as a base for social action:

Begun as friendly households in parts of the city where social problems were greatest, with the idea of dispensing hospitality and collecting factual material about "how the other half lives," they soon found themselves formulating statements of needs—even methods of supplying these needs. The resident workers were not merely reporting to the rest of society as they originally intended, but they were stimulating their neighbors to cooperate in the battle to secure equal privileges for the economically dispossessed, the educationally deprived, the physically handicapped, and those discriminated against because of race, foreign birth, nationality, or religion (7, pp. 2–3).

There was another institution that offered striking resemblances in its approach to the same immigrants: the political machine operated with the same pragmatic style, although its moral perspective was different from that of the settlements. We have discussed these similarities in another paper (3), but Banfield's account of how the ward leader mediated between the neighborhood and city hall is worth noting here:

One or two evenings a week he is available to all comers in his office. People come to him to inquire about welfare payments, to get their relatives into public institutions, to get something done about neighborhood nuisances (the garbage has not been collected from an alley or a policeman is needed at a school crossing) and to make complaints about the police or other city departments (1, p. 119).

In any event, both of these institutions were overtaken by the huge increase and bureaucratization in welfare and government programs in the 1930s. The wardheeler was faced with changes in political organization and an expanding social welfare bureaucracy. The dispensing of services by a person involved in the total life of the neighborhood was replaced by formal and rule-bound agencies, and these "natural mediators" were lost as an organizational force. Similarly, the increasing professionalization of social service caused many of the settlements to concentrate on services for children and youth through group work and recreational programs. Gans (4) has pointed out that this produced a greater emphasis on serving the more "mobile" youth and his family, motivated as they are to take advantage of such "character-building" efforts.

These social changes also created a neighborhood that was different from that formed by the early immigrants. Primarily, the difference lay in the increasing differentiation of the lower class itself; many authors have described the variety of life styles and perspectives of lower-class families, with differences cutting across ethnic lines. Herbert Gans (4) named four types:

Mobiles, Routine Seekers, Action-Oriented, and Maladapted. S. M. Miller (6) identified the various family types as Stable, Consistent Copers, and Inconsistent Copers. Madeline Engle (2) combined these and delineated five categories: Strivers, Consistent Copers, Inconsistent Copers, Reliefers, and Hold Overs (Residuals). The basis of all these typologies is the relationship between the lower-class families and the various public and private bureaucracies and organizations of modern society. Thus, the "Mobiles," "Stables," and "Strivers" are those of the lower class who are church-going adults with low-paid but steady jobs, who have "achieving" children, and who know how to use the various "character-building" agencies in the neighborhood. They are, in many respects, similar to the settlement's original clients, the immigrants. On the other hand, the "Maladapted," and the "Inconsistent Copers" are those families who are the most isolated from the bureaucratic structures of education, employment, welfare, and the settlements themselves.

These differences within the lower class isolate the subcultures from each other and create a situation in which the neighborhood no longer functions as a unit. Social action by the "mobiles" will not necessarily benefit the more isolated families; in fact it hardly ever does. And because the mobiles are the most politically active, politicians connected with the neighborhood will most often direct their concerns to the aspirations of this group. Thus, we have a situation in which the best gets better and the worst gets worse. The problems of low-income neighborhoods therefore become increasingly connected to the plight of those families at the very bottom of the lower class. If the settlements are to serve in these neighborhoods, they must develop strategies that will enable them to help alleviate this isolation and its effects. This chapter will describe the efforts to develop such a strategy by one agency in one such community.

THE SETTING

The Wesley Community Centers were founded in San Antonio, Texas, in 1909 and served the early Mexican immigrants who came to this country during the period of the Mexican revolution. In their poverty these Mexicans were similar in many ways to the European immigrants then moving into other parts of the country. Over the years the neighborhoods served by the Methodist centers began to change and develop the characteristics discussed above. The centers had attempted to reach out to the problem families in various programs, but this was not done systematically until after the unification of the three Methodist centers of San Antonio in 1958. Soon after the unification the Wesley Community Centers began a program designed to reach out to the conflict gangs in the neighborhood. Out of this effort evolved the Wesley Youth Project, financed by the National Institute of Mental Health as a program for working with conflict gangs among low-income Mexican-Americans.

First devised as a delinquency-prevention program, the Wesley Youth Project began to change as it became obvious that we were dealing with the more generalized problems of poverty. There was a staff tendency to resist this new direction, since it seemed so far away from the Project's initial intention, and the concern with "poverty" seemed to involve a commitment too vast and global. However, the new direction grew from the realization that causes as well as symptoms must be addressed by a service agency, even though the "solution" of poverty could not be reached within the foreseeable future. Our own change began when we realized that the hard-core poor were disadvantaged in their efforts to negotiate solutions to the problems that continually affected their lives, either in their own neighborhoods or in the community-at-large. The more "affluent" were relatively successful in negotiating society's institutions; they paid their taxes, contributed to

United Funds, voted, held organizational offices, and supported social causes.

Like the more affluent, the hard-core poor had some definite ideas about what is right and wrong, although these might differ drastically in certain respects; smoking marijuana and having sexual adventures before the age of sixteen might be intolerable to the affluent but commonplace to the poor. The very poor differed, too, in that they were far more likely to distrust agencies, to think that all politicians were crooked, and to be certain that it does absolutely no good to fight city hall. What was common to both the poor and their more organized neighbors was the desire to be somebody and to possess the material things that connote status.

Although it is important to guard against the tendency to generalize too broadly about the "culture" of the poor, our own efforts to understand the lower-class Mexican-American neighborhood brought us to recognize three family types, somewhat similar to the classifications described above. First, there is a "mobile" working class that lives in comfortable houses and owns most of the modern conveniences. There are several motives that keep them in the neighborhood: many of their close relatives live there; living expenses are comparatively low; it is close to their work; and they feel emotionally tied to the neighborhood in which they grew up. The mobiles are generally looked up to by the rest of the neighborhood; if, however, they display their possessions too boldly, or if they hold themselves aloof, they could be unpopular. Other neighborhood families often call the mobile family "Agringado," or "overly-Americanized." Sometimes—but not too often—the mobile family becomes dissatisfied with being a big frog in a small pool, and it then moves to a middle-class neighborhood.

Next, there is a stable, working-class population, composed of the poor-but-honest, whom we saw mowing the lawns and removing the garbage of the more affluent. They are the hard-working, poorly paid, tradition-oriented families, who maintain extended family ties and move only with great difficulty, if at all, into the next class. Only a few of their children complete high school. This group identifies itself as "La Raza," or "the people."

At the bottom of the lower-class Mexican-American neighborhoods are the hard-core problem families, who fail in almost every family task, whether by middle-class or any other standards: their health is poor; the children are not controlled; the houses are drafty and dirty; work is hard to find and harder to keep. Marriage occurs at an early age and there are many children. In general, the hard-core poor are the fatherless welfare families; the males are loosely connected to the female-headed household and are associated in "action-oriented" peer groups. In these neighborhoods the hard-core poor are the most isolated and the most despised.

We have some general ideas about why these families are so despised by their own people, but these need to be developed in more detail. We know that we meet with strong rejection when we point out the plight of the very poor to the mobiles in the low-income neighborhood. Perhaps they are too close to the problem to deal with it securely. Perhaps we are asking them to be understanding of people who have been family enemies over an extended period. In any event, we found that the poor themselves were most prejudiced toward the very poor—even more rejecting of them than are the affluent of society. The hard-core poor are, of course, rejected by perfect strangers as well—welfare workers, public health nurses, school principals, and other professionals.

The neighborhood worker is thus in an ambiguous situation from the beginning as he moves into work with the very poor. The neighborhood is willing to let the settlement deal with these difficult, depressing problems, but as the staff member begins to work the neighborhood resentment mounts as he spends more of his time with "those ungrateful and worthless people." These hostile and bitter reactions were particularly strong when we showed interest in the "hoodlums"—trouble-some youngsters largely from the multiproblem families. We received immediate reactions from neighborhood people and from the agencies and schools as well. A professional said:

These people don't want to help themselves. The only way you can get along with them is to coddle them and what you will probably do is teach them they can get away with anything. However, I don't want anything to do with them; you can help by keeping them out of my hair.

And a local school principal generalized thus, from a specific family to the neighborhood itself:

Juan is bad and it's no wonder with that mother of his. She has had children by half a dozen different men. She's immoral and wouldn't listen to us. I told her: Don't have any more babies. But they don't listen to you—they blame us; we can't do anything for this neighborhood.

FINDING A NEW DIRECTION
FOR NEIGHBORHOOD WORK

From the sheer necessities of the work itself, we were forced to move toward the principle that *the integration of neighborhood and community must begin at the point of maximum damage.* Our workers found their attention constantly drawn to the weaker links in the chain; they concluded that the hard-core poor are the essence of the social problems in a slum neighborhood. The problems of the very poor exhibited on a grand and compelling scale the status anxiety and unequal opportunity that were universal handicaps in all such neighborhoods. And they acted as strong negative forces impeding the neighborhood's overall tendency toward acculturation and integration within the larger community. From this it followed that solutions would begin only as the residents, the social agencies, and the educational institutions moved to accept these hard-core problems as their own.

Thus, we found that our work must focus directly not only

on the problems of the poor themselves but also on the task of helping the larger neighborhood and the community to accept these problems as partially the products of their own activity. Our general direction then became one of mediating the relations among individuals, groups, and their society. Neither of the large, popular alternatives made sense in our context: we could neither restructure entire personalities nor place a crowbar at the point of greatest leverage—the base of the whole social structure. But while we could no more affect "total society" than we could "total personalities," we could get at what was in between—families, gangs, schools, neighborhood organizations, and struggling individuals. Our responsibilities began with people who were unable to express their needs to their neighbors and their community, and extended to the groups who needed to be responsive to those needs.

The mediating function played itself out in specific practice situations, each of which required the greatest skill we could muster: we became involved in crisis events affecting the hard-core families; we worked closely with the institutional representatives involved in the various crisis situations; and we involved neighborhood families in comprehensive neighborhood organizations that could define the issues for the larger community and call attention to the problems of the families at the bottom. Let us describe for you some of the problems that emerged and the practice strategies we employed.

THE CRISIS SITUATION

The neighborhood worker became a significant person in the lives of his families only to the extent that he was able to take on the world view of the poor and was able to prove himself useful to them. It meant finding the pace and direction of individual poor people without becoming totally immersed in their many problems and their expectations of failure. Crisis situations provided excellent vehicles for involvement. Most of the troubles were silent and hidden: the unwed teen-ager who realized she was pregnant; the drug addict hustling to support his habit; and other similar predicaments. Some of the crises were violent and immediate, such as the neighborhood feud that erupted into a shooting, and the marijuana party that came to an end when a car smashed against a telephone pole. Such situations required an enormous amount of effort by the poor because of their lack of resources to negotiate in their own behalf; and during such moments of agitation and confusion their attitudes of distrust and suspicion were momentarily discarded:

Worker is getting into his car at 6:00 p.m. after visiting with the mother of a young alcoholic. As he prepares to leave he is asked by the mother to "do something" about a distant relative who is "dying" a few houses away. The worker and woman enter a run-down shack where an older woman lies in bed, semiconscious and moaning softly. She is surrounded by neighbors, none of whom wish to take responsibility for doing anything; they cannot realistically assess the situation . . . (her condition turned out to be a diabetic coma). Because of the late hour the usual resources are not available. An hour passes before an ambulance arrives and before Charity Hospital's staff agrees to accept patient. The next day an older woman who was in attendance during the crisis situation visits the worker and asks him to serve as her parole advisor.

The worker is with several addicts at an ice-house, which is located on a busy thoroughfare. One of the addicts, Ruben R., is on the verge of seeking treatment at the Public Health Service Hospital. As the worker talks to Ruben about this, a couple walks up and asks for information. They see the worker and then leave. The girl appears to be in her late teens. She looks frightened and uncomfortable. Ruben explains: "That's a bad deal. She is one of my sister's friends. That man gave her her first fix last night. It won't be long before she's hooked and is out hustling for the bastard. She's young, man." The worker and Ruben exchange looks. The worker feels angry and helpless. After awhile Ruben shrugs and then begins telling the worker why he wants to postpone hospitalization for a few days.

Crisis situations emerged from relationships both within the neighborhood and with the surrounding community. Prime sources of conflict in the neighborhood were family tensions, peer group relations, and misunderstandings between age groups. The most frequent sources of difficulty in the larger community were unemployment, police interventions, and medical emergencies, and school frictions:

Monday, I passed L.'s house and she hollered at me. I asked why she hadn't gone to school. She said she had a cold and a stomach ache. I found out later on she had been suspended. The teacher had told her to move to another chair; she had said "who." The teacher said "your grandmother." L. let loose and started cursing the teacher. She was sent to the Dean. She also had it out with the Dean.

In discussion L. says that it is very difficult to control her temper and that the teachers have labeled her as a trouble maker and she is blamed for everything even though it is not her fault. L. got back into school, but was suspended again for speaking Spanish.

Later the worker conferred with the assistant superintendent of schools, and they effected a transfer to another school at L.'s request. Still later L. fought in the street, left school again, and the worker subsequently worked with her in terms of her perception of what was happening to her.

Frequently the workers moved into crisis situations involving employment and relations with employers. In the following example the client was a former addict who had spent 2 years in prison and had now been fired from his job through an irresponsible act:

I opened the telephone conversation by identifying myself and my relationship to the client. After the preliminaries I asked Mr. T. if M. G. was a good worker. Mr. T. replied. "Yes, he is, he's been quite good, on time, works hard." Then I asked if M. G. liked to work. Mr. T. replied, "Yes." I said, "That's what he tells me; he likes the work there and is very disappointed about leaving."

At this point I tried to focus on the facts of M. G.'s case and why he had taken off to Laredo with his friends, leaving the company in the lurch. Mr. T. responded with a comment about this type of person. "Yes, I've been dealing with them for 40 years. I was in the Military Police." We go on trading arguments about people like M. G. However, in turn I get Mr. T. to talk further about his role as a "psychologist" at the plant, that is, about some of the personnel problems of the employees. He tells many stories about trouble he has had and how he has helped his workers; and about a few failures who really had troubles and whom he has had to fire. . . .

My work centers on individualizing M. G. (Mr. T. constantly refers to him as "those guys") and separating M. from his two friends that worked with him. I also try to show Mr. T. how disappointed I am in myself because I am failing M. G.

Mr. T. slows down some by talking in terms of M., at the same time he bawls me out (in a fatherly kind of way) for protecting M. by assuming responsibility for him. Towards the end we began talking about Mr. T.'s success cases, those who are borderline cases, those that respond and behave differently. Those that give Mr. T. trouble are those who provide much satisfaction to him because "they begin to act like men."

Although crises in the neighborhood occurred frequently and called for continuous intervention, there were also brief, periodic lulls, of what we came to call *pre-crisis situations*. During these periods our workers had the opportunity of cultivating their relationships both within the neighborhood and with representatives of the community-at-large. The work with institutional representatives during the pre-crisis periods was valuable primarily because the worker was not then advocating any specific action for the poor. Within this neutral framework he could develop his service reputation among the school teachers, policemen, work supervisors, medical personnel, welfare workers, judges, and public officials in his area. Workers visited school officials to discuss school and neighborhood problems, contacted potential employers, and kept up a consistent effort to keep their institutional representatives receptive to the needs of the low-income group. Where such relationships were weak, institutional negotiations were constantly at the crisis level, bearing on whether Juan should be permitted to re-enter school, getting Maria's grades up to par, or getting José's job back. In the following, the worker forms an ongoing relationship with an important neighborhood person:

Mrs. Gonzales is a young school nurse who has operated in the neighborhood for several years. Frustrated by the inconsistency of the residents and the limited time and resources provided by her agency, she tended to reject those who did not immediately respond to treatment plans and follow-up care. Following a casual meeting in the waiting room of the local charity hospital, the worker and school nurse were able to discuss mutual problems with particular families in the neighborhood. Worker used this opportunity to introduce the nurse to his contacts among hospital personnel. Knowing the day of the week that the school nurse is at the hospital, the worker drops by and drinks coffee with her. Most of the conversation is about appropriate goals for particular individuals and how medical problems are related to other social problems. Through such experiences the nurse has learned the value of limited goals and has felt freer to engage herself with the troublesome families of the neighborhood.

NEIGHBORHOOD ORGANIZATION

A further focus for staff work was to help establish vehicles through which the poor could take collective action on their problems. Such organizations might not initially, or perhaps even eventually, culminate in militant social action; but they would provide a medium for developing the skills with which the poor could negotiate with the various sectors of the larger community. These groups provided experience in collective action as they brought together the various subgroupings within the neighborhood.

This aspect of our work was designed to attack one of the major handicaps of the poor, namely, their lack of participation in formal organizations and community activity. Without such participation their interests are either completely ignored, or else they are represented by groups that serve them inadequately. And, since the poor generally do not understand bureaucratic behavior, they are tempted to perceive the institutions of the larger community as conspiring against their interests. These attitudes of distrust and suspicion, however well-founded, have served to isolate our families and discourage them from taking advantage of the social benefits of education, medical care, and consumer information. The feelings also spill over into self-hate, producing recriminations toward each other and toward the most disadvantaged people in their own neighborhoods.

The workers' moves toward neighborhood organization began with their first efforts to involve themselves in neighborhood life and learn its patterns—who was related to whom, which families had the most positive or negative influences, which group perspectives generated which individual acts, and which people were most approved or disapproved of by the various neighborhood groups. In the process the worker established himself (again, like the early wardheeler) as a person to be trusted; he usually became a part of several peer groups, extended families, and "religious" families (compadre systems). From his growing familiarity with these systems and other social, civic, and church associations, he would fashion his first steps in building a local, neighborhood organization. The major strategy was to combine the various family types— the "mobiles," the "poor-but-honest," and the "troublemakers," or hard-core poor. To insure further cross-representativeness within the neighborhood, Wesley workers tried to involve those family members who had communication links to other families and individuals by ties of blood and friendship.

The effort to strengthen and make explicit the solidarity and identity that could bind the neighborhood together was not easy: the mobiles tended to dominate the organization, use it for their own purposes, and discourage the "troublemakers" from joining; the stable working-class members came to meetings out of a sense of personal loyalty to a neighbor or to the worker; and the worker himself, in his anxiety to succeed, often rejected the hard-core group. What was saddest and most ironic, however, was the sight of hard-core family members discouraging other hard-core members from becoming part of the neighborhood organization:

One neighborhood meeting ends on the note of engaging the older ex-gang boys as group leaders for the neighborhood's third and fourth graders. Two of the possible candidates are mentioned by name. The older sister of Tony J. is at the meeting. As the meeting is adjourned the group drinks coffee together. Then the mother of nine illegitimate children, including three seductive daughters, mutters in a loud voice about how she wouldn't trust Tony J. to walk her dog, because he and his friends raped her oldest daughter 2 years ago. This was peppered with a string of curse words. Tony J.'s sister replies, charging both the girl and her mother with being a bunch of 50-cent prostitutes. Worker separates the two almost immediately, but he is unable to calm either one. As a result both women don't attend further meetings and insist that they will not rejoin the organization until the worker guarantees the other one will not be there.

Nevertheless, the task of making the neighborhood organization representative of the area rather than an expanded peer group of selected individuals had to be faced. The worker's principle concern was to mediate the legitimate interests and social problems of those most unable to represent themselves. Often, the worker had to become closely involved in an extremely difficult family situation, while at the same time considering the larger strategy of helping the family become a part of neighborhood organizational life. Many frustrations had to be overcome before the family was ready to join with others to work on neighborhood issues:

I received a phone call from Rose, the eighteen-year-old wife of a twenty-year-old ex-convict. Rose is an older daughter from a multiproblem, third-generation welfare family. I have been trying to encourage members of this family to go to the neighborhood organization for weeks.

Rose, with deep anger and force, tells me of the many abuses her husband, Tomás, has put her through lately. The discussion turns to the precipitating crisis, since I know these fights and "picking" behavior are common between Rose and Tomás.

Rose reveals that she called because Tomás's constant yelling and complaints are driving her nuts. It all started 2 days ago when she lent her family 5 dollars from Tomás's small pay check. This leads Rose to talk about leaving Tomás and living with an aunt. This idea is quickly dismissed when I asked her if this is the same aunt who is on dope and who wants Rose to be a prostitute. Rose concludes this by saying: "I don't want to end up with any animal getting on top of me." Then she adds: "Besides, I'll just get over to her house and think." I responded: "You'll just think of Tomás?" She replied "Yes." At that point Rose began to cry softly. "You want to do right, but then you do things that get you into trouble." I asked, "Tomás doesn't understand what really is going on, does he?" She said, "No." "And the big thing he is missing?" I probed further with: "What is it he really doesn't understand?" She answered: "About those kids. My little brothers and sisters. They're the ones I'm trying to help. Not my mother, not my sister. They shouldn't have to suffer because there's not 5 dollars to give them. But no, Tomás just bitches and bitches because there's no money left for him to go to work, so he has to walk and he wouldn't have a lunch." I responded: "So you're on the spot right now because you want to help your people and Tomás acts like you shouldn't do that, but yet it's something you feel you have to do."

The conversation turns to sharing Rose's "side of the story" with Tomás when he gets home from work. Rose's anger has drained itself out by this time and she says the main thing right now is that Tomás should cut out his bitching.

Several hours later Tomás, Rose, and the worker meet. Tomás ventilates his anger and frustration with Rose because she is always goofing off and giving more attention to her family than to him. After 15 minutes of explanation Rose admits Tomás is right about the stack of dirty clothes on the crib and halfway expresses her willingness to wash them.

I quickly supported this, and she promises to do them the next day. At that point both of them admit how boring it is to live in two small rooms and always be scraping along on pennies and nickels. I mention the benefits of getting out as a family and having fun together. I go on and talk about the dance that the neighborhood organization is giving Saturday night. I invite them to be chaperons at the dance.

Tomás and Rose came to the dance and I engaged them in conversation with another young couple who point out the benefits and fun of belonging to the neighborhood group.

As issues arose at the meetings, the neighborhood organization gave the poor a medium in which to express their sense of futility and powerlessness and to try on the contrasting feeling of mastery and control:

After considerable discussion of a frustrating episode about addicts who are stealing the neighborhood blind, the ex-treasurer of the neighborhood organization remarks: "I thought this was why we have meetings like this—to do something about things we are afraid to do alone." There are agreeing comments and glances. I picked up, saying: "There are several things you can do, depending on what you want to do." I outlined some possible courses of group action, told them about the special department of the police that handled drug addicts. . . .

The organization also served to distribute information about the neighborhood and about bureaucratic behavior that they found alarming. In a recent experience, city inspectors checked neighborhood houses—in response to the neighborhood organization's request—to determine whether safety codes were being followed. The red tag left by the inspector indicated that he would be along to check a particular feature, as for example the electrical system. This was interpreted by some residents to mean that the house would be condemned and they would be forced to move. Members of the organization picked up this rumor and, with the worker's help, interpreted to the neighbors the actual significance of the red tag.

INSTITUTIONAL CHANGE AND
COMMUNITY IMPACT

All of the activities described above called for continuous community involvement and ongoing work with institutional representatives—school teachers, principals, police officers, welfare workers, and others. Institutional change actually began in the pre-crisis and crisis situations. The function of mediation thus further implied that such changes would multiply if the low-echelon practitioners most directly involved with the families were given more discretionary power as they moved about the community.

We found that the settlement could not operate from an isolated position within its own neighborhood, for the neighborhood itself was linked to the general community in many ways. By the very nature of its organizational patterns the settlement was tied to the community through its board of directors, advisory committees, volunteer groupings, and other vehicles through which a wide range of citizenry identified with the services of the neighborhood agency. In our work, for example, an advisory committee composed of representatives from various community sectors helped us obtain jobs that would otherwise have been unavailable, and they provided support when the neighborhood people addressed the problem of the slum landlords.

There also were a number of existing community groups—civic clubs, church groups, professional organizations, and social clubs—in which staff members involved themselves as participants. One such group was interested in the public image of Mexican-Americans, as projected in the communications media. Many Mexican-American leaders were involved in this work, and they have been instrumental in helping our workers develop a wide array of community contacts. San Antonio is fairly pluralistic, and such group activity created linkages with a range of organizations and subgroups. Such

ties became highly relevant for issues that were of crucial
concern to neighborhood groups.

As these issues were raised—by neighborhood organizations,
individuals, or groups outside the neighborhood but concerned about it—our mediating stance was not one of attacking for the sake of attacking but of raising the issues to a level
where dialogue and negotiation could proceed. Some of these
issues were highly controversial; others were not. The problems ranged over a wide spectrum: organizing a delinquency-
prevention program, sponsoring a new service, taking action
on neighborhood improvements such as street lights, housing,
and street repair, and organizing a cleanup campaign or a
block party. The experience with local issues often stimulated
interest in wider ones, such as voter registration, slum clear-
ance, minimum-wage laws, and other social legislation.

As workers involved themselves in the community, they
came face to face with the polarizations of power among the
various community groups. This frequently took the form of
struggles for control rather than attempts to solve problems.
Furthermore, as the settlement organized the poor it found
that their new power was interpreted in the context of traditional power alignments; the question was repeatedly raised
as to which side we were on. We found that this polarization
process created states of risk for the agency; we came to
classify these risks as "high," "low," or "medium." The high-
risk issues were those that threatened the very support and
resources of the agency itself, as when we came to grips with
problems in the school system and the possibility was raised
that our funds might be cut. In this situation it was necessary
to lean heavily on the agency's moral and ideological commitments: when board members raised the issue of staff being
used by certain political elements, the director reminded them
of Jesus's involvement with all kinds of people, even publicans
and prostitutes. Ultimately the line was held, and the agency
was able to effect marked changes in some school regulations

and in the working relationship between the agency and the school.

A low-risk issue was one in which the agency's status could not easily be affected, as when the staff raised questions about the functioning of a local poverty program that had become as rigid and bureaucratic as any traditional welfare or educational setting. In this case no one connected with the program had the power to affect Wesley, and negotiations were considerably less precarious as the work proceeded on the crucial issues.

An example of a medium-risk issue emerged from the concern of a neighborhood organization about enforcement of the housing code and the future of an urban renewal area. In this situation the agency courted little danger from the landlords, who were connected with the political segment that could not hurt the agency; but there were elements of risk in our negotiations with the city administration. In the process our role was fortified by joint meetings between neighborhood people, city councilmen, and housing inspectors, as well as by the clear evidence that the neighborhood was willing and able to do something about its problems.

IMPLICATIONS FOR AGENCY STRUCTURE

The mediating function described here requires a generalist and flexible organization that is structured to seek out the bottom layer of the lower class, establish relationships with these families, and work with their most difficult problems. The workers' dual focus on both community and client puts them into different power relationships with their employing agency; simple and direct lines of authority are not very appropriate; non-bureaucratic forms of administration have to be created. The outreaching nature of the workers' activities involves them with both those who have a direct voice in agency policy and the clients for whom the workers literally create eligibility as they go along. The open-endedness of the service calls for a continuous process of decision-making in the field on questions of eligibility and direction. Furthermore, the ongoing evaluation of worker expertise and efficiency is based on a quick succession of events in the field. It is hard for administration and supervision to keep itself informed and make necessary judgments unless there is a very open and direct system of communications within the agency. Such requirements preclude the traditional, hierarchical lines of accountability.

Several types of administrative strategy were developed at Wesley to meet these requirements. Most important among these was the flexibility of authority roles among staff members with specific functional tasks. Even the agency's Director was responsible in some of his program roles to an area co-ordinator or the administrator of a service—as, for example, the Neighborhood Youth Corps. Another important strategy was to maintain a process of open and direct staff confrontation on all important administrative rules and decisions.

There also was a deliberate attempt to recruit a staff with a variety of work-styles and professional allegiances. Our assortment of personnel could be characterized as including representatives of a variety of orientations: clinical, political, religious, welfare-supportive, indigenous lower class, matronly, educational, student-radical, and student-square. A further ecumenism, as well as some spirited engagements on certain moral issues, was created by our effort to build in a humanist environment made up of staff members with Catholic, Jewish, and a variety of Protestant orientations. Finally, it was important to involve clerical and maintenance staff as closely as possible in decisions dealing with agency program and policy. Elliot Studt has discussed a similar arrangement in her concept of the "staff-work group" (10).

With such a wide assortment of backgrounds, interests, approaches, and assignments the Director found it necessary to use a number of *ad hoc* group approaches to facilitate communication and the flow of decision-making. When there was a serious split between the VISTA group and the regular staff, a series of meetings between the volunteers and the administration restored the balance; a similar mode of confrontation has been used from time to time since then. Temporary groupings have been created with other staff clusters as these have become necessary.

CONCLUSION

In summary, the impact of the hard-core poor on the social resources of a low-income neighborhood has forced us at the Wesley Community Centers to address ourselves to the needs of the most deprived families as well as to the formation of vigorous neighborhood organizations composed of a wide range of family types. Since these needs have been neglected for decades, we think of what we are doing at Wesley as a revolutionary process—a conception shared to some extent by the more able neighborhood residents and those in the larger community whose ignorance and neglect of these problems we are constantly pointing out.

We suggest that these priorities are basic to the function of any settlement house working in a slum neighborhood. We maintain that the traditional settlement groups should take a lower priority or should be conceptualized as stepping stones to the building of neighborhood organizations. The so-called "character-building" activities can be important as a technique in what we have come to call "career deflection," where people from the different family types can combine to create an influence toward responsible and legitimate activity. One of our strongest neighborhood organizations grew out of our Golden Gloves boxing team; it is staffed almost entirely by volunteers and includes ex-gang boys and squares, pre-adolescents and young married adults, school dropouts and steady job holders. This organization crosses many boundaries and is now in the process of raising funds not only for its own activities but for those of the agency as well.

We have projected here a methodology that we have termed *mediation;* and we would suggest that this applies as well to the overall role of the social worker. Siporin (9) has called this the "community role," as distinct from various "situational roles"; our concept is similar also to Schwartz's (8) description of the function of the social worker. In our conception, the social worker stands between his individual client or group and other individuals and groups in an effort to create or restore "reciprocity" among the various actors, with reciprocity defined as mutual action, exchange, or support.

Further study is needed of the various roles required of the worker as he carries out the agency's mediating function. For example, the movement toward reciprocity cannot assume a relationship of equality between the client and his systems; one of the first mediating tasks may then be to find a role designed to equalize the relationships involved. For this reason we have described certain "situational roles" that have tended to be partisan to the poor and we have entertained similar considerations with regard to "advocacy" and "actionist" roles (5) on certain community issues. We have also explored the "double agent" role, in the sense that this puts the worker into close communication with both sides of an important community issue and brings him knowledge and insight into the perspectives and operational strategies of both sides. Still another role seems to be that of "catalyst," in which certain experiences are created that will serve to initiate a process of problem-solving by the residents. And the worker may act as "organizer" when it is necessary to maintain the pace of collective functioning at the neighborhood level.

All of these roles may be necessary to set the framework of mediation between equals, and they call attention to the importance of social change and modification of certain institutional behaviors. At the same time, however, other roles— "group leader," "compadre," "family counselor," and more— imply influence and control with regard to client behavior. Here the worker serves as a professional technician trying to enable the poor to determine and work out alternative courses of action. Thus, the mediator stands at the point of *conflict* (a lack of reciprocal relations) and can be an agent both of client control and of social change; in fact, to be effective he usually *must* be both.*

This range of roles is now being studied, and we are looking forward to providing a more detailed description of the worker behaviors required to carry out the mediating function. Using such chronological accounts of practice and devices as the "Problem-Solving Interaction Sequences," ** we are trying to develop some typologies that will be useful to the field. We hope in this way to develop a deeper understanding of, and a broader agency interest in, the strategies that will strengthen the work of the settlement with a population in great need of its help.

REFERENCES

1. Edward Banfield and James Q. Wilson, *City Politics* (Cambridge, Mass.: Harvard University Press, 1963).
2. Madeline Engle, "A Reconceptualization of Urban Lower Class Subcultures," Juvenile Correction Project, Department of Sociology and Anthropology, Fordham University (January 1966), mimeographed.
3. Buford E. Farris and William M. Hale, "Responsible Ward Healers: Neighborhood Workers as Mediators," paper presented at the National Conference on Social Welfare, Chicago,

* For a fuller description of the implications of this point, see: White, Farris, and Brymer (11).
** The P.S.I.S. is the nexus of several lines of behavior by several different persons, each operating according to a particular role set, in the context of his past relationships.

Illinois, May 1966, and revised for the Symposium of the Texas State Council of NASW (November 1966), mimeographed.

4. Herbert Gans, *The Urban Villagers* (New York: The Free Press, 1962).

5. Charles F. Grosser, "Community Development Programs Serving the Urban Poor," *Social Work*, Vol. 10, No. 3 (July 1965), pp. 15–21.

6. S. M. Miller, "The American Lower Class: A Typological Approach," *Social Research*, Vol. 31, No. 1 (Spring 1964), pp. 1–22.

7. Lorene M. Pacey (ed.), *Readings in the Development of Settlement Work* (New York: Association Press, 1950).

8. William Schwartz, "The Social Worker in the Group," *The Social Welfare Forum, 1961* (New York: Columbia University Press, 1961), pp. 146–77.

9. Max Siporin, "Private Practice of Social Work: Functional Roles and Social Control," *Social Work*, Vol. 6, No. 2 (April 1961), pp. 52–60.

10. Elliot Studt, "Fields of Social Work Practice: Organizing our Resources for More Effective Practice," *Social Work*, Vol. 10, No. 4 (October 1965), pp. 156–65.

11. Orion White, Buford E. Farris, and Richard Brymer, "Bureaucracy, Efficiency, Rationality, and Social Change" (Spring 1967), mimeographed.

[5: THE HOSPITAL]

The Social Worker as Mediator
on a Hospital Ward

HAROLD LIPTON and
SIDNEY MALTER

A CONSIDERABLE BODY of literature has been developed on the "therapeutic milieu" or "therapeutic community" as a treatment modality in the psychiatric hospital (4, 6, 14). The concept has been defined as ". . . *a scientific manipulation of the environment aimed at producing changes in the personality of the patient*" (4, p. 5). The findings derived from the pioneering studies on the significance of interacting social systems and ward culture in the mental hospital field (2, 9, 12) are gradually being applied to the medical institution, and some beginnings are being made in practice in a few hospitals. Very little has been written, however, about the actual problems of practice. In this chapter we shall describe one such beginning, with particular reference to the role of the social group worker engaged in introducing the concept and the reality of the "therapeutic community" on a hospital ward for paraplegic patients. The authors will examine some of the practice issues, problems, and skills required in working in a setting in which the atmosphere is often charged with conflict as patients and staff members attempt to perform their respective roles. The conflict may find expression around such matters as the quality of the food, the level of medical and nursing care, or other aspects of the daily living situation in the institution.

We are indebted to Weiner for exploring the implications
of the basic idea that the social worker in the medical-hospital
setting can assume the task of working with the hospital, the
administrative staff, the ward, and the patient; he views all of
these systems as appropriate subjects for his professional interventions:

It is suggested that the social worker in a hospital work to affect
the values and norms of behavior of both staff and patients through
the use of the group method. The thesis is developed that a hospital as a total entity, as well as each ward, seriously affects the
patient's attitude toward illness, his self-image, and discharge plans.
This occurs through interactions of patients with each other and
with staff in the normal course of daily living. The objective is to
illuminate this process and subject it to positive social change
[13, p. 58].

There have been many applications of the group work
method in the medical institution, going under a variety of
names and intended to meet different needs. The names given
to such programs have ranged from group activities to group
psychotherapy, and they have been utilized in work with the
aged, with children, with specific diagnostic categories, and
with the relatives of patients (5). The work of Abramson,
Kutner, and their associates at the Albert Einstein College of
Medicine of Yeshiva University is particularly relevant, since
it concerns the application of the therapeutic-community approach in a general hospital as an especially functional rehabilitation service. They emphasize the role of the group worker
in that context, and point out that the aims of the therapeutic
community in rehabilitative medicine are: (a) to involve
patients and staff in a general therapeutic milieu; (b) to develop the patient's social skills by deliberately creating opportunities for social interaction; (c) to preserve the patient's
ties with family and community; and (d) to create a treatment
plan consistent with the patient's past and his anticipated post-
hospital role (1, 7).

Medical social workers have traditionally concerned themselves with the social and emotional impediments to patient rehabilitation and with the patient's reintegration into community living. They have used counseling methods and direct manipulation or mediation of the familial or community environment to make hospital discharge possible. If the medical social worker is now to be concerned with the hospital milieu as well, because of its profound influence on the patient's self-concept and treatment course, then it becomes appropriate to exercise a similar mediating function with respect to the social forces impinging on the patient within the institution. In the complex nature of hospital structure, these forces derive from the interactions of the several layers of staff hierarchy with one another and with the patient. As a mediator the social worker helps the patient enter into the role of the patient and utilize the medical services provided, and he helps the staff perform their therapeutic roles vis-à-vis the patient.

Accepting this rationale for utilizing the therapeutic-community approach, we will proceed from theory to practice and present some of the issues that emerge when the group worker is newly introduced to the medical setting and endeavors to initiate a program that involves not only the patient population but also the medical and para-medical staff.

THE AGENCY SYSTEM

The Bronx Veterans Administration Hospital, as a center for the treatment of spinal cord injuries, has two wards within the Physical Medicine and Rehabilitation Service, with a total of ninety-six beds for the treatment of paraplegics and quadriplegics. These are patients who have suffered lesions to the spinal cord, resulting in paralysis or weakness of the legs, or paralysis of the legs and upper extremities. The extent of the disability will depend upon the level on the spinal cord at which the lesion has occurred. Paraplegics have paralysis of

the legs and quadriplegics have paralysis of arms and legs.*
Often these patients are not only unable to walk, but they also
suffer from loss of sensation, bladder and bowel control, and
sex function. In addition, they are subject to recurring medical
problems such as urinary infections and bed sores (decubitus
ulcers). The more seriously stricken quadriplegics have to be
dressed, fed, washed, and tended in every respect, since they
literally cannot lift a finger to help themselves. Despite such
massive disability, many paraplegics and even some quadriplegics have considerable rehabilitation potential and can be
helped to leave the hospital and lead productive lives in the
community once they have learned how to live in a wheelchair. Still, they must continue to be dependent upon others
for many of the activities of daily living that "whole" people
take for granted. They suffer the constant fear of humiliation
because of their lack of bladder and bowel control, and they
suffer the ultimate insult to a young man's ego—the loss of sex
function (7). Feeling themselves to be so massively deprived,
hurt, and dependent, it is not surprising that they become
depressed and withdrawn, drink too much at times, succumb
utterly to whatever satisfactions they can derive from their
dependence on the hospital culture, and act-out in other ways
that are unacceptable to most of the hospital personnel.

The paraplegic population of the hospital tends to fall into
three main categories: (a) the newly injured, who require
active medical treatment and rehabilitation training; (b) the
successfully rehabilitated, who return to the hospital on occasion for minor treatment; and (c) the long-term chronic
patient who has not been able to leave the hospital because of
social, psychological, or economic, rather than medical reasons. It is the latter group that has constituted a problem for
the staff—they use the sheltered hospital environment to receive continued custodial care. They frustrate any attempt to

---

* We will use "paraplegics" as the generic term, regardless of the extent of the disability.

secure their discharge by presenting needs that are consistent with the function of a domiciliary institution but inimical to the function of an acute medical-treatment facility.

If we consider that the emotional impact of the paraplegic disability and the regressive modes of behavior that it imposes must have an ego-damaging effect of serious proportions, then we can see that the paraplegic's condition in the hospital is not too different from that of the hospitalized psychiatric patient (3, p. 154; 8, p. 443). Both need help to negotiate the hospital system, and both need to develop the ego strength to leave the hospital and face the hazards of community living.

The paraplegic patient is very dependent on the nursing assistant for the most intimate personal care, and he is also dependent on the nurse for management of the daily routines of ward life. The staff's workload on the paraplegic section is very demanding, and at the same time the patient is often perceived as being surly and ungrateful. The medical staff, who are at the head of the hierarchy of treatment disciplines, are credited with providing excellent medical care. But the effect of this care is diminished by their cold, impersonal approach, and their inability to communicate appropriately with patients. Nursing assistants and nurses have, in fact, resisted assignments to these wards because they have felt abused by the patient and unappreciated, while the patients have complained of real or fancied instances of neglect. The long-term chronic patients, whose personal pathologies complicate their adjustment within the hospital culture as well as outside, tend to transmit their pessimism and dissatisfaction to the newer patients—patients who need instead to be encouraged by the example of persons who have been successfully rehabilitated. As a result the atmosphere is conducive to all manner of interpersonal difficulties and disturbances in patient-staff relationships that detract from proper therapy and discharge-oriented goals.

The clash of patients and environment in our hospital came

to a head when the patients sent a letter of complaint to the authorities in Washington, alleging instances of inadequate care. This brought about the appointment of a social-scientist consultant to study the "structure and function" of the Spinal Cord Injury Section and examine the communications gap between patients and members of staff. The ensuing investigation explored patient grievances, staff problems, and the patient-staff system (7). The recommendations that followed from the study could be grouped into two areas:

1. There should be administrative rearrangements to eliminate specific grievances, such as a shortage of nursing assistants.

2. A program of improved psychosocial therapy should be instituted to overcome dependent, lethargic, and stagnant patient attitudes.

It was recommended that a social worker experienced with groups, or a group-trained psychologist, be employed to implement the psychosocial program. This, it was hoped, would provide a forum for patients to work on matters affecting their daily lives in the hospital, encouraging them to take responsibility for some activities currently being managed by staff and opening avenues of communication between patients and staff. As patients become organized into groups in order to work on common tasks, as they experience themselves being able to solve problems and take actions in their own behalf, and as they learn that they can have a positive influence on their own milieu, it is expected that there can also be significant development in ego strength and a new capacity to face life more independently.

And so, with the foregoing goals and expectations, the group worker entered the scene. It was agreed that initially he would form patient groups in order to help them express their dissatisfactions and channel their energies toward more constructive use of self and toward resolution of their difficulties. It was hoped that problem areas could be identified and resolved at a ward level, with a reduction of patient-staff animosities.

Translated into functional terms, the worker would consider both the patient subsystem and the staff subsystem as objects of his concern. Because the common ground between patient need and hospital service had become obscure, the worker would have to try to redefine these areas of concensus, and he would have to help both components of the total hospital system if positive social change were to occur.

The worker's theoretical approach was based upon William Schwartz' unique conceptual framework of the function of the professional. Schwartz states:

. . . the general assignment for the social work profession is to mediate the process through which the individual and his society reach out for each other through a mutual need for self-fulfillment. This presupposes a relationship between the individual and his nurturing group which we would describe as "symbiotic"—each needing the other for its own life and growth, and each reaching out to the other with all the strength it can command at a given moment. The social worker's field of intervention lies at the point where two forces meet: the individual's impetus toward health, growth, and belonging; and the organized efforts of society to integrate its parts into a productive and dynamic whole [11, p. 154].

THE WORK WITH PATIENTS

The job of the group worker began by his "tuning-in" on the reactions there would be to his presence on the ward. As can be imagined, he could anticipate the suspiciousness of the patients, the hostility of some elements of staff, and the inertia that is characteristic of any complex bureaucratic organization. The key beginning issue was how to establish himself and gain acceptance for the mediating function he had to exercise between patient groups and staff. By encouraging patients to become rebels and act in their own behalf he was in danger of threatening the sacred medical-nursing power structure. There were staff members who felt criticized and feared loss of control. And, on the other side, while many patients were eager to try to change the atmosphere on the ward, there were others who resisted "making waves," or being perceived as rebels.

The worker was also concerned with how the patients' physical disabilities would affect him—the worker—emotionally. Would they make him very uncomfortable? The worker realized that if he felt some discomfort, he would somehow have to cover up his feelings and eventually work them out before he could be helpful to the patients. He looked for patients' fears about trusting him with their complaints—fears that he would try to change them somehow—and he hoped that they would become interested in and curious about his function on the ward. The following contact occurred in one of the rooms on the worker's second day at the hospital. It was rather typical of the early contacts that took place:

. . . I introduced myself to the several patients in the room. J. asked me to sit down and talk. I sat on the edge of his bed and he sat in his wheelchair. I said I was a social worker who was assigned to the ward and I was there to help. J. said, "So you are here to help? Maybe you can help with a tip on a horse at Yonkers?" I said, laughing, "The last time I went to the races I lost 40 dollars." Others in the room laughed. J. said he could see I could not help with that. He then said, "You *can* help me. See that wire on the table—bring it over here." I got it and he showed me how to manipulate it so that the bottom loops fit on his fingers and the top loop held a cigar. I lit it for him. E., a patient in the next bed, said, "So, will you be here to give us a crying towel or to give us financial aid?" I said, "Neither." He said, "The social workers here help with stuff outside of the hospital but none of them seem to help with anything inside of the hospital." I said, "I know that. And the hospital realized that some kind of help is needed inside as well as outside of the hospital. So they hired me to see if I could help." E. asked, "What can you help with?" I said, "I'm not sure

. . . I'll need your help with that—but maybe I could help get you something, or help if you have some complaints about the service here." J. said one has to be careful about making complaints because of "reprisals." E. said, "Yes, you know when you are dependent on somebody and you make a complaint against him then he could take it out on you." I said, "I know. Sometimes it could be scary or risky if one complains." J. said again, "Yeah, you got to watch out for reprisals." Another patient said there was no sense in complaining. I asked if it felt hopeless to complain. E. asked, "What about the PVA? * We used to be able to complain to them." "I'm not coming here to change the PVA or change the ward. I'm here to try to help. However, one problem with the PVA is that it only meets once a month and if you have a complaint you might have to wait a month or so for something to happen. Maybe I could help speed things up a little." There was a silence. I said, "Of course it will take a while before you trust me." J. said, "It's not that we don't trust you—but if complaints are made, pretty soon they will want to know names—and then reprisals." I said, "If there are complaints that you want kept in confidence, I won't say anything."

Among the themes that appeared in this contact were early testing on the part of the patients, fears that the worker would try to change them, and lack of confidence in using the worker in making complaints. The fear of "reprisals" seemed to run deep, and the worker might have attempted to work more on spelling out the meaning of these reprisals. The worker wasted no time however, in beginning to define his function, and this seemed to be helpful in terms of the patients beginning to trust him and use his help.

The First Patient Ward Meeting. After many individual contacts with the worker on the ward the patients began to ask when group meetings would begin. A meeting was arranged during the worker's second week at the hospital. He

* Eastern Paralyzed Veterans Association, an organization of paraplegic veterans whose representatives meet regularly with hospital administrative staff.

realized that most patients still did not understand his function and that they did not trust him yet. He could anticipate
that the patients would try to get the worker "on their side"
rather than have him function as a mediator. These themes
would have to come out before the patients could begin to
use him to work on their complaints. Thirteen patients were
present at the first ward meeting:

I began the meeting by saying, "It might be helpful if I start out
by explaining why I am here. I have done this with many of you
individually but I think it may help to go over it again here. I
am here because there are lots of problems on the paraplegic wards
that have been brought to the attention of the hospital by the PVA
and by the patients themselves. A large part of my job is to try to
help with some of these problems." D. interrupted and said angrily, "The reason you are here is because of the pressure put on
the hospital by the PVA. The hospital did not hire you out of the
goodness of their hearts. So you were really hired by the hospital
in response to the pressure from the PVA." I said, "But I was hired
by the hospital." He did not respond. I said, "I think that behind
what D. is saying is a question that may be bothering most of the
patients—that is, Whose side will I be on—the patients or the
staff?" Some patients nodded. Others smiled. I said, "The answer is
neither." There were some curious looks on the faces of patients.
I continued, "Well, I think that if I am going to be helpful around
here I will need to be in good with the patients and also in good
with the staff." D. said, "Yes, like a mediator." I said, "Exactly."
Nobody challenged this position. Somebody asked, "What are you
going to help with?" I replied, "That largely depends upon what
the patients want help with." B. took it from there when he complained about the air-conditioner being broken for weeks in the
therapy room on the first floor. What followed was a gripe session
which included complaints about the air-conditioner, dirty hospital
grounds, rooms being too hot or too cold, a lack of volunteers on
the ward, a lack of male nursing aides, call lights not being answered, the switching of aides from the ward, and temporary aides
not giving proper care to paraplegics.

After this fast and furious outpouring there was a lull. I said, "Well, it seems that there are a couple of problems around here. What would you like to work on first?" I read the list and the patients wanted to work on the problems dealing with the nursing assistants. The patients felt that Mr. H., the nursing supervisor, was the one to talk to. I said, "Well, I could let him know about some of your aggravations—or else I could try to arrange a meeting for you to talk with him. What do you think?" Immediately the answer was, "We'll talk to him." Another patient said, "Yeah, let's get the answer right from the horse's mouth." R. said, "Sounds great—but will you be able to talk to him?" "Why not?" asked K. I said, "I heard that a lot of the patients worry about getting in trouble for making complaints." K. said, "That's true." Someone agreed with K. I asked, "What do you think would happen if complaints are made?" Some fear of retaliation in the form of neglect was expressed, but the patients decided to proceed in setting up a meeting.

As expected, the worker was being tested here about "what side" he was on. The worker's ability to reach for this concern and his directness about his function seemed to speed up the process of helping patients to work on their complaints. The men began to work, at first on the "safer" issues, and then they focused on an important one—the shortage of nursing assistants. The worker was not satisfied with the expressed opinion of the patients that they were ready to tackle this problem. He knew that there was more ambivalence present than was being expressed. He reached for the negatives (the fears), and thereby made the group work more full—more real. The patients, beginning to feel some strength as a collective force, decided to go on with their work of confronting a ward authority with their shared problem.

It took more than a few contacts with patients before they really began to develop confidence in the worker. The patients tested him in many ways. It was necessary to interpret the mediating function again and again. An individual contact with a patient may be helpful in illustrating how the worker further explained his job. The following occurred 2 days after the first patient meeting:

A patient approached the worker on the ward and said, "You're in with the guys—but the only worry is that if you hang around with the staff too much you will get 'tainted' by them." I asked if he meant that I will side with staff in case of an argument between patients and staff. He said, "Yes." I said that I used to worry about that. But my experience had been that when in the middle between tenants and landlords I was able to help the tenants more when I was also helpful to the landlord. I gave an example. I said, "Suppose a tenant asked me to get a little something from the landlord —say a paint job. Now if I was helpful to the landlord he might say OK. But if I was not helpful or was nasty to the landlord he might very well tell me and the tenant to go to hell." D. laughed. I said that although I had not worked in a hospital before, the same thing might apply. D. said, "I think I get it." I said, "I think it is a hard thing to really get and I think it will be a matter of concern to patients for a long time—until they get to trust me some more." Before D. left I said that I could talk this over with the guys at meetings again.

The above excerpt illustrates the worker trying to use a frame of reference familiar to the life of the patient (tenant-landlord work) when explaining the mediating function. As the patient still did not trust the viability of that function completely, the worker did not attempt to solve the issue on the spot; he held out for more work on the subject at a later time.

THE WORK WITH STAFF

At the same time as the worker did his best to interpret his role to the patients he simultaneously began the same process with the staff. At a meeting with the ward staff (doctor, case-worker, nurses, and aides) he mentioned that his job was to try to be helpful to both patients and staff. As he listened it seemed clear that the staff's only expectation of him was that he begin work with a group of patients in order to motivate them to leave the hospital. While this could be viewed as the ultimate goal of the rehabilitation process, it could not be the worker's sole function, and it was certainly not his immediate task in dealing with suspicious patients. The worker had to make it clear that he was not the "discharge agent" for the hospital:

. . . I said, "You know, I'm not a magician. I'm sure that I will be able to help some patients leave the hospital, but I have no easy solutions. And if a patient really wants to stay here and if he really has no means of leaving, then I certainly can't 'motivate' him to want to leave. However, once the doctor decides, and tells a patient that he will be discharged, I may be able to help him to live with that reality. But remember, I have no authority to discharge anybody. . . ."

In this example the worker indicated that he had no ready answer for the staff's problem about discharging patients. While he showed appropriate assertiveness in explaining what he could not be immediately expected to do, he missed an opportunity to explain what he *was* there for. (He made the mistake of assuming that staff already knew.) This lack of explanation and lack of reaching for the staff's concerns about the worker's function made for considerable lack of trust and much testing of the worker by ward staff members.

When it seemed that a meeting between a ward nurse and the patient group would be mutually beneficial, the worker approached the nurse. The worker felt it would help if he would explain to the nurse what issues and feelings the patients might present to her. He attempted to reach for her self-interest in meeting with patients, and tried to be sensitive to any resistances she offered vis-à-vis the proposed confrontation:

. . . I mentioned that the patients might invite her to a meeting to talk over various nursing matters. She said she didn't see the need for such meetings—that she should be given a chance to do her job. I said, "I have the feeling that you feel I am criticizing you for not doing a good job." She listened. I said, "I'm not here to criticize anybody. I'm sure that no matter how good a job you do the patients will have some complaints." Miss B. said, "I'm afraid that the patients' meetings may snowball." I asked her what she meant. She said, "After last week's patient meeting one of the paraplegics was yelling in the hall, 'Now we don't have to be afraid no more—now we have something to say.'" I laughed and said, "Miss B., you must be worried about a revolution." She said, "Yes, and I feel that the patients don't run this place and should not." I said, "Of course not. But how about their having a little something to say about what happens to them around here?"

She did not answer. I said, "Miss B., I know you don't trust me yet, but I'm really not here to create a revolution. I'd really like to help and I think that if patients and staff talk over their differences it might be helpful to all concerned. Let me give you some examples. If patients could express some of their aggravations to you about nursing aides or poor equipment, and you could do something to help, I think the morale of the patients might be a little better and they might be a little easier to live with. Let's say a patient complains that he is left lying in bed in one position too long. If the patient brings this to your attention and you could correct the situation, then the patient's skin is healthier and he could get out of here faster. . . ." Miss B. said, "The patients can always complain to me individually." I said, "If they can that's fine. But the fact is that many are afraid to do this for one reason or another and they need the group to enable them to speak up."

Miss B. said, "Well, I don't know." I said, "There's no question about it. This type of involvement means a lot of work for you and I know you are very busy. Also it may be hard for you to meet with patients who are angry, but I really feel that if you did, it would be to your advantage as well as theirs. Maybe you would like to think about it some more. I'll be glad to talk about it again with you anytime. . . ."

This encounter with the nurse shows that she felt very threatened by the prospect of patient meetings and her involvement in that process. It also reveals that the worker was not sufficiently sensitive to her anxiety about meeting with the patients. The worker was overidentified with the patients' wish to have the confrontation and thereby placed a demand on the nurse that was too great for her to handle at the time; consequently, a battle of wills was set up between the nurse and the social worker. This did not enhance the working relationship between them, and it did not help in the nurse-patient relationship.

THE PROBLEMS OF CONFRONTATION

There are many demands that the worker must meet and tasks he must perform if he is to help the parties engaging in confrontations of various kinds to get their work done. A number of them will be discussed below.

Preparing a Nurse to Meet with Patients. When the patients had problems that they wanted to present to an administrative nurse, she agreed to meet with them. The worker reached out to her in order to prepare her for the meeting. The following exchange took place in her office:

I met with Nurse A. this morning and tried to prepare her for the complaints and feelings she might expect today in her meeting with the ward patients. When I mentioned that a problem for the patients seemed to be the shifting around of nursing aides, she said she wished she could keep them on the ward. She said, "They can't wait until they get off the ward." I asked her why. She said, "Because of the heavy work load and the constant demands and complaints of the patients." She added, "Of course I would not tell that to the patients." I asked, "Why not?" She looked blank. I said, "I think it might be helpful to the patients if they knew why many aides don't want to work there. But I think that if you tell them the truth they will be more likely to trust you. . . ." I informed Miss A. that many of the patients were very angry about the way things were on the ward. I asked, "How will you feel if they express a lot of anger toward you at the meeting?" Miss A. assured me that this would not be a problem for her. . . .

In this example the worker's reaching out to the nurse was interpreted as a sign of concern for her feelings. The nurse was caught off guard by the worker's suggestion to "level" with the patients. (However, she used the worker's idea when she met with them, and it helped the communication to be real.) The nurse was not thrown by the complaints and anger that the patients expressed to her, partly because she had been prepared for it. This helped the nurse feel that the worker could be relied upon to assist her in interpersonal dealings with the patients.

Keeping the Affect Real. One of the worker's prime tasks in helping a passive group deal with a powerful authority figure is to work toward keeping the affect and the issues real. The group and the authority figure may have a tendency to "cool out" the anger because of the anxiety it evokes. They may feel impelled to avoid issues and tend toward "not making waves." The worker may have pressure on him to fall into the same trap—but he must not. His task is to bring out the conflicts, not to suppress them. For unless the difficult issues are faced there can be no mutual benefit in the face-to-face confrontation. The worker in this hospital had had some difficulties in handling this problem area, but he learned quickly that it did not help when he joined in the "conspiracy to avoid." The following is an example of the worker helping patients to face the issues as they prepared for a meeting with the Hospital Director:

The patients angrily went over the issues they wanted to present to the Hospital Director. They had no difficulty in expressing their feelings or in finding items to gripe about. I said, "Sounds like you guys are getting ready for a big battle tomorrow." B. said, "That's the way it feels to me." G. said, "We'll tell him." I said, "It's obvious that you are angry and that's the way you ought to sound tomorrow." The patients looked at me. I asked, "Do you know why I say that? Because if you don't sound angry your words will come unnatural and you will be hiding your real feelings. And if you do sound too cool—if you hide your anger—Dr. S. will probably think that things are going pretty well for you around here." Patient L. said that if a patient complained too much he would be put out on the street. I asked if this had ever happened. He said that it had several years ago. I said, "I met with Dr. S. yesterday and he assured me that there would be no retribution from him if patients complained. But if you're not sure about it suppose you face him with this issue at the start of the meeting." L. said he would do that and others thought it was a good idea. . . .

In the group meeting the patients seemed somewhat frightened by the worker's suggestion not to hide their feelings of anger when they met with the Hospital Director. On the other hand, they seemed somewhat assured by the worker's having anticipated their fears and his having already spoken to the Director about them. Having decided to express many of their real complaints and feelings of anger, the patients were able to sound a note of seriousness—of urgency—when they confronted the Director. The sense of urgency they expressed seemed to be a factor in the Director's taking remedial action.

Identifying with Both the Patient and the System. If the worker takes sides in a conflict encounter—if he advocates for either the client or the system—he becomes dysfunctional in the mediating role. He cannot then be useful as a third party or bridge between the client who is struggling to be the recipient of better service and the system that is striving to give better service. Thus, he interferes with, rather than enhances, the natural client-system symbiosis. Sometimes the worker may make the mistake of advocating for the patients. This happened at a meeting between patients and a supervisory nurse, and is illustrated below:

Both the patients and Miss D. seemed to avoid the topic in the first few moments. I suggested that it would be helpful if both sides put their cards on the table. B. then asked directly why the Junior Red Cross girls were not allowed on the ward. The answer was that Nursing Service must decide where the girls can be most useful and it was decided that they could be more useful on other wards. B. said he thought that the girls could be useful up here. Miss D. said angrily that she felt that the girls could be more useful elsewhere. There was silence. I asked why. Miss D. looked at

me with anger and did not answer. I said, "Miss D., I think that
it might be helpful if you gave some reasons so that everybody will
be able to understand better." She didn't answer. I said, "Miss. D.,
I think the fellows have some ideas that the drinking and socializ-
ing might have something to do with it." She said, icily, "Mr.
Lipton, I will not assign them to the ward." There was a loud
silence. I said, again putting my foot in my mouth, "Well that
settles that—except I guess the feelings of the patients are not
settled." Patient Y. said, "Yeah, we got left out again. . . ."

The remainder of the meeting was distinctly unproductive
and much of the blame for that could be attributed to the
worker. The prime problem that prevented him from exer-
cising his mediating function was his anger at the nurse's
apparent rigidity. When he could not discipline that anger he
sided with the patients and could not be sensitive to the
nurse's problems. Had he been functioning as a mediator he
would have suggested that the patients and the nurse move on
to other areas of mutual concern. (The worker apologized to
the nurse when he realized that he was perceived as being
both arrogant and overidentified with the patients.)

Bringing the Patient and the Staff System Together. As was
pointed out in the previous example, the role of the social
worker can have an important bearing on patient-staff confrontations. In the following illustration the worker was prepared to help both sides in a conflict situation. This occurred
when the patients heard that the doctor was going to transfer
six long-term patients to their ward:

The patients became so angry with the doctor that he seemed im-
mobilized for a moment. The worker yelled, "Calm down. With
everybody yelling at once, Dr. D. cannot answer anybody. Let's try
something else." The patients calmed down a little and the dialogue continued. A stalemate developed with neither side showing
any signs of budging from its position. The worker asked of the
doctor, "Could you transfer a few of the patients instead of all of
them?" He thought for a moment. The patients verbalized some
interest in this suggestion. He said, "No, I want to transfer all of

them." The frustrating battle then continued. The worker said, "Let's move on to the five items on the agenda. We can get back to this later." Both sides welcomed this plan and agreement was reached on each of the five issues. The worker said, "We're not doing so badly. We only have the one remaining problem." The doctor and the patients were unable to resolve their conflict. The deadlock remained. The worker said, "Maybe we can't do any more on this today. What's the next step—would you like to work on this again soon?" Neither the patients nor the doctor wanted to meet again on the issue. . . .

In this example the worker's intervention helped to calm the patients enough so that the doctor could continue working with them. The suggestion to transfer a few of the patients was an attempt to reach a compromise agreement but was acceptable only to the patients. However, it seemed worth risking. By the worker's action in moving the work to the five other problems, areas of mutual concern were addressed, and agreements were reached. When work on the one remaining problem seemed to be too difficult to handle, the worker helped to relieve each side of some of its frustration by tabling the issue.

The worker did not let the matter rest, since both parties were still upset. He discovered, by talking informally with the patients, that they were told by their nurse that she would resign if the transfer of long-term patients was effected. The worker then returned to the harried doctor early the next morning:

"You know in the meeting yesterday I could not understand the reason for the patients being so angry about the transfer." He said, "I don't know why they made such a big deal about it either." I said, "I think I found out why. Apparently the nurse is very upset about the transfer. She likes the idea of having active patients on her ward and feels that the patients you have in mind are those that can never be discharged. She said she would quit if the transfers are made, and this upset the patients on the ward." He said, "Oh, I wasn't aware of that." The doctor was quiet. I asked what he was thinking about. He said he still wanted to transfer patients but did not want to lose the nurse. I said, "I think that if you include the nurse in your planning—if you ask her for her cooperation you can work something out with her. Then you will have no problems with the patients either." The doctor made a note to meet with the nurse.

In the above encounter the worker reached out again to try to uncover the key concern of the patients. Unable to verbalize the problem at the meeting for fear of causing trouble for their nurse, the patients did share their worry with the worker. The worker then reached out to the doctor and helped him to realize his error—he had left the nurse, a power figure on the ward, out of the decision-making process.

Helping the Doctor to Understand and Respond to the Emotional Needs of the Patient. One patient was confronted by the need for major surgery for a condition unrelated to his paraplegia. The worker discovered that the patient was extremely fearful of the operation and was unable to verbalize his concerns to the doctor. In trying to help the patient to express his fears and questions about the treatment to his doctor, the worker learned that the patient was on the verge of leaving the hospital against medical advice even though his life depended upon the operation. The following interchange with the doctor took place in the informal atmosphere of the dining room:

The doctor played down my concern about the patient. He said, "You tend to blow things up too much." I said, "But doctor, listen to what the patient himself is saying. He told me that he wants to talk to you but always freezes up when you approach him." "But I just talked to him today," said the physician. I said, "He wants you to level with him about his treatment. If you simply tell him that he will be okay without a full explanation he may not believe you, and he is even thinking of leaving the hospital. He also asked me to ask you if you or the surgeon would draw a diagram of the expected treatment and tell him what he can expect to happen. He is afraid that he will lose his jaw in the operation." The doctor said, "That won't happen." I asked, "Could you tell him that?" The doctor said he would.

The doctor's full and unhurried bedside chat with the patient was instrumental in easing some of the patient's anxieties about his treatment. The worker's sense of urgency and his persistence in the face of the doctor's resistance seemed to be the key factor in the patient's receiving the emotional and factual information he needed in order to face the operation.

Reaching for the Self-Interest of the Nurse. In an interview with one quadriplegic patient the following themes came through: he was angry at not getting turned over in bed at frequent enough intervals during the night; he was unable to verbalize his problem directly to the nurse; he was generally passive with authority figures; and he was interested in opening a business at such time as he became able to leave the hospital. The patient decided to try to assert himself to the nurse about his "turning" problem and asked the worker to help explain his problem to her. The problem for the worker was how to bring the problem to the attention of the nurse in order to collaborate with her in the treatment of the patient. In the past the particular nurse involved often became defensive and hostile when the worker brought complaints about her service to her attention. At the same time she was very interested in helping patients to reach their maximum rehabilitation potential. The following conversation took place in the office of the nurse:

I told the nurse that I was working with L. this morning and that he has a problem. "He said he does not get turned enough at night" (worker explained the details). "But he has a problem in asserting himself—he is afraid to tell you about the problem. In fact he said he never has really been able to complain or argue with adults. But the interesting thing is that he wants to go into business and *that* involves learning to speak up for himself. I suggested to L. that it might be helpful if he could learn to speak up for himself here, and that you would be the one who could help him with his

nursing problem." The nurse said, "Sure—if he is going into business he has to learn to open his mouth to people. What should I
say to him?" The worker replied, "Try something." She said, "Suppose I say to him something like this: 'Mr. Lipton told me that you
are not getting turned enough at night. If that happens I am just
as concerned as you are about it. I want you to tell me about these
things if they happen. . . .'"

In this example the worker's reaching for the self-interest
of the nurse—her strong desire to help in the rehabilitation
process—was instrumental in effectuating a worker-nurse collaboration. The worker, by sharing the patient's problem with
the nurse, was able to help the nurse grasp the significance
of her involvement in the rehabilitation process. The nurse did
not regard the worker intervention as merely presenting another complaint. Rather, she saw his intervention and her own
role in terms of their joint professional efforts to help a patient
to prepare for his life outside of the hospital.

SUMMARY

In the beginning months the bulk of the worker's time and
energy was spent in helping with patient-staff conflicts. As
time went by the content of the group meetings subtly changed
from gripe sessions to constructive work on the problems of
ward life. The patients began to appreciate the realities of
staff shortage, fund limitations, and other administrative problems. The staff, both on the ward and in administrative positions, became more sensitive to the psychological effects the
ward atmosphere has on medical treatment and rehabilitation.

When the patients became weary of focusing on complaints,
social and recreational activities were suggested. The patients
asked for a cook-out on the hospital grounds and expected
that the worker would organize and run it. When the worker
made it clear that he would help, but not run the picnic *for*
them, the patients' energies went into planning and organizing
the event. The significance of the outing lay in the fact that

it was the first patient-sponsored and executed project, whereas in the past the patients had passively accepted recreational activities brought to them by outside organizations. Similarly, groups of patients have been helped to plan parties, outings to restaurants, nightclubs, auto shows, athletic events, and even fishing trips on the ocean, thus demonstrating to themselves the possibility of deriving satisfactions away from the all-protecting hospital. Gradually, many began to relate to the emotional aspects of their massive disability and sought out the worker to discuss their problems and tasks in individual as well as in group sessions. While it is not possible to catalogue all of the work involved, it should be noted that groups for newly injured patients, discharge planning, and groups and monthly meetings for the relatives of the patients have been institutionalized as part of the ongoing hospital program. The frequency and quality of staff meetings have improved, which furthers the therapeutic potential of the team approach for the patients.

The issues, tasks, and problems that the worker faces each day are difficult to understand and to deal with. A high level of skill, sensitivity, and energy is required to assist the patients and the staff system to live more satisfactorily with each other. Some of the skills and tasks of the mediation function are: (a) the worker must reach out to both of the major subsystems in the hospital—the patients and the staff—despite the resistances encountered; (b) he must define and clarify his function to all parties in the setting in which he is working; (c) he must attempt to bring the client and other subsystems together, keeping the affect and issues real, in order to work on exploring the common ground between the patients' need for a functional service and the staff's need to integrate the patients into a productive system of treatment; and (d) he must be able to identify with—to advocate for—both the patient and the staff, in order to be of help to both parties.

The concepts and processes described in this chapter are

not new to social work, and they are undoubtedly familiar to others who have attempted to introduce a therapeutic milieu in an institutional setting. A great deal more work is needed, however, in understanding the specific practice demands and skills needed to assist both patients and the staff to achieve the primary goal of maximizing the patient's rehabilitation potential within the very culture that purports to prepare the patient for the larger society in which he will ultimately live.

REFERENCES

1. Arthur S. Abramson, *et. al.*, "A Therapeutic Community in a General Hospital: Adaptation to a Rehabilitation Service," *Journal of Chronic Diseases*, Vol. 16, No. 179 (February 1963), pp. 179–86.
2. William Caudill, *The Psychiatric Hospital as a Small Society* (Cambridge, Mass.: Harvard University Press, 1958).
3. Rose Laub Coser, "A Home Away from Home," in Dorian Apple (ed.), *Sociological Studies of Health and Sickness* (New York: McGraw-Hill, 1960), pp. 154–72.
4. John Cumming and Elaine Cumming, *Ego and Milieu* (New York: Atherton Press, 1962).
5. Louise A. Frey (ed.), *Use of Groups in the Health Field* (New York: National Association of Social Workers, 1966).
6. Maxwell Jones, *The Therapeutic Community* (New York: Basic Books, 1953).
7. Bernard Kutner, "Report of a Study of the Spinal Cord Injury Section, Bronx Veterans Hospital, December 17, 1964," Bulletin No. 133, 1965.
8. Talcott Parsons, *The Social System* (Glencoe, Ill.: The Free Press, 1951).
9. Robert Rapoport, *The Community as Doctor* (Springfield, Ill.: Charles C. Thomas, 1960).
10. A. Rosenblatt and V. W. Trovato, "Evaluating a Medical Symptom with Paraplegics," *Social Casework*, Vol. 41, No. 3 (March 1960), pp. 128–39.

11. William Schwartz, "The Social Worker in the Group," in *The Social Welfare Forum, 1961* (New York: Columbia University Press, 1961), pp. 146–77.
12. Alfred Stanton and Morris S. Schwartz, *The Mental Hospital* (New York: Basic Books, 1954).
13. Hyman J. Weiner, "The Hospital, the Ward, and the Patient as Clients: Use of the Group Method," *Social Work*, Vol. 4, No. 4 (October 1959), pp. 57–64.
14. Harry Wilmer, *Social Psychiatry in Action* (Springfield, Ill.: Charles C. Thomas, 1958).

Group Work with Adolescents in a
Public Foster Care Agency

JEAN B. PETERSON *and*
CALVIN H. STURGIES

OUR AIM in this paper is to present and discuss our work with groups of adolescent girls at the Division of Foster Home Care of the Bureau of Child Welfare of New York's Department of Social Services. We view our group work with teen-age foster children as an effective way of helping troubled young people grapple with some of their difficult life problems; it is also a productive new way of serving children in a large and complex public agency.

FROM THE LITERATURE

During the past several years the field of public welfare has been the setting of many approaches to the use of group services. Fenton and Wiltse (17) broke new ground in this area with a program of twenty-five group service experiments in thirteen county welfare departments in California. They worked with a wide range of client groups: applicants for public assistance, unemployed older workers, alcoholics, prospective adoptive parents, foster parents, adolescent girls, and others. The problems they found were characteristic of similar programs: the need to clarify the relationship of group work to casework skill; the struggle to differentiate between "educational" and "counseling" groups; developing a clear sense of group purpose; and others. Literature in the field has been produced by Federal coordinating and program agencies, such as the Bureau of Family Services (6, 19, 26) and the Bureau of Public Assistance (5) of the United States Department of Health, Education, and Welfare. Public-private collaborations have also produced some interesting accounts (2, 3, 18, 22). And the list of individual articles, reports, and technical papers on group work practice in public welfare is growing rapidly (1, 9, 13, 14, 20, 21, 24, 27).

A panoramic overview describing group services programs in public welfare around the country was presented in the October 1968 issue of *Public Welfare,* and an exploratory study of significant factors in the initiation, success, and failure of group services in public welfare appeared in a subsequent issue of the same journal (16).

The specific antecedents of our work with groups include a series of presentations, reports, and articles for publication about the group services program of the Bureau of Child Welfare, primarily from our own Division of Foster Home Care. Two accounts dealing with the Division's use of groups with foster parents (12) and adolescent boys (7) first appeared in the Bureau's own publication. Later, staff members presented papers at the 1967 Annual Forum of the National Conference on Social Welfare (4, 15); two accounts were subsequently published (8, 10), and Schwartz's story of the consultative work done over a 4-year period with staff, administrative, and client groups in the Bureau of Child Welfare has appeared in the aforementioned October 1968 issue of *Public Welfare* (23).

THE AGENCY

The Bureau of Child Welfare of the New York City Department of Social Services is a large and complex operation, serving over 22,000 children both in its own facilities and in those of voluntary agencies in New York City. The Bureau's eleven separate divisions offer a wide range of services; among them, The Division of Foster Home Care is charged specifically with the responsibility of placing children in foster homes, supervising their care, and providing them with services essential to their successful development.

The organizational plan of the Division revolves around nuclear units, consisting of from three to five caseworkers with a Unit Supervisor at their head. These units are in turn combined into clusters of three and four, to be administered by a Case Supervisor. The use of this unit-based structure constitutes an unique feature of our recent work with groups of adolescents.

The agency has been offering group services for some 8 or 9 years. One of the most difficult and frustrating problems faced by those involved in these programs has been that of coordinating services and relevant communications between caseworkers and group worker, for the workers were usually scattered widely in different supervisory units throughout the agency. Heavy workloads, lack of uniformity and field days, and difficulty in working through several different supervisory lines made group conferences and worker collaboration difficult to build in. Our innovation was to form groups that were entirely unit-based. That is, the group members were drawn from the caseloads of the five workers in the same unit, all working under the same supervisor.

The idea of forming unit-based groups sprang from the unit itself, growing out of its common problem-solving work. It was felt that this focus would simplify the problems of communication between caseworkers and group worker and reduce the anxiety of caseworkers who often felt threatened by the groups and resisted the group worker's efforts to build a relationship with "their" children. With a unit-based program, the social worker who served groups would be a familiar co-worker and a peer. As the unit-based idea was put into practice, discussion of the groups became part of the ongoing agenda of weekly unit meetings. All unit members were thus involved closely in each phase of the group process and gained knowledge about the group work process itself.

GROUP FORMATION AND THE "TUNING-IN"

Group formation began with a review of the unit's case population. Each worker discussed under supervision the appropriateness of individual referrals, and each child was discussed at a unit meeting. The caseworkers assumed total responsibility for initial discussion of the proposed group services with the girls and their foster parents and the unit meeting was used to discuss possible reactions and resistances that might be encountered in this preparation process. The outcome of this work was the formation of two groups of adolescent girls, ages twelve and fifteen through seventeen.

Prior to any formal discussions with the girls we extended invitations to their foster parents to come to the agency to discuss group services. The two parent group meetings thus held were led jointly by the group worker and the unit supervisor. The foster parents had an opportunity to meet the worker who would be seeing their children in the group, to ask questions, and to express concerns about the program. In both sessions with the foster parents the group members quickly moved from the specifics of the adolescent groups to some of their own common problems and concerns in their roles as foster parents; they gave clear evidence of their need for, and ability to use, group services in their own behalf.

All of these steps helped the unit, and the group worker in particular, to "tune-in" to the girls as individuals and as group members, to anticipate the emotions and concerns they would bring to the group. This was a kind of "preliminary empathy" through which the worker "tries to use prior knowledge to anticipate clues that will be thrown away so quickly, and in such disguised forms, that the worker will miss them unless he is somehow 'tuned' to the client's frequency." *

* See Chapter 1 in this book, p. 14.

This "tuning-in" process was more than an essential part of group formation; it was an ongoing aspect of our work with the groups. As indicated, regular unit meetings were devoted to bringing each other up to date on what was happening in the emotional and active life of each girl. As crises arose in the life of a group member, workers fed back information so that individual and group services could be sensitized.

The group worker's written records of group meetings also contributed to the ongoing feedback processes. A combination of summary and process recording was used, and records were distributed to all unit members, as well as to various administrative and supervisory personnel, to be used for training purposes. Recordings were used extensively in collaboration and discussion within the unit. The group worker's review of her own records and her use of them in supervision to help her focus on concrete practice problems were vital to her work. An attempt was made to treat group recordings with the same confidentiality and care as case records; however, the relationship between the two has remained unclear, and effective means have yet to be found for incorporating the group accounts into the permanent files.

BEGINNINGS: THE PROBLEM OF "CONTRACTING"

In the first meetings with the girls the chief focus of the worker was on developing with them a consensus as to the terms of the "contract," or purpose, and the ground rules of the group. This contract was not something completely established at the first meeting. The girls' struggles to understand and collaborate in the contract-making process continued throughout the life of the groups. At the first meetings the girls were tense and anxious, uncertain of themselves, each other, and the worker. Most had come reluctantly, only under pressure from their foster parents and case workers. They had no real understanding of what the group was all about. The worker began by recognizing their discomfort in the new situation:

After more silence, I recognized the difficulty of talking in a new situation and suggested that perhaps some of them had not wanted to come . . . giggles from the group. I said I knew Dora and Vicky hadn't really wanted to come . . . they nodded. The girls began participating around this piece of common reality—that they were here because someone else thought it was a good idea. . . .

Initially the girls gave very little verbal response to the idea of a group for sharing common concerns and helping each other with problems. Interaction began around the normal interests of adolescents—what schools they attended, where they lived, and whether they had common acquaintances. After a few meetings they began to warm up to each other, the worker, and the idea of sharing problems. Yet there were concurrent moves to escape serious grappling with difficulties. In the fifth meeting of the younger group the following interaction occurred after one member attempted to change the purpose of the group into one of "telling funny stories":

I said that I had never said it was easy to be the kind of group we said we were. Talking openly in a group about things that really worry you was very hard to do. Gloria said, "That's it, I don't want to talk about problems because it's hard for me." . . . Dora said that she didn't tell other people personal things because "they tell your business" to everyone. All the girls strongly agreed, citing personal experiences. . . . I summarized, saying, "so you're saying it isn't safe to talk to people because you can't trust them not to use what they know in a way that hurts you." Nods. Wanda said that it was different with different people. I asked what made it feel safe to talk to some people and not to others? What kind of people was it safe with? Vicky said it was safe to talk to me. I nodded and asked quietly if she knew why it felt safe. She looked away, shrugged and said, "I don't know . . . you don't go and tell everything."

There is evidence here of a growing relationship between the worker and the girls. Recognition of the difficulty of the work they were doing helped the girls move in this meeting into a deeper level of sharing about the fear of real intimacy, and from there they moved to a discussion of ways in which they coped with their fear of trusting and opening up personal feelings to others.

The demand for work, which at the outset came primarily from the worker, began to be expressed by the girls themselves:

When Dora and Vickey arrived, Wanda's face perked up. When they were settled, I said, "Well, ladies, let's go to work." After a pause, Wanda asked who had the "problem of the day." Everyone laughed . . . Vicky spoke up, saying she had something to talk about; something that had happened to her last week.

They also began to show their stake in the group's purpose by pressuring nonverbal members to contribute to the discussion:

I asked how they felt about those things. Dora and Wanda started squirming and joking. Gloria asked Dolly why she never talked, saying she wanted to hear her talk. The other girls agreed and everyone looked at Dolly. I said that they were sort of putting her on the spot now, which didn't make talking any easier. Dolly gave a half-nod. I asked her quietly if she had the same kinds of conflicts with her parents. She nodded.

MAJOR WORK THEMES

The content of the groups' work ranged over a wide variety of topics, but focus returned again and again to a few central concerns about which the girls showed considerable anxiety. Mainly, these involved their feelings about their foster care status and their confusions about their identity; their struggles to deal with their angry and strong love feelings; their peer relationships; their sexuality and relationships with boys; their feelings about race and being black; their complex relationships with the foster parents; their relationship to the agency and its social workers; and their fears of psychiatric referral. Limitations of space do not allow us to show the full range of work done on all these concerns. Through a few excerpts taken from group records, we will try to give a sense of how some of these themes arose and what they looked like in action.

Being "Foster". The reality of their foster care status was difficult for the girls to face. For most adolescents in foster care the struggle is carried on alone. They are often unable to open up this area of feeling either with foster parents or with caseworkers; they are also ashamed to talk about it with their friends, thus cutting themselves off from their most natural source of support. In a group composed entirely of foster children, meeting at an agency whose business is foster care, adolescents are freed from the need to hide the fact that they are "foster." Through sharing their feelings they can learn they are not alone in experiencing them and can gain strength from a common bond of mutual support:

Jerry said soberly that being "foster" was awful. I asked her to talk more about what she meant. She said foster children never were treated the same as real children. In her house she always felt different from the others who were natural children. Real children didn't have all those strange feelings. Shirley said she had a real mother who visited, and living with her would be better. Jerry said she had a mother too, but she knew she was better off where she was. It would be worse with her mother because she drank too much and used to beat her. That was why the court had taken her away. . . . Shirley continued that being "foster" was awful because it wasn't like a family. . . . When her foster mother jumped on her she had no one to go to and talk to except her sister. I asked the others who they had. Jerry said, "No one." Carrie said "No one." Dinny said, "No one." There was a deep silence. After a few minutes I said, "You all have a lot of sad feelings . . . they're sad and angry feelings, like it's your fault somehow. But it isn't your fault. It's true that the world gave you a dirty deal." After more silence I said that there wasn't really anything that could take those feelings away. They were real feelings and they hurt. But sometimes it helped to talk about them with other people who felt the same. Shirley said that it helped not to be the only one.

Race. All of these girls were black and grew up, for the most part, in New York City's black ghetto areas. The worker was white and this made race-consciousness an inevitable and almost constant element of the group dynamic. The worker tried to project an open, relaxed acceptance of racial differences, although she herself was not entirely comfortable with her differences. An early attempt by a group to deal directly with the subject of race is illustrated below. In this excerpt the girls were struggling with conflicts between Black and White, conflicts between generations, feelings about their own blackness, and their immediate feelings about their relationship to the white worker:

Vicky shared being very angry at a white teacher who made subtle, derogatory comments about Afro haircuts, clearly implying the superiority of straightened hair. From their anger at this, the girls moved into discussing Afros. Wanda and Vicky had both tried their hair natural. Vicky mentioned her mother made her change it back. I said that it seemed to me they must get caught in a bind between their parents' feelings about naturals, Black Power, etc., and the feelings of friends, black teachers, community leaders. All the girls responded with nods. Vicky described feeling strange when she used to go to dance lessons in Harlem. She felt embarrassed that she was the only one on the streets with straightened hair. Everyone had naturals, African clothes, etc. But she didn't like those African shirts. Dora spoke angrily about being "brainwashed" by her Afro-American history teacher and a white teacher with a black husband who was always talking about what good care he took of her. She then, with obvious identification, told of a friend who went to a Black Power rally, where the speakers were yelling about how bad it was to straighten your hair and to try to be white. She was the only one there with straightened hair. The girls all emphatically verbalized feeling like running and hiding in that situation. I said that even deciding what words to use must be a problem, because different people felt differently about "colored," "black," "Negro." Vicky described her ambivalence about the word "black" by recounting another school incident. I said she seemed to sometimes feel it was like "nigger" and to sometimes feel it meant pride and self-respect. She nodded and then said with frustration that she wasn't even sure what "nigger" meant, asking if it meant an "uneducated person." . . . I said race was a hard thing to understand and that white people got confused too about all those different words. I wasn't sure exactly how they felt about them and it was hard to know which ones to use. At this point Dora began joking nervously. Vicky said, "Be quiet, Miss Peterson's talking." . . . I said that it was very hard to talk about these things, especially since I was white and they were black. They didn't really know exactly how I thought and felt about race and I didn't know too much about how they felt either.

Sex. Concerns about boy-girl relationships and many aspects of sexuality permeated the discussions and constituted one of the most significant work themes in the group life. The younger girls were able to express some of their underlying feelings and questions about the physiology of sex:

Gloria sighed and said she wished she were a boy. Dora nodded and said boys didn't have all that trouble. General consensus that periods were a mess. I asked if any of them had any physical trouble with their periods (cramps, etc.). Several indicated they did, and all the girls expressed how bad it was to have cramps at school. Wanda expressed her feelings about how messy and awful using Kotex was. There was general agreement and discussion about feeling "dirty" and "nasty"; hiding their periods from other family members, being embarrassed that boys could tell at school when they had their period. Vicky announced that she didn't use Kotex, but used Pursettes. She was the only girl who used any kind of tampon, and the others clearly had questions and anxieties about this. Wanda made a face and said she was "scared of using those things." Gloria remarked that she didn't know where her "hole" was. She wasn't even sure she had one. Laughter. I said that most girls were scared at first about using tampons and worried about how to put them in, whether they would get lost or stuck, etc. They giggled and nodded as I expressed their fears. I then suggested it might help if Vicky talked about it and they asked her questions. She said she had figured out how to use them herself, with no instructions or help, after finding some in her sister's bureau. She grinned and said, "Well, it took a long time to get it in the first time," when I remarked it must have been hard and scary. Wanda asked with concern whether it hurt and if you could "feel it in there." Gloria said she had thought you had to be older to use it.

The worker moved here to give some information about menstruation and the use of tampons, answering openly and specifically the girls' very intent and eager questions.

Boy-girl relationships were dealt with in the groups on many levels. The girls shared feelings of anger and resentment that most boys didn't seem to care about them as people, but just wanted to "mess you up" and "get you pregnant." In the older group, where the girls had begun to develop more involved individual relationships with boys, one member was helped to live through the painful feelings of "breaking up." In another session, the worker's explanation of what a hymen was, and its actual and supposed relationship to virginity, triggered the following very serious discussion.

The girls reached a consensus that it was impossible to talk to most adults about anything related to sex because they immediately judge you as "bad" and see sex as evil under most conditions. I said clearly that almost everybody has mixed-up feelings about sex, and that all teen-age girls think about it a lot, imagine what intercourse is like, etc. It didn't make them bad or different if they did. I then asked how they felt, what they thought or imagined about it. This freed Vicky to say openly that she had had intercourse before. She was warmed up to talk about her worry about this. I said that even if Dora and Wanda had not experienced intercourse, they had a lot of feelings and questions about it, too, which I thought they could help each other talk about. Wanda said, "Okay, let's help Vicky." Wanda was quite threatened by the subject, however, and had difficulty staying focused. I supported her by saying that the whole business of sex was very scary and confusing to talk about and it was just as hard to listen to others talk about it. . . . Vicky verbalized her feeling of great relief at "telling" and "getting it out." Wanda referred again to the unaccepting attitude of most adults. I said that I hoped the group was a place where they could talk straight about themselves and be listened to without being told they were "bad." Everybody had to make decisions about how to behave sexually every day, and each person made her own decisions. Being told you were "bad" didn't help any. What might help was talking about how you feel about the decisions you make, what consequences the decisions might have, etc. . . . Vicky was then able to express having felt stupid, embarrassed, and scared of her boy friend finding out she was a virgin. She was very anxious about the possibility of pregnancy, and when I asked what she was doing about it she indicated he had used a condom. I very firmly stressed the risk she had taken. She nodded and said it "wasn't worth it." Wanda mentioned "the pills" and there was quite a bit of discussion about what was in them, how they worked, etc.

Peer Relationships. Problems in relationships with friends was a regular part of the groups' business. The following incident shows how one of the younger girls focused directly on this kind of work:

Vicky said she wanted to fight Louise, but if she fought in school and got in trouble she was afraid she wouldn't graduate. She said she didn't want to fight at 3:00 because then her friends would all jump in and she wanted Louise "all to myself." At the same time, she didn't want to fight her because she was afraid she would really hurt her—she was that mad. I clarified her conflict as being between acting on her strong immediate feelings and controlling them because of realistic consequences that would hurt her. She saw this and could also express her fear that she might lose control and do something she really didn't want to do. She specifically turned to the group and asked, "How can I avoid fighting Louise?" . . . She again expressed her fear of really hurting Louise. I asked the group if they had ever really hurt someone in a fight. All the girls nodded. Several incidents were cited. I asked how they had felt about it while fighting and afterward. Vicky said she had told the girl she was sorry, and she really had been. The others shared this feeling. Vicky said she didn't want to fight at 3:00 because her friends

would gang up on Louise . . . she would really get hurt. . . .
Someone remarked that she felt sorry for Louise. I asked if they
had ever been the one who was ganged up on. They all nodded.
Vicky said that she talked big about fighting, but she was really
scared whenever she did. She acted brave and said she wanted to
fight on her own, but she really always made sure all her friends
knew when and where she planned to fight so she wouldn't be
alone . . . Vicky said soberly that it really was bad when kids—
especially boys—ganged up to fight, because people really got
hurt. Wanda and Dora chimed in, adding that kids started carrying
knives, etc., and when the gang fights started they used them.

Foster Parents. This problem of dealing with anger came up
over and over in relation to many different content themes:
conflicts with peers, siblings, social workers, teachers, self,
and most particularly, the foster parents. The width of the
generation gap, in terms of sexual mores and ideas of "proper"
social behavior, can be seen in the following excerpt:

I asked what their mothers thought was the proper way for girls
their age to have to do with boys. Dora blurted out angrily, "We
should run whenever we see one!" Vicky added sarcastically that
they certainly "shouldn't talk to one, 'cause you'll get pregnant. . . ." She remarked "How are we supposed to learn about
boys and sex if we're locked up 'til we're eighteen. Then all of
a sudden we can do anything we want. We'd really get in trouble
then." . . . "Parents still act as if it's the olden days! And . . . the
first thing on their minds is that all we want to do when we get
our period is go out and have a 'good time' and get pregnant,"
asserted Gloria. Vicky said quietly that when her mother kept saying that it sometimes made her feel like going out and doing it,
but that wouldn't be any good. . . . Dora said she just tried to
forget what her mother said until afterward when she went to a
party because she wanted to have fun.

The angers and frustrations felt by the girls in relation to what
they viewed as the moralistic and restrictive attitudes of their
foster parents sometimes reached an intensity that was fright-

eningly difficult for them to cope with. This is evident in the following excerpt, when the younger girls begin to risk exposing their aggressive fantasies:

Vicky said she knew it wasn't nice to think such things, but when her foster mother had been unpacking things beside the window in the new apartment she had wanted to push her out the window. She and Dora, her foster sister, giggled tensely. They both began saying that they were "horrible," the things they talked about sometimes, indicating other fantasies of hurting and punishing their foster parents. I said I didn't think that was so horrible—everybody wished things like that would happen to people they were mad at sometimes. Dolly responded to the other girls' fantasies by giggling, hand to her mouth, and rocking in her chair. She gave a very slight nod when I asked if she sometimes thought things like that. I said again that I didn't think wishing things like that made them horrible; and just thinking of them wouldn't make them happen.

Feelings of Love and Loneliness. On the other side of the coin, there was the yearning, the inchoate need for love and intimacy. The worker helped the girls begin to share these feelings as well:

Vicky said, with feeling, that she didn't think she knew what love was. . . . I gently asked them to try to talk about what it was. Wanda said she knew what it was, but she couldn't explain it. . . . Vicky said she thought she did know, after all, but she couldn't say. I urged her to try it. She said with difficulty that love was when you were willing to do anything for somebody, and when you thought about them all the time. Then she said softly that she didn't think she'd ever loved anyone, or that anyone really loved her. After saying this, she seemed to withdraw. Gloria said she didn't love because she just thought about herself all the time. The group fell silent. I said that the things they'd been working on were some of the hardest things to talk about—feelings of not understanding love, not loving, and feeling unloved. . . . It was scary and it hurt to feel those feelings. . . . Vicky had quietly begun to cry. The others noticed this as I said I thought Vicky was feeling the sad and lonely feelings about love more than the others now. . . . I asked her quietly if she knew why she was crying. She nodded. When I asked her if she wanted to talk about it she shook her head. I nodded acceptance of this. After a silence she sighed and said, "You know, Miss Peterson, sometimes I really feel like committing suicide." I said that I knew it was very, very frightening to feel like that. The things we were talking about, especially feelings about not being loved and not loving anyone, are the things people cry about more than anything, the things that hurt the most.

The worker at this point helped other group members to share with this troubled girl similar experiences of feeling lonely, depressed, and unloved, of feeling like committing suicide. In this way she was given support and helped to see that her own strong feelings were not "crazy" or entirely different from those of others.

These groups have gone through several periods of transition—addition and subtraction of members, changes in meeting time and place, a slight restructuring of the group over the summer—during which the worker had to help the girls adjust to the changes and resettle into a culture of purposeful work. When the time comes for endings, for termination of the groups, she will be called upon to help the girls' feelings of intimacy that have grown and continue to grow in the group. She will have to help the girls prepare for and face the painful loss of this intimacy and prepare to continue in other ways to work on the "unfinished business" of the life problems they, for a time, worked on together in the groups.

SKILLS OF THE WORKER

Throughout these excerpts runs the continuing theme of the strengths and weaknesses of the worker's use of herself and the ways in which she tried to help these girls use each other. We have described how, at the time of group formation, unit meetings were used as a device for helping the group worker "feel into" the lives of the group members, and how this process was continued throughout the life of the groups, through formal and informal communications between group worker, caseworkers, and supervisor. We have spelled out the specific tasks involved in the contracting phrase, and excerpts have shown how the worker detected when purposeful work was being evaded and, reaching for the negative side of their ambivalence about the group, helped the girls express and work through some of their doubts about the contract. In each of the work themes discussed, aspects of the worker's attempts at skill are illuminated: how she helped the girls clarify problems and partialized them into manageable pieces; how she continually tried to reach for and legitimize expression of feelings, both positive and negative; how she shared from her own fund of information and experience where this was useful; how she shared her own feelings about the groups' struggles, allowing her own value perspective to express itself honestly; and how she helped the girls relate to each other, supporting and reinforcing their efforts at mutual aid.

A device that both worker and girls found helpful in opening up new areas of common effort and increasing spontaneity was the psychodramatic technique of role-playing. The girls related quickly and easily to the acting-out of problem situations and relationships. The following example from an early group session shows how the use of role-playing allowed the girls to expose feelings about race, welfare, cursing, jobs, marriage, and sex, feelings they had previously kept well controlled and hidden:

Vicky said that "fourteen feels like nothing." In exploring this and what age they thought would "feel like something," I suggested we all pretend it was 5 years from now and we had met on the street and were having coffee together. They moved easily into this dramatic play, enjoying it immensely. They also seemed much freer than usual to make spontaneous comments. For example, when Dora was kidding around, Gloria snapped, "Act your age not your color." This brought a brief silence, then Gloria asked what "acting your color" meant; that she had heard people say that. Dora and Vicky commented that prejudiced people thought Negroes always acted stupid. Also, in surveying what each girl was doing as an eighteen- or nineteen-year-old, joking comments about being on Welfare and "on the streets" emerged quickly. There was also more freedom in cursing openly. As we talked as in 1974, we discovered that Dora was a movie star and secretary. Gloria was taking a trip in space and holding four jobs (couldn't decide) as a secretary, movie star, nurse, and teacher. Vicky asserted that she was married and had a baby.

The worker here stepped out of the role-play situation and was able to help the girls to move into work on feelings about marriage and sex with more openness and depth than they had reached at this point in the life of the group. Through individual role-reversal with foster mothers, social workers, or parts of the self, several of the girls were able to give expression to feelings they had been unable to reach in group discussion. The worker's use of these techniques was based on the methods of Robert W. Siroka and Ellen K. Siroka, developed at their Institute for Sociotherapy in New York City (25).

SOME CONCLUSIONS

Concrete results are difficult to measure, but in several individual cases the groups' helpfulness was evident. Two foster siblings, aided by the awareness that other group members also had serious conflicts with their foster parents, opened up to a social worker for the first time and bared some of the painful stress they were under in their foster home. One of these girls also used her group as a vehicle for asking for psychiatric help. In the older group, a member underwent a series of crises, including several severe clashes with her foster mother, running away from the foster home to her natural mother, and two court hearings. Throughout this chaotic period she actively used the group to reveal her almost uncontrollable, pent-up anger. Expessing the negative side of her strongly ambivalent feelings toward her caseworker in the group helped enable her to maintain and deepen her relationship with that worker, a tie that was vital in supporting her through these crises. This youngster has been discharged from care and is now on After Care Service, and her maintenance in the group is an important part of her after-care treatment plan, giving her a continuity of relationship with the agency, which she needs at this time.

Generally, the girls' involvement with their caseworkers has been extended and deepened, and they have used the group to role-play some of the areas of concern they have hesitated to discuss with their caseworkers.

The members have developed some confidence and skill in self-expression and have begun to deal more directly and realistically with the role of the agency in their lives. The experience of sharing feelings related to their "foster" status as well as their common problems as black adolescents would seem to give them some help with the difficult and often lonely task of struggling to achieve independence and identity. They have learned in some measure to place more value on the open sharing of feelings, both joyful and painful.

On the negative side, there were instances in which girls felt threatened by the group discussion and dropped out, expressing to their caseworkers a dislike of being "reminded" of their foster care status, of problems, and of painful feelings. Normal teen-age rebellion against authority is magnified in the adolescent's relationship to the foster care agency because of the depth and pervasiveness of that agency's control over his life. Attendance at group meetings in some cases became a focus for the acting-out of this rebellion. Even when the child's motivation to attend the group was strong, many ambivalent feelings about the agency and the worker were present.

The foster parents have also in some cases used group attendance as an arena for expressing their resistance to the social workers' close involvement in the lives of their foster children. Feelings of inadequacy in handling the innumerable problems of parenting an adolescent often threaten foster parents' feelings of self-worth. A common defense against such feelings is denial of problems and conflict. Since preserving this defense involves a continuing pretense to the agency of "so far so good" and "everything's okay," these foster parents are further threatened by the thought that their adolescents might reveal conflict areas to either the caseworker or group worker. The group meetings are particularly threatening, as foster parents have less control over the situation and less opportunity to give "their side." A common fear of foster parents is that of being "ganged-up on" by the teen-agers and group worker. These fears were recognized and discussed in the preliminary meetings of group worker and supervisor with the foster parents. However, those who feel most threatened by the agency tend also to be those who fail to attend these opening meetings or to express their fears. The fears appear instead as exaggerated objections to meeting times, traveling distance, and time away from studies.

All of these factors make follow-up work by caseworkers a very important part of a group services program in this type of agency. Far from being a work saver, having a child enrolled in the group often adds considerably to the problems the caseworker must handle with both the adolescents and their foster parents. We have no doubt that this effort repays itself in service to the childen and their foster families.

Group work is still in many ways itself a "foster child," lacking equal treatment to casework, the "real" child. The caseworker remains known in agency vernacular as the child's "regular" worker. Within the unit-based structure we were able to equalize this relationship somewhat in improved processes of communication and collaboration. In the Division of Foster Home Care, as in most public welfare agencies, statutory requirements, financial limitations, and workload coverage problems tend to force evaluation and development of group services programs down on the list of agency priorities. The literature cited clearly verifies that our agency is not alone with this problem. Certainly, careful thought would have to be given to the feasibility of assigning caseloads and unit loads on the basis of age, geography, commonality of problems, or other criteria of group formation. Yet, if group work is to be adopted into full "sibship" with casework in public welfare, serious consideration must be given to restructuring agency services in a way that facilitates rather than complicates this relationship. Our model of unit-based group service offers an opportunity to deal with the most prominent obstacles to the integration of individual and group services.

REFERENCES

1. American Public Welfare Association, *Potentials for Service Through Group Work in Public Welfare* (Chicago: The Association, 1962).
2. Lillian E. Barclay, "A Group Approach to Young Unwed Mothers," *Public Welfare*, Vol. 27, No. 3 (July 1969), pp. 253–60.
3. Janice Bowen, *A Study to Determine the Feasibility of Developing a Demonstration Project in Group Care for Young Children within the New York City Department of Welfare* (New York: New York Fund for Children, 1966).
4. Florence E. Boyd, "Work with Adoptive Parents and Recruitment," paper presented at the 1967 Annual Forum of the National Conference on Social Welfare, 1967, mimeographed.
5. Bureau of Public Assistance, *Training for Service in Public Assistance* (Washington, D.C.: Department of Health, Education, and Welfare, 1961).

6. Bureau of Family Services, *Helping People in Groups: Six Background Papers from the Workshop on Group Services* (Washington, D.C.: Department of Health, Education, and Welfare, 1965).

7. Woodrow W. Carter, "A Group Counseling Program in BCW," *Staff Development News*, Vol. 2, No. 3 (Fall Issue, December 1964), p. 4.

8. Woodrow W. Carter, "Group Counseling for Adolescent Foster Children," *Children*, Vol. 15, No. 1 (January–February 1968), pp. 221–27.

9. Edith M. Chappelear and Joyce E. Fried, "Helping Adopting Couples Come to Grips with their New Parental Roles," *Children*, Vol. 14, No. 6 (November–December 1967), pp. 223–26.

10. Adolin G. Dall, "Group Learning for Foster Parents: In a Public Agency," *Children*, Vol. 14, No. 5 (September–October 1967), pp. 185–87.

11. Adolin G. Dall, "Instituting Group Work Services for Foster Parents," paper presented at the 1967 Annual Forum of the National Conference on Social Welfare, 1967, mimeographed.

12. Adolin Dall and Seymour Fass, "Use of the Group Method with Foster Parents," *Staff Development News*, Vol. 1, No. 2 (September–November 1963), pp. 1, 5.

13. Louis B. Dillow, "The Group Process in Adoptive Home-Finding," *Children*, Vol. 15, No. 4 (July–August 1968), pp. 153–57.

14. Hans S. Falck, "Helping Caseworkers Use the Social Group Method," *Public Welfare*, Vol. 22, No. 2 (April 1964), pp. 125–29.

15. Seymour K. Fass, "The Institutionalization of Group Services through Supervision and Administrative Practice," paper presented at the 1967 Annual Forum of the National Conference on Social Welfare, 1967, mimeographed.

16. Ronald A. Feldman, "Group Services Programs in Public Welfare: Patterns and Perspectives," *Public Welfare*, Vol. 27, No. 3 (July 1969), pp. 266–71.

17. Norman Fenton and Kermit T. Wiltse, *Group Methods in the*

Public Welfare Program (Palo Alto, Calif.: Pacific Books, 1963).

18. David Kevin, "Group Counseling of Mothers in an AFDC Program," *Children*, Vol. 14, No. 2 (March–April 1967), pp. 69–74.

19. Marjorie Montelius, *Working with Groups: A Guide for the Administration of Group Services in Public Welfare* (Washington, D.C.: Bureau of Family Services, Department of Health, Education and Welfare, 1966).

20. Murray Ortof, "Group Services to Families Receiving ADC," in *Group Method and Services in Child Welfare* (New York: Child Welfare League of America, 1963).

21. Barbara Reigel, "Group Meetings with Adolescents in Child Welfare," *Child Welfare*, Vol. 47, No. 7 (July 1968), pp. 417–18.

22. Santa Clara County Welfare Department and Family Service Association of Palo Alto and Los Altos, *Reducing Dependency in AFDC Families through the Use of Group Treatment* (Palo Alto, Calif.: the Department and the Association, 1964).

23. William Schwartz, "Group Work in Public Welfare," *Public Welfare*, Vol. 26, No. 4 (October 1968), pp. 322–70.

24. Louise P. Shoemaker, "The Use of Group Work Skills with Short Term Groups," in *Social Work with Groups, 1960* (New York: National Association of Social Workers, 1960).

25. Robert W. Siroka and Ellen K. Siroka, "Encounters with Psychodrama in a Therapeutic Community," in Leonard Blank (ed.), *Encounter: Confrontations in Self-Other Awareness* (New York: Macmillan, 1970).

26. Harleigh B. Trecker, *Group Services in Public Welfare* (Washington, D.C.: Bureau of Family Services, Department of Health, Education and Welfare, 1964).

27. Louise C. Youngman, "Social Group Work in the AFDC Program," *Public Welfare*, Vol. 23, No. 1 (January 1965), pp. 25–31, 59–61.

A Group Approach to Link Community Mental Health with Labor

HYMAN J. WEINER

DAY HOSPITALS, halfway houses, foster homes, and a variety of other sociotherapeutic approaches, usually coupled with medication, have achieved some success in keeping the mentally ill outside the hospital. Residing outside a hospital, however, is not necessarily synonymous with participating in community life (3). For many patients, living in the community has little meaning unless it also involves being able to function as productive members of the labor force.

Unfortunately, however, the mental health field finds itself isolated and estranged from the world of work. For too long these two social networks have passed each other like ships in the night, each losing out by lack of real contact with the other. As a result of this situation the mental patient is usually left to his own resources in overcoming the barriers to finding and holding a job. Some, independently or with professional help, do mobilize sufficient strength to achieve this goal. But for each successful candidate all too many fall by the wayside.

There is, however, a pilot venture that is attempting to link the world of work with a mental health service in the men's

Reprinted from *Social Work Practice, 1967* (New York: Columbia University Press, 1967), pp. 178–88. Slightly edited.

clothing industry in New York City. In dealing with a group of business agents * as official representatives of the labor union, a group work approach was employed to help union officials and mental health professionals examine the way they were dealing with mentally ill workers and test new methods of coping with the problem.

Grants from federal agencies * * made it possible to establish a mental health program at the Sidney Hillman Health Center. The center is an outpatient medical facility co-sponsored by the New York Joint Board of the Amalgamated Clothing Workers of America and the New York Clothing Manufacturers' Association. The union members whom it services comprise thirty thousand clothing workers, consisting primarily of three ethnic groups: Italian, East European Jewish, and Puerto Rican.†

The content of and the approach to the group sessions grew out of an appreciation of the overlapping needs of the union and the rehabilitation program as they both sought to deal with the emotionally ill clothing worker. It was clear that maintenance of employment or return to work required the intimate involvement of those who had direct contact with the workers and control of job opportunities.‡ What was less clear, however, was identification of the needs of the industry, and particularly of the trade union, that might be satisfied by cooperating with the mental health program. There were three potential keys to gaining union commitment and participation:

* A business agent is a full-time, paid union official who services the membership on problems of grievances, change of jobs, and so forth.
* * The demonstration program is supported, in part, by grants from the National Institute of Mental Health (MH-1523) and the Vocational Rehabilitation Administration (RD-1453).
† For further discussion of the mental health project in the men's clothing industry, see Hyman J. Weiner and Morris Brand (12) and John Sommer (10).
‡ The union operates a labor bureau which, in effect, serves as the exclusive hiring hall for the men's clothing industry in New York City.

1. The union is under pressure to maintain an experienced labor force for the industry.

2. The union's tradition and its community image as a socially responsible pacesetter make it hospitable to pioneering programs.

3. The union is in the market for new personal services that will help maintain the loyalty of its membership.

Union officials must deal daily with the mentally ill clothing worker. In spite of their desire to alleviate the personal suffering and the industrial problems that result from the disability, their efforts are not always successful. It was this fact that set the stage for a dialogue between the union and the mental health program.

Ten business agents were assigned by the union leadership to meet regularly with the mental health staff. The project director, a social worker with group work experience, was instructed by the union president to "tell them what to do so that they can help the members." The mandate was for a didactic educational program. The director, who was to lead the group, subsequently won the right to set up a workshop rather than a lecture format. This was especially significant in view of the fact that an authoritarian leadership approach to problem-solving had cultivated a pattern of passive behavior among the business agents. In addition to a style of dependent group participation the specific "charged" nature of the mental health issue contributed its own dynamics to the situation. Genuine interest in finding new ways of coping with the mentally ill was all but neutralized by the fear of approaching such a delicate subject, particularly in the presence of psychiatrists. Another potential source of resistance to participating in the group was the union's suspicion of social workers, which was summarized by the late Albert Deutsch:

They had little use for the busy-bodies and crackpot reformers who often dominated voluntary social work, bent on moralizing missions, often debasing their own religious faiths by crude attempts to bribe the poor into their particular creeds with the crumbs of charity (2, p. 290).

The group, comprised of mental health professionals and business agents, moved through three phases in developing trust and a way of working together. These phases overlapped and continued to assert themselves, each with a dominant quality.

The classic group attitude of reliance on authority—"Tell us about mental illness and what to do about it"—characterized the initial period. This was exacerbated by the desire on the part of some of the professionals to relieve their own anxiety by playing the role of expert.

This search for useful agenda, which finally developed when the group and its purpose were brought into focus, illuminated the real differences in perception held by the two parties. It became evident that the business agents believed they were assigned to be "mental health aides." They saw this as a new and time-consuming role, bearing little relationship to their functions as union officials. A record of the first group meeting includes the following:

As they entered the room there was a good deal of kidding among themselves about their assignment. . . . Behind this joking, the agents' interest in the new role seemed intermixed with considerable anxiety about what they would do.

Their anxiety was well founded, for, assuming that they were to act as mental health aides, or "subprofessionals," they truly lacked the knowledge and skill such a task demanded. Some of the mental health professionals challenged the notion that business agents could become "aides." It was pointed out that expertise existed on both sides. The business agents knew the world of work and, moreover, had a tremendous amount of experience in dealing with mental health problems on the job. It was this ability that they could contribute to the group —not a watered-down, fear-ridden, subprofessional role.

Although the professionals harbored some doubts, they expressed an expectation that expertise would be shared. This idea was viewed with considerable skepticism by the business agents, who were also uncomfortable about their limited formal educational backgrounds. Both sides grew more appreciative of their mutual contribution as actual job problems of emotionally ill clothing workers were discussed.

During this first period the role of the group leader began to be clarified. Though he was a member of the mental health team, his function as workshop chairman, with the responsibility of keeping the parties working at the problem, became an accepted part of the emerging group culture. In many ways he resembled the "stranger" as described by George Simmel:

. . . distance means that he, who is close by, is far, and strangeness means that he, who is also far, is actually near. His position as a full-fledged member involves both being outside it and confronting it. He is not radically committed to the unique ingredients and peculiar tendencies of the group and, therefore, approaches them with the specific attitude of "objectivity." But objectivity does not simply involve passivity and detachment; it is a particular structure composed of distance and nearness, indifference and involvement (13, p. 404).

Phase two was marked by further exploration of the special contribution that each could make. Discussion within the group and activity outside of it proceeded along parallel rather than integrated paths. Among the cases brought before the group during this period, the history of Mrs. Ritter * is typical. The business agent was called to the shop by her employer, who complained that after many years of competent service as a ticket sewer Mrs. Ritter was mixing up her work. As a result the entire shop was being disrupted. After talking with the worker, the agent recognized that she had an emo-

---

* Here, as in all case histories in this book, the names are fictitious.

tional problem and suggested she "go to the union health center and talk it over with someone." Simultaneously, he alerted the mental health program.

Mrs. Ritter did not arrive at the health center, and the case was discussed at the next group meeting.

The business agent was surprised to learn that Mrs. Ritter had not contacted the mental health program. He reported further that she had walked off the job without an explanation to the employer. Several of the union officials suggested that the health center send a letter to the worker asking her to come in. At this point, one of the professionals asked what might have happened if there were no mental health program. A few agents replied that such a worker often disappeared from the industry. Another indicated that sometimes the business agent called the worker, letting her know that she was in danger of losing her job. One agent challenged the notion of direct contact with the worker. He warned that "if you get involved with the mentally ill, they always accuse you of being crazy." He went on to say that "our job is to let you [the professionals] know who's in trouble, then it's up to you to take over."

Mrs. R's own business agent disagreed, saying that "Good ticket sewers are hard to get, and since she was the only one in her factory, the boss wants her back to work." He said he felt comfortable telling her the truth, that she would lose her job if things remained as they were. One of the professionals suggested that reaching out to her might show union interest in her welfare and help start the process of getting her back on the job.

It became clear to the group that there was a merging of interests of union, management, and the mental health program in relation to this worker in trouble. The group encouraged the business agent to approach Mrs. Ritter on the basis of protecting her job rights, a point of entry with which he felt comfortable because it was consistent with his traditional duties. Subsequently, he accompanied the worker to the health center and introduced her to the mental health program administrator.

Let us consider some of the dynamics of the group experience up to this point. The group leader's primary task was to place the situation consistently before the two parties. He encouraged a discussion of the differences within the group, always focusing on what might be done to help the patient-worker. Attention to these specific tasks helped reduce the guarded self-protective quality of the two "camps." In this workshop atmosphere alliances became fluid. Subgroups formed, reflecting specific action lines in a particular case.

At times the business agents would retreat into a demand for more general mental health information so that they could "understand" the problems of the mentally ill. The leader alerted the group to the danger of entering the trap of didactic lecturing. Gradually, the sharing of relevant knowledge for dealing with a specific case became accepted group behavior. This, in turn, often touched off interesting discussions of a general nature but was utilized less often as a way of avoiding dealing with the job at hand. In the case of Mrs. Ritter, for example, the psychiatrist pointed out how kindness and "being on the worker's side" helped mitigate some of her suspiciousness and contributed to her willingness to accept help. This led to a lively discussion about paranoid behavior and its possible causes.

Testing new ways of coping with mentally ill workers and searching for knowledge became intertwined. The pragmatic style of the union representatives served to remind the professionals that knowledge had to "pay off" on the firing line. It should be noted that group movement occurred not only as a result of change in the business agent's behavior; the professionals, too, in dealing with actual cases, gradually began to appreciate the valuable experience and expertise of the union official in his own area. The mental health workers developed a deeper comprehension of the job demands in a clothing factory. This permitted new insights into the way psychopathology and a particular work situation interlocked.

Thus, mutual problem-solving—finding new ways of coping with old problems—marked the entry of the group into the third phase.

The clarification of roles reduced the tensions of both parties and led to a workable division of labor with each contributing what he could do best. During the first two phases the parties made few demands on each other, while the third phase was marked by mutual demands. To the surprise and discomfort of the mental health personnel, the business agents began to inquire about plans for patient treatment of the mentally ill, frequency of visits to hospitals, and so on. They became secure enough in the group to raise questions of "quality care." They complained that not enough treatment time after working hours was set aside for patient service and that it often "took too long for results to show." Some of these demands resulted from a lack of understanding of the treatment process. Others were realistic complaints about administrative procedures to which they were not accustomed in the industry. The mental health program did extend its clinical hours (7). At the same time, the questions provided an opportunity to discuss the nature of the therapeutic process.

During this third period the professionals began to make demands on the business agents that had implications for union policy and practice. The group's discussion about the case of Mr. Loberto illustrates the resulting strain on the collaborative process and the steps taken toward resolution. The patient, a long-time worker in the industry, was referred to the mental health program after he dropped out of work. During the treatment process it became clear that one of the factors contributing to his separation from the labor force was his feeling of being underpaid. Despite his paranoid symptomatology, Mr. Loberto had what might be considered to be a realistic grievance, and he was encouraged to raise the issue with his business agent. The following selection from a group record describes what happened:

Mr. Loberto's business agent became angry when the problem was raised in the group. He said that he should be grateful for what he's getting, because he is slower on the job. He then turned to the professionals and indicated that this was strictly a union matter and that they should not get involved. The social worker working with the patient indicated that it is difficult to help a suspicious person like Mr. Loberto if one doesn't try to separate the real complaints from the false ones. At this point the group seemed to drop the subject and go on to another case. The group leader reminded them that the earlier difference of opinion was not discussed. Another business agent suggested that though the worker was getting slower he may have a legitimate grievance. He added, "I know Loberto is a real nudge but maybe you can work it out somehow." The patient's business agent, somewhat upset, agreed to meet with the patient and his social worker and try to resolve the problem.

At the next meeting the business agent reported that the worker did, in fact, have a legitimate grievance, and it was resolved at the factory. This event was used to illustrate the benefits resulting from a trusting relationship in which members can feel free to "make demands of each other and disagree."

The leader concentrated on ways in which each party, by identifying and working on overlapping needs, could implement its own organizational goals. In this vein, William Schwartz believes that:

The worker's search for common ground is expressed in two major forms of activity. One is his efforts to clarify the function of the group and to protect this focus against attempts to evade or subvert it—whether by the agency, the group, or its individual members. The other is represented by consistent efforts to point up for the members those areas in which they feel, however faintly, an interest in the social objects which confront them (9, p. 20).

In the process of helping institutions reach out to each other, the problems of individual people illuminate organizational policies and practices. Each case of a person in trouble can be viewed as an opportunity to consider institutional as well as personal inadequacies. Searching for common ground invariably leads to identification of divergent as well as convergent interests. If the respective parties manage to sustain their face-to-face confrontation, new solutions to individual and institutional problems begin to emerge. An example of this process is the relationship between the union grievance machinery and the collective bargaining procedure. The grievances of individual workers are transformed into policy issues at collective bargaining sessions.

For the trade union, like most membership organizations, mutual aid is the *raison d'être*. This significant feature is also the major theme of an effective group process. Thus, the union setting provides a fertile and potentially congenial field for the practice of social work, and particularly for utilization of the group approach. Bertha Reynolds, who established the United Seamen's Service during the Second World War, commented that it led to a "different *quality* of work with people who feel that a service belongs to them because they belong" (8, p. 1). This social work service with the National Maritime Union proved to be ahead of its time. After the war, another avant-garde program was initiated by the Welfare and Retirement Fund of the United Mine Workers of America (5). Service to the mentally ill miner and his family was an integral part of its comprehensive medical care system. It was not until the 1960s that other unions followed in the footsteps of these pioneering ventures. Currently, social workers with the United Auto Workers (4) and the Retail Clerks Union (11) programs are engaged in providing services and building bridges between labor and the community mental health field.

This development is in keeping with recent interest in involving the consumer of a service in its planning and execution. There are a number of practice issues, however, that must

be studied as social work moves into the new terrain of work
with membership organizations. Among them are the problems
of entry and confidentiality.

Perhaps the most salient practice issue requiring examination is that of entry into a going concern. It is not unusual for
membership organizations to be suspicious of social workers
and other members of the helping professions. One way of
initiating a dialogue is to attempt to help the system deal with
the mental health problem where it feels the pinch. For example, each mentally ill union member with a problem of
maintaining his job or returning to work is a potential link
between a labor union and a mental health program (1). The
question for the social worker is: Will the membership association allow me to take part in its problem-solving process?
Identifying specific tasks through which the "mutual aid
society" can help a member with emotional problems is the
basis for initial collaboration. After a while the social worker
will develop an appreciation of each union's unique history,
style of service to its membership, and awareness of internal
difficulties.

The issue of confidentiality also requires reappraisal. Trying to develop a working partnership is always a hazardous
undertaking. It is difficult to participate in the rehabilitation
of the mentally ill if the partners do not have equal access to
information. The professional is often the recipient of "secrets"
from the patient. The union representative, on the other hand,
may also serve as the depository of confidential information.
If the business agent and the mental health professional are
to work together, however, they must have at least a common
base of knowledge about the individual whom they are attempting to help. In the program with the Amalgamated
Clothing Workers it was found that a worker would usually
permit mutual disclosure between union officials and professionals when he felt that both parties were working in his
behalf.

The mental health movement is interested in establishing meaningful ties with significant institutions in the community. The labor movement, in its quest for improved benefits for its members, has become more responsive to their mental health problems (6). The utilization of a group approach is one means by which to begin to merge these particular institutional interests.

REFERENCES

1. David N. Daniels, "New Concepts of Rehabilitation as Applied to Hiring the Mentally Restored," *Community Mental Health Journal,* Vol. 2, No. 3 (Fall 1966), pp. 197–201.
2. Albert Deutsch, "American Labor and Social Work," *Science and Society,* Vol. 8, No. 4 (Fall 1944), pp. 289–304.
3. Howard Freeman and Ozzie Simmons, *The Mental Patient Comes Home* (New York: Wiley, 1963).
4. Melvin Glasser, "Prepayment for Psychiatric Illness," in *Till We Have Built Jerusalem* (Washington, D.C.: National Institute on Rehabilitation and Health Services, 1966), mimeographed.
5. Lorin E. Kerr, "A Labor-Health Program for Rehabilitation," *Journal of Rehabilitation,* Vol. 28, No. 4 (July–August 1962), pp. 17–19.
6. Arthur Kornhauser, *Mental Health of the Industrial Worker* (New York: Wiley, 1965).
7. Robert Reiff, *Issues in the New National Mental Health Program Relating to Labor and Low Income Groups* (New York: National Institute of Labor Education, 1963), mimeographed.
8. Bertha C. Reynolds, *Social Work and Social Living* (New York: Citadel Press, 1951).
9. William Schwartz, "The Social Worker in the Group," in *New Perspectives on Service to Groups: Theory, Organization, Practice* (New York: National Association of Social Workers, 1961), pp. 7–29.
10. John Sommer, "Labor and Management: New Roles in Mental

Health," *American Journal of Orthopsychiatry,* Vol. 35, No. 3 (April 1965), pp. 558–63.

11. Phillip S. Wagner, "Psychiatry for Everyman," *Psychiatry,* Vol. 30, No. 1 (February 1967), pp. 79–90.

12. Hyman J. Weiner and Morris Brand, "Involving a Labor Union in the Rehabilitation of the Mentally Ill," *American Journal of Orthopsychiatry,* Vol. 35, No. 3 (April 1965), pp. 598–600.

13. Kurt Wolff (ed.), *The Sociology of George Simmel* (Glencoe, Ill.: The Free Press, 1950).

A Function for the Social Worker
in the Antipoverty Program

DAVID HEYMANN

A GLANCE at the brief history of the "antipoverty" programs will show that social workers have frequently found themselves caught in the battle between the poor and the institutionalized power interests. Unlike most of the traditional social services directed to poor people, the newer community action programs have been doing battle with other social welfare establishments, ranging from the local welfare department to the office of the mayor. Although these are fought in the interests of the poor, the community action programs are often the butt of political counterattacks that result in drastic curtailment of funds. As each program withers and dies the professionals move on to new settings, but the ghetto residents are once again left without the services they need.

The antipoverty programs were designed to differ from traditional community approaches in some important respects, as Frank Riessman and Martin Rein have pointed out:

The traditional planning approach derived its legitimacy from social and economic élites. It was assumed that they acted in the "best interests" of the *total* community. . . . The harmony of community interests rather than conflict and vested interests was the accepted orthodoxy. In contrast, the new approach derives its legitimacy from political government and may be more directly responsive to the consumer, to the electorate, and to public opinion than the élites were. In the lexicon of politics interest groups are recognized. The political process accepts conflicts as natural . . . [20, p. 6].

Thus, the very existence of these federally sponsored programs is a sign of recognition that the specific interests of the poor are often in conflict with the interests of established social institutions. The antipoverty program has a difficult role to fulfill in working directly with clients who are the main recipients of services from *other* social agencies. The program, standing directly between client and social agency, is in a key position to facilitate or to disrupt the provision of social services to the poor. Community action programs exist as potential aids and potential threats to traditional welfare institutions serving poverty areas. The tension is further heightened by the fact that programs are at once a part of, and yet separate from, conflicting groups, whether they are tenant organizations, school systems, welfare departments, police, or local landlords. Beck has commented on this from the perspective of a program administrator:

There are sharply conflicting claims placed on the administrator of the anti-poverty program by the various groups and organizations that are both recipients of service from the program and dispensers of service to it. These groups and organizations must be viewed as organs that induce change, and yet they themselves must be changed. . . . A basic problem concerns the need to stay in the good graces of representatives of established power while remaining true to essential organizational purposes [2, pp. 103–104].

This polarization of interests between clients and institutions has been a running theme in the field of social work. During the last 30 years social casework has tried to solve this dilemma by focusing almost exclusively upon the psychology, or psychopathology, of the individual client (19, p. 14). Strongly influenced by Freudian concepts of psychoanalysis, traditional casework methods have often been directed toward helping individuals gain insight into their own behavior in order to cope with environmental pressure. Eventual social change was seen as a hoped-for result of successful individual adjustment. Gordon Hamilton states: "The case method addresses itself to individual adjustments and solutions, but the meaning of these cases taken one by one may prove to be of far-reaching significance" (14, p. 15). Hollis defines the casework task as alleviating ". . . some of the pressure of poverty, on the one hand; on the other hand, it attempts to undo, or to help the individual overcome, the damage his personality has suffered from years, or even a lifetime, of grinding and humiliating deprivation" (15, p. 464).

The therapeutically-oriented approach has been more closely suited to the needs of the economically stable middle class than to the everyday struggle for existence experienced by the poor. Hamilton states: "Causes of unadjustment which are broadly economic will be seen as such . . . while stresses which lead to 'more personal search and action,' whether or not the economic factor is involved, come within the casework objective" (14, p. 15).

As a result, the 30 years have seen a gradual movement of caseworkers from public to private agencies and away from the poor. This disengagement from the poor has been reflected in a growing tendency to discriminate between the psychologically "accessible" and the psychologically "inaccessible" and the accepted classification of many lower-class clients as "hard to reach" or "multiproblem."

The preoccupation with individual psychology has been criticized by both clients and social work practitioners (6). Cloward and Epstein claim that the casework method systematically excludes many of the persons most in need of help (8). Schorr suggests that casework is not effective even when properly applied to "motivated" clients (21). Brager claims that casework is an inappropriate method in work with the poor (4). Miller argues that casework is moralistic and inherently degrading (17), while Specht writes of the case-

worker's sense of inadequacy in dealing with problems of social policy formulation (23). Thus, much of the recent literature dealing with the problems of poverty has turned away
from the individual client and toward institutional reform,
social action, and social policy.

On the other hand, social workers in antipoverty programs
have tried to resolve the dilemma of conflicting interests between clients and institutions by focusing primarily upon the
ills of the "system." The growing body of "social action" literature in the social work journals points to an increasing
tendency of social workers to identify with the ideology and
tactics of the various social action movements. Richard Cloward and Frances Fox Piven, two of the foremost proponents
of social action in the field, have called for "a strategy which
affords the basis for a convergence of civil rights organizations, militant anti-poverty groups and the poor." Thus, "by
the internal disruption of local bureaucratic practices, by the
furor over public welfare poverty, and by the collapse of current financing arrangements, powerful forces can be generated
for major economic reforms at the national level" (10, p. 510).
In "The Case Against Urban Desegregation," Cloward and
Piven recommend the development of separatist Black institutions akin to the ideology of the Black Power movement (11).
Daniel Thursz claims that social workers must learn the elementary steps involved in mounting a social action offensive:
"It is the professional thing to do to participate in civil disobedience when civil disobedience is the only route to social
justice" (24, p. 19).

The theme that runs through most of the social action writ-
ings, and is evident in the work of many of the antipoverty
professionals, characterizes the traditional welfare institutions,
public and private, as the enemies and exploiters of the poor.
As with the more militant civil rights groups, helping clients
is seen as being synonymous with destroying or "overthrow-
ing" the institutional system. Traditional efforts to "change

the poor" have now become attempts to "change the system." But what the social worker actually *does* in effecting such changes is rarely defined in the social action literature. Cloward and Piven never address themselves specifically to the question of the social work role in change efforts. Thursz naively assumes that "professionalism" and a code of ethics can solve the difficult task of developing a working definition for the professional worker in the antipoverty program:

Today, there are many who wish to speak for the downtrodden, the oppressed, and the poor. . . . The greatest strength that the social worker brings is his professionalism and adherence to a code of ethics that does guide his behavior and states that the professional gives precedence to the needs of others over his own interest [24, p. 17].

As seen by the administrators of the established institutions that provide social services, the generalized social action stance taken by social workers in community action programs has created an image of a disruptive force. However, antipoverty programs are typically dependent upon the institutional systems that they are trying to change. For better or for worse, a program cannot function long without attempting to meet its basic obligations toward the fundamental institutional structures with which the poor and the program must deal. This fact is often ignored in the literature as well as in the daily practice of professionals in such programs. After perhaps 6 months to a year of "fighting the system" social workers become indignant when their program is not refunded or when serious questions are raised with regard to the program's functioning. Pearl and Riessman, in discussing nonprofessionals working in HARYOU and Mobilization for Youth, raise an important question: "The question arises as to whether the government (and most private foundations) will long continue to support organizations that 'bite the hands that feed them'" (18, p. 200).

Fighting the system raises ethical issues as well. The social work profession derives its legitimacy from its socially sanctioned responsibility to help fulfill certain unmet needs of individuals and groups within the system. The unresolved issue is: *How does one remain responsive to both the client system and the institutional system, especially when there are elements of conflict between them?* This question must be resolved if the programs are to meet their legitimate responsibilities to the funding source(s) (that is, sanctioning bodies) as well as to the poor. The position that the government, as the funding agency, is the enemy of the poor has proved unworkable for these programs. A new frame of reference must be found if social workers are to find a place for fruitful work within the public sector.

A FUNCTION FOR SOCIAL WORK

It is possible to conceptualize the antipoverty program as having *two* clients—the traditional welfare institutions and the poor. The social work role becomes one of helping the poor to demand badly needed social services, while helping the social agency to meet these demands from its clients. The worker can focus upon the interaction between the individual (or group) client and the social agency. From this perspective the social worker does not choose sides; instead he focuses his work on those areas of mutual interest to both the suppliers and consumers of social services.

The rights and needs of the poor must thus be articulated together with the function of the social agency. The fact that most agencies act ambivalently toward fulfilling their publicly designated tasks often obscures the fact that social agencies need clients, just as clients need the schools, welfare agencies, and other services. The ambivalence of agency toward client and client toward agency usually results in an ineffective and fragmented service-delivery system. The function of the antipoverty program is to improve service delivery—helping to connect clients with agencies and agencies with clients, and working with both individuals and institutions on the obstacles that create gaps between the need and the provision of help. Riessman and Rein define a similar function for Community Action Programs:

What distinguishes the CAPs from the traditional American and the European approaches is their commitment to respond to both the supply and the demand side of the service equation, and in so doing to help reduce the fragmentation, increase the coherence of the welfare system, and facilitate the more human and equitable distribution of resources [20, p. 8].

A similar conception of the social work function in antipoverty programs has been developed by Buford Farris. In his work with delinquent gangs Farris found that as much time was spent in working with institutional representatives as with the gang members themselves (12). Farris characterizes this work as "mediating" problem relationships. This role is based upon the proposition that a person, his subgroup, and the larger society are all dynamically interrelated and interdependent, and that most social problems stem from a faulty and specifically unproductive relationship between the individual and his society. Schwartz writes:

The social worker's field of intervention lies at the point where two forces meet: the individual's impetus toward health, growth, and belonging; and the organized efforts of society to integrate its parts into a productive and dynamic whole. . . . Placed thus in Bertha Reynolds's old phrase, "between the client and the community," the social worker's job is to represent the symbiotic strivings, even where their essential features are obscured from the individual, from society, or from both [22, p. 7].

Attempts by workers to use this frame of reference create certain practice problems, the most important of which begin with the questions: Who defines what is helpful for both sides? What guidelines does the worker have for finding the common ground? Here, as in all effective social work practice, the guidelines begin with the clients' definition of need. The worker may begin simply by carrying messages between parties or arranging meetings where each can express his wishes, needs, and arguments. After this initial step the need for the worker (or third party) is dependent on the form and intensity of the negotiating process. A tenant group may need help with internal problems, such as fights among members or other obstacles blocking movement. A welfare worker may be unable to respond to client demands without support from the antipoverty worker. The work with both parties focuses on the process of negotiation, using specifically defined tasks and concentrating closely on what each party is saying rather than on global generalizations and abstract goals.

THE SYSTEM'S STAKE IN MEDIATION

The welfare departments, schools, hospitals, landlords, housing authorities, and others have in common the fact that they are not adequately providing the services they are explicitly charged to provide. Any complex, modern institution has at least a partial stake in maintaining its *status quo.* Brager writes:

Social science theory leads to pessimism regarding the likelihood of commitment by welfare organizations to the promotion of change. Banfield notes in his study of civic associations involved in controversy that large bureaucratic organizations are neutral in character. Organizational decision-making arises out of their maintenance and enhancement needs [1].

Organization theory—and the experience of a considerable number of Community Action Programs—points to the sacrifice by organizations of commitment to efficiency. Causes and objectives lose in the competition with administrative convenience and environmental peace. Public relations replaces public benefit * [5, p. 62].

* Pearl and Riessman (19, p. 200) claim that "any social agency tends to have a vested interest in the *status quo.* . . . [Thus, they conclude] we must re-align the pressures that now foster empire building and maintenance of the *status quo* so that they will become just as power-

On the other hand, there are forces that move the agencies toward change. The most potent of these is the dissatisfaction of both clients and workers. To avoid unrest and rebellion the traditional agencies must begin to provide more adequate services to the poor. In responding internally to its professionals and externally to its clients the agencies are being compelled to move. Rent strikes, marches, and sit-ins in the schools, welfare centers, and housing projects have demonstrated that agencies will be worse off if they do not respond to the demands for change being made on them. At the same time, the unwieldy welfare apparatus is often as frustrating to agency workers as it is to the clients. High rates of job turnover in welfare institutions may be due to a persistent sense of failure and subsequent feelings of inadequacy and hopelessness.

The problems of practice then move to the question: Will the institutional representative—landlord, school official, or welfare supervisor—accept help from the worker, who is somehow identified with the dissatisfaction of the angry tenant, delinquent student, or welfare recipient? The worker is often seen as a leader of the dissatisfied poor in spite of his attempts to explain and demonstrate his third-party role (and that of his antipoverty program). This initial distrust contributes to the difficulty; but the suspicions of a landlord or welfare worker toward the social worker are in essence no different from the initial resistance of any client toward any helping person. The institutional representative may begin by rejecting the worker; but as the poor, with the help of the antipoverty program, gain experience in obtaining their rights, the institutional representative finds his role becoming increasingly difficult. Mounting client pressures force agencies to

---

ful implementers of a change system as they now are resisters to change." *Also*, for further discussion of the lack of commitment by social welfare organizations to the promotion of change, see: Richard A. Cloward and Frances F. Piven (9).

admit their need for help. And, because of his key position and knowledge of the situation, the antipoverty worker can place himself in a strategic position to help both sides. As the pressure becomes more intense, the social worker repeats his offers to help in mediating or negotiating the conflict.

In the following illustration a social worker offers help to a landlord about to face a rent strike. This landlord had previously been suspicious and angry at the rather militant activities of the worker and the antipoverty program in helping tenants apply legal pressure to force him to repair their apartments:

I said that I guessed he was over a barrel. If he didn't get the building fixed, things would get worse for him; and the problems and red tape in fixing the building seemed insurmountable. The landlord, Mr. T., said rather sadly that it was true, that he knew things would just get worse if he didn't do it. I told him that one of the reasons I had come to see him was to let him know that the Department of Welfare was thinking of putting the building on the Spigel Act (cutting off rents completely) because the building wasn't repaired and a hazardous condition still existed. I said that I wanted to let him know so that he could get the building repaired before he lost any more rents permanently. I also mentioned that some of the tenants were thinking of applying for rent decreases. Mr. T. actually thanked me for this information in a warm manner. He began to complain that no matter how much he tries, he always gets the worst end of things. . . .

Here the worker is providing needed information and support in helping the landlord develop his own solutions to a difficult situation. As in labor disputes, where management invariably needs a channel of communication with striking unions, the landlord or agency official may not like the social worker, but eventually he must have information and help in understanding and meeting client demands.

Later, at another conference with both the landlord and superintendent of the building, the worker is let in on some interesting information. He then analyzes his impressions of the encounter and his own style of work in this area:

Mr. T. began complaining about what a pain this building has been to him and how much hard work with little reward it is. I said I guessed he was sorry he bought it. He brought out all the books showing me all the repairs he had made and how much work he has done in that building. He went on for 15 minutes, apartment by apartment, pointing out each repair he had done and how no one appreciates it. He kept saying that he was sorry he ever started the whole thing in the first place. I mentioned that I bet he couldn't get rid of it and that he must be really stuck—"screwed." He quickly objected, saying that he had many offers from buyers lately and that "something is going on in the neighborhood—at least there are rumors." Mr. T. continued talking about the buyers for the building and finally said that he would settle for 45,000 dollars—1,000 dollars off the assessed valuation—for the building and the vacated hotel on the corner. He asked if Mr. D. was still anxious to buy the building and I said that I would surely ask him and let him get in touch with Mr. T. Mr. M. muttered that he was not so sure the building was going to be sold and T. said that "that is our business, we will discuss that when Dave isn't around." There was a rather awkward silence and finally T. said, "I want to tell you something confidentially—this is off the record. Mr. M. has invested in part of the building. He has an interest in the building and that's why I never come around anymore and he seems to be solely responsible. We are truly partners now but there is no need for the tenants to know this." I grinned at Mr. M. and said that I guess *he* really was the boss. He became very defensive and said that he doesn't act that way even though the tenants accuse him of it and won't listen to him. Mr. T. began to ask me again why people don't want to listen to Mr. M. anymore. I said briefly that, as I told him earlier in the year, there comes a time where people become so angry because of the conditions that they live under that words simply don't count anymore. I emphasized that whether or not this was just or unjust, if people feel that way they simply will not listen. Mr. T. reiterated that everyone seems to be against him but that all he can do is wait for the red tape to clear so he could do what he should.

I offered to get in touch with the Buildings Department for the contractor (instead of the landlord doing this) in order to hurry the process. Mr. T. said that "Now I was talking" and he would tell the contractor to call our office tomorrow. As long as he could avoid scandal he was all for getting things done as fast as possible. He mentioned that he appreciated my patience and then said that he understood that I was "leaving them." We spoke for a little while about my new job and Mr. T. expressed regrets that he could not do all he wanted to to help the addicts in his neighborhood because his business took so much time. Mr. M. and Mr. T. thanked me for coming.

Impressions and *Analysis:* It seems that the only way Mr. T. can accept help (like anyone else) is to feel that the helper is on his side. The difference between him and most of my other clients is that he simply manipulates and co-opts to a greater degree and more obviously. Since I did not oppose him or point out the contradictions in what he was saying, as I usually have done, I imagine he felt that he was convincing me of what he was saying. Thus, he actually began to confide in me.

Another reason that he seems to have trusted me more than in the past is that he knew of the talks I have had with his superintendent (now his partner) and that Mr. M. has probably told him that I was sympathetic. I think that Mr. T. has known all along that there are ways in which I could be useful to him, but he simply could not trust me enough to let himself accept this help. . . .

My style of work with Mr. T. changed at the meeting. In the past I had tried to force him into "being honest" before I would help him. The constant confrontation and pointing out of contradictions caused him to see me as his enemy (not unrealistically). I realized that if he was to use me at all I would have to listen to his "blusterings" as much as I would have to listen to anyone's defensive statements about themselves. In other words, I tried to let Mr. T. work in his own way. Many times during the meeting I wanted to say to him: "You can really cut the bullshit; you can get as much by being honest with me and it will be a lot easier for both of us." I realized, however, that it would be a lot easier for me but impossible for him. Mr. T.'s style (generalized as the "landlord style") is to act like the world is taking advantage of him and so gain a rather exploitive control of the situation through seeming weakness. Specifically, he tries to win people over through sympathy for his plight, and then uses them to satisfy his needs.

I found that by confining myself to the area of mutual need between tenants and landlord (getting the repairs made would lessen the anger and fear of the consequences of tenant action), I was able to work more freely, since I did not have to "fight" or take the tenants' side against the landlord. It is interesting that the landlord also stayed within this range of mutual need. I have finally convinced him (probably through my work with Mr. M.), that in certain areas I am impartial. . . .

THE CLIENT'S STAKE IN MEDIATION

The poor also need mediators, or third parties, in their dealings with institutions or agencies. A rent strike, grievance meeting, or even a phone call to the landlord is not always easily accomplished. The time period between perceiving a problem and taking action toward its resolution is often characterized by anxiety and turmoil. Frequently the ghetto resident is faced with pressures and obstacles that inhibit his problem-solving activity. Legal procedures, the filing of complaints, and formal meetings are unfamiliar activities, and talking with neighbors about common problems may be a new and awkward experience for many people.

The social worker can be quite useful in these areas by enabling tenants to talk with each other as well as with institutional representatives with whom they must deal. In the following excerpt the worker supports an angry and fearful tenant in speaking to the building superintendent concerning apartment repairs:

I said that I knew Mr. M. (superintendent) was not the easiest guy to get along with, but when I was gone she would have no one to do it for her, and it might be easier then, if she could try now. Mrs. B., an extremely nervous and weak woman, was unable to speak.

I said that if she wanted I would go with her and talk to him. There was another pause, and she finally said that she would go talk to him, and it was good that I could go with her because she would feel much less nervous.

We went to visit Mr. M. three times, each time finding him not at home. At first, Mrs. B. sent her child to knock at the door, but by the third time she knocked herself, although a little timidly. Finally Mr. M. answered and invited us in. Mrs. B. stood there speechless and Mr. M. began fidgeting with a piece of paper. I said that Mrs. B. had come to explain to him some of the repairs that she wanted made in her apartment. Mrs. B. then started to speak fluently in Spanish, explaining the things that had been promised but were not done. As she spoke, Mrs. B. seemed to gain strength; she took him to her apartment and angrily showed him all the violations, holes, falling plaster, and leaking pipes. . . .

In this example the worker does not take the problem away from the client but asks her to try to deal with it with the support of his presence. Mrs. B. is able to express her anger and becomes more free to act than previously. Tenants need a worker who can understand the ambivalent feelings of fear and anger and yet is able to move with them as they assert themselves. Conflicts between tenants, a person's fear of speaking in a group, or general feelings of hopelessness and despair must be brought out and dealt with by the worker. Only in this way can the obstacles toward movement be identified and challenged:

Mrs. L. said that she had, at first, been very afraid to participate in the rent strike because her family had told her you don't do those things in this country. But by my support of her, and frequent visiting with the tenants, she had gradually come to realize that she did have rights, and that if everyone stuck together she would not feel so afraid. She spoke about how she had slowly realized that the landlord was cheating her and didn't really care about her;

how alone she had felt; and how good it was to find that her neighbors were with her in doing something about this terrible situation.

As the people begin to support each other, the worker can help them recognize both their common strengths and the obstacles that lie in their path. And as the process evolves, the clients grow in their ability to move into negotiation with other systems. In this process the worker-mediator must learn to play his third-party role consistently, maintaining his interest in the communication between clients and other systems. In the following the worker holds his role up to scrutiny of the tenants before they move into meeting with the landlord:

I explained that at the meeting between tenants and landlord I would be in the middle, between both sides. Mrs. N., a tenant, thought that was a good idea since "my husband flies off the handle, and the landlord also gets mad. Maybe with you there, we can get something done. . . ."

Mrs. N. recognizes the worker as a person who, because of his function, can aid tenants and landlord in controlling their angry feelings, and this service is seen as a helpful tool in negotiation. The ghetto resident usually has the feeling that no matter what he says, he will not be heard. The social worker can be of great use in helping a person master his feelings of helplessness—not only by helping him speak but by guaranteeing an active but objective stance in pursuing the free flow of communication. A tenant, after a heated meeting with the building superintendent, illustrates this concept when he tells the worker "I am happy the meeting went so good, and it was because you stayed on *both* sides, and didn't take sides."

The worker will find that as both parties begin to trust him and understand his role, he will be freer to move about:

I said to the tenants that they must wonder how I worked, since I seemed to be talking to everyone, on all sides, all the time. I said it must seem strange that I expected them to confide in me, and yet talked to the landlord, tenants who weren't on rent strike, and welfare investigators. Everyone thought about this, and finally Mr. Q. said he didn't care what I did or who I talked to because he knew I helped the tenants.

THE WORKER AND THE "NATURAL MEDIATOR"

I have referred to the building superintendent as an institutional representative with whom clients must deal directly. School teachers, hospital aides, child care workers, and others have similar positions within their agency systems. They are closest to the client; they are most often the lowest in status in their institutional hierarchies; and their function is to provide the actual service of the agency.

Because they supply the direct service and are within immediate reach of the client, these institutional representatives bear the full force of the client's angry feelings toward the agency. They are most often blamed by higher agency members for service level problems. The literature on bureaucracy documents the fact that the communication tends to be increasingly negative as it moves down the staff hierarchy (3, 16). Goffman, in another context, suggests that deflecting hate is a latent function of the lowest-level staff: "It is this group that must personally present the demands of the institution. . . . They can come, then, to deflect the hate . . . from higher staff persons . . ." (13, p. 114).

In the housing context, the building superintendent is caught between the agency system and the client system, and any malfunctioning in either of these systems complicates his job. Thus he has a vested interest in satisfying the client as well as the agency: the building superintendent, who usually *lives* with his "clients," must see to it that the tenants receive services, while the landlord receives rent. Lower-level agency staff also have a high stake in proper agency *and* client functioning, for they bear much of the burden if dysfunction occurs. The direct service member of the hierarchy may thus be seen as the *symbiotic link* between service agencies and the poor. In his proper role he embodies the concept of mutual interest and mutual need between systems. At a meeting between tenants and a building superintendent this concept of mutual need is dramatically highlighted by the superintendent's opening speech:

We have been living in this building for almost a year, and it has been hard for all of us. The thing that you tenants don't realize is that I need your help as much as you need mine. We are all Puerto Ricans, and we all live in this place together—we must get along or else everyone is unhappy. I have many problems in running this building, trying to make it better for everyone, including myself. (The superintendent began to elaborate all of his problems and efforts at keeping the building in shape during the past year. He meticulously went over each incident, what he did, and the trouble he was facing.) I want you people, my neighbors, to realize that I am not a bad person and that I really try to make this place better for everyone. But I need you to help me, as you need me to help you.

I can't keep the hall clean if you send your kids down with garbage and they accidentally drop some. This causes rats to come, and they get into my apartment as well as yours. If I don't fix your apartments, you get angry and yell at me, and make things unhappy for me. But if you knock at my door and yell late at night, it makes me angry and makes you unhappy. We are all Puerto Ricans and live together, and we need each other.

With this vested interest in effective functioning on both sides of the service equation, the superintendent actually becomes a kind of *natural mediator*. Helping this natural mediator function in his difficult position is *synonymous with helping both parties*—in Riessman's terms both the "supplier" and the "consumer." The superintendent, caught between conflicting loyalties to landlord and tenants, is in a similar position to the CAP staff member caught between the "city" and the poor. As with the struggle of the antipoverty program to define its third-party role, these institutional representatives must also deal with the basic problem of helping two conflicting parties with a common stake.

As part of his own third-party role the social worker must concentrate on helping these natural mediators fulfill their task of providing direct service to both parties, even while the worker continues to mediate the struggle between the institution and the poor. The natural mediator can serve as a communications channel between tenants and landlords or clients and welfare officials. In learning to deal with the natural mediator the poor are learning to deal with systems that vitally affect their lives. It may be that helping the natural mediators cope with their working situations will enable both tenants and agencies to continue to find common ground long after the Community Action Programs themselves have disappeared. In the long run, the objective is to create social roles through which our institutions can be helped to accept the challenge of change, even *while* the poor are helped to present the challenge.

REFERENCES

1. Edward C. Banfield, *Political Influence* (New York: The Free Press, 1961).
2. Bertram M. Beck, "Knowledge and Skills in Administration of Anti-Poverty Program," *Social Work*, Vol. 11, No. 3 (July 1966), pp. 102–106.
3. Peter Blau and Richard W. Scott, *Formal Organizations* (San Francisco: Chandler, 1962).
4. George Brager, "Institutional Change: Perimeters of the Possible," *Social Work*, Vol. 12, No. 1 (January 1967), pp. 59–69.
5. George Brager, "Motivation—a Social Worker's Perspective," *Education for Social Work with "Unmotivated Clients,"* Brandeis University Papers in Social Welfare, No. 9, 1965.

6. Scott Briar, "The Casework Predicament," *Social Work*, Vol. 13, No. 1 (January 1968), pp. 5–11.

7. Case Record, University Settlement, New York City, April, 1966.

8. Richard A. Cloward and Irving Epstein, "Private Social Welfare's Disengagement from the Poor: The Case of Family Adjustment Agencies," in Mayer N. Zald (ed.), *Social Welfare Institutions* (New York: Wiley, 1965), pp. 623–44.

9. Richard A. Cloward and Frances F. Piven, "Politics, Professionalism and Poverty," paper presented at the Columbia University School of Social Work Conference on "The Role of Government in Promoting Social Change," Harriman, New York (November 1965), mimeographed.

10. Richard A. Cloward and Frances F. Piven, "The Weight of the Poor: A Strategy to End Poverty," *The Nation* (May 2, 1966), pp. 510–17.

11. Richard A. Cloward and Frances F. Piven, "The Case Against Urban Desegregation," *Social Work*, Vol. 12, No. 1 (January 1967), pp. 12–21.

12. Buford E. Farris, Jr., "A Neighborhood Approach to 'Mexican-American' Gangs." Progress Report Submitted to the National Institute of Mental Health, October, 1966.

13. Erving Goffman, *Asylums* (Garden City, N.Y.: Doubleday, 1961).

14. Gordon Hamilton, *Theory and Practice of Social Casework* (New York: Columbia University Press, 1951).

15. Florence Hollis, "Casework and Social Class," *Social Casework*, Vol. 46, No. 8 (October 1965), pp. 463–71.

16. Robert K. Merton, *et al.*, *Reader in Bureaucracy* (Glencoe, Ill.: The Free Press, 1952).

17. Henry Miller, "Value Dilemmas in Social Casework," *Social Work*, Vol. 13, No. 1 (January 1968), pp. 27–33.

18. Arthur Pearl and Frank Riessman, *New Careers for the Poor* (New York: The Free Press, 1965).

19. Bertha C. Reynolds, "The Casework of an Uncharted Journey," *Social Work*, Vol. 9, No. 4 (October 1964), pp. 13–17.

20. Frank Riessman and Martin Rein, "A Strategy for Anti-Poverty

Community Action Programs," *Social Work,* Vol. 11, No. 2 (April 1966), pp. 3–12.

21. Alvin L. Schorr, " 'Mirror, Mirror on the Wall———,' A Review of 'Girls at Vocational High,' " *Social Work,* Vol. 10, No. 3 (July 1965), pp. 112–13.

22. William Schwartz, "The Social Worker in the Group," in *New Perspectives on Services to Groups: Theory, Organization, Practice* (New York: National Association of Social Workers, 1961), pp. 7–29.

23. Harry Specht, "Casework Practice and Social Policy Formulation," *Social Work,* Vol. 13, No. 1 (January 1968), pp. 42–52.

24. Daniel Thursz, "Social Action as a Professional Responsibility," *Social Work,* Vol. 11, No. 3 (July 1966), pp. 12–21.

The Skills of Child Care

DAVID BIRNBACH

A RESIDENTIAL TREATMENT center for children is a total institution in which all aspects of the child's life take place in the limited arena of the institution's own grounds (10). Its function is to offer the individual child a number of related experiences that are designed to help him regain some control over his life and the circumstances surrounding it. The unique feature of residential treatment is the group living situation, in which the child spends the greatest part of his time in the institution.

In order for the institution to meet its commitment to the community it must provide the basic services necessary to sustain children in a living situation in a manner that is beneficial for children, and it must do so in an orderly and effective way if it is to perform its other therapeutic functions. There are daily living routines to be followed, and the living unit must meet some standards of orderliness, structure, and conformity to rules and regulations. In other words, before the teachers, psychiatrists, psychologists, and others arrive in the morning, the children must awaken, dress, make their beds, clean their rooms, wash, eat breakfast, tend to necessary morning chores, gather their schoolbooks, and arrive at their destinations on time.

Similarly, life goes on for the children after the teachers, social workers, and others have gone home for the day. They do their homework, play, relax, eat, shower, and prepare for bed. While these tasks may appear to be trivial or menial, in actuality they are vital to the function of the institution and to the well-being of the children. The group living unit must be maintained as an integrated system, and this requires dealing with the many problems that arise as the result of interaction among children with various emotional problems, and between children and adults who supervise them.

Ideally, residential treatment is designed to integrate the tasks of daily living with those of direct treatment. In practice, however, we have tended to split the tasks of treatment into those dealing with the mind and those dealing with the body. The culturally downgraded task of dealing with the child's body has gone to the child care person. Child care is frequently viewed by other disciplines as a necessary but menial set of tasks—a holding action to maintain the child for more significant treatment intervention elsewhere.

Where the tasks of daily living and direct treatment are separated, and the custodial function of stable and orderly group living becomes an end in itself, the worker in child care performs the necessary tasks commensurately. In fact, the dichotomy between treatment and "routine living" can lead to conditions where if two children are assigned to clean a floor and the stronger one bullies the other into doing all the work, the staff response may be, "I don't care *how* the job gets done, as long as it gets done well." If the child were to say, "You care more about having a clean floor than you do about me," the worker, if he were being honest, would have to admit that the child was correct. If the child care worker views himself merely as a custodian or manager and does not deal with human relationships, it is more than likely that the transactions between the child and the agency staff, and between the individual and his small society, cannot contribute to the overall treatment objectives of both agency and client—their symbiotic relationship. Third parties are then required to help the child express and deal with his feelings, to mediate between the systems, and to unlock them from unproductive encounters in which they then become engaged.

The ways in which staff and children live together, the rules and customs they develop, must be consistent with the treatment goals of the institution and beneficial for the individual children in the institution. In this very basic sense child care is the essence of residential treatment.

PROBLEMS OF CHILD CARE

The child care worker has the task of managing the group living situation and working with the children who are a part of it. He is the operational person who has the direct responsibility for supervising and organizing the regular aspects of the children's daily lives—and for the therapeutic ways in which these become a part of the child's overall treatment.

At the same time that the institution presents its demands to the child care worker to regularize the lives of the children, each child is also presenting his individual demands. In effect, the child tells the worker that he wants his individual needs met as *he* perceives them. He will attempt to convince the worker that his demands are more important than the requirements of the institution; he may balk at rules that restrict him and procedures that are arduous.

The child care person is thus the man-in-the-middle—positioned directly between the agency and its needs for structure, and the client and his needs for individualization. At times the needs of the two systems appear to be in opposition to each other, and the worker then feels the pressure to establish his identity by polarizing the demands and siding with either one or the other.* The polarities are varied: the child *or* the rule; the individual *or* the group; say "yes" *or* "no"; structure and discipline *or* feelings and understanding; punish

* Major credit for the formulation and clarification of this concept is owed to William Schwartz, who served as Group Work Consultant at Hawthorne Cedar Knolls School over a 3-year period.

the child *or* listen to the child; my feelings are more important *or* the child's feelings are more important; be easy-going *or* be tough; get the children's respect *or* get their love; indulge the child *or* deny the child; be an authority figure *or* be one of the boys; be permissive *or* be repressive; and there are others.

The child care person, trying to decide whom he represents, finds himself irresistibly drawn toward the making of "choices"—as though the choices were real. He can address himself to the *instrumental* tasks of discipline, strict limits, and running a "tight ship," or he can concern himself with the *expressive* tasks of listening, empathizing, and exploring feelings (18). The expectations generally are that if he is "tough" he will gain the children's respect; if he is "nice" he will gain their love. If we carry these modes of functioning to their logical limits, the worker must strive to develop skills that will allow him either to win the child or to conquer him. In one sense the conflict here portrayed is whether the worker will adopt a "mother" image or a "father" image—the former representing giving, warmth, love, and affection, and the latter representing strength, rules, and firmness. It may be the polarizing process itself that has led us to regard the child care worker as a kind of parent substitute. The child care person functions as an authority agent of the institution to a greater extent than most other staff members, and he also has more opportunities for real involvement with the children. The job is so difficult precisely because the worker is in such close emotional proximity to the child at the same time that he has major responsibility for his management. Themes of *intimacy* and *authority* are in constant and intense interplay with each other.

To complicate matters even further, the worker also brings to the job needs and requirements of his own that serve to determine the ways in which he will handle problems and resolve conflicts. He may have a strong desire to be liked by the children. He himself may resent rules and regulations. He may feel insecure about being the "boss" and telling children what to do. He may feel that if he does not set very strict limits the children will take advantage of him ("give them an inch and they'll take a mile"). It may bother him if a child puts his feet on the furniture or wears his hair too long. He may enjoy the delinquencies and pranks of some children, secretly gratifying some of his own needs. He may be afraid to talk to children about problems for fear that he may say the wrong thing.

As he performs the roles of disciplinarian, judge, consoler, mediator, and advisor, the worker's senses are continually bombarded with stimuli that are designed to beguile, convince, seduce, disarm, anger, or even hurt him. His situation is one in which he attempts to be responsive to a child's feelings at the same time that he must deal with how he feels about the child's actions. For example, when two children stole their child care worker's car and inadvertently drove it into a ditch, the worker found himself in an extremely complex situation. He wanted to find out what had caused the children to take the car—he was concerned for their safety; he had to meet administrative demands that such behavior not be tolerated, and that serious punishment be meted out to the transgressors; he needed to come to terms with his own feelings about the children stealing *his* car; and he had to work with them on how they would continue to live together. He had to consider all of these factors as they were impinging on him *simultaneously*.

The professional task in the group living situation is to find the viable and operational connections between the institution's needs for a "tight ship" and the client's needs to develop autonomy and to negotiate within and among the various systems with which he must come to terms. As the worker finds these connections, his job increasingly becomes one of performing both instrumental *and* expressive tasks, of maintaining the tight ship *and* individualizing, as he goes about working with the children within the organizational structure and auspices. This is a difficult task and one that the worker never quite feels he has mastered; but it is the road along which lies the development of real professional skill and identity.

What I have proposed, then, is that the nature and the problems of the child care role in the residential treatment setting create complex demands of a professional order that establish the need for personnel with considerable professional discipline and skill.*

THE LITERATURE ON CHILD CARE

There is an extensive literature on residential treatment, but there is little recorded material to illustrate the details of the helping process in child care practice. Let us look at some of the reasons for this.

First, there has been little agreement about what it is that child care workers are supposed to do and, therefore, the work processes they should be recording. This notion is understood by Hromodka, who conducted a systematic field study of the role, functions, and qualifications of child care workers in twelve institutions in the mid-Atlantic region (14). He found that very rarely was there a job description of the child care job. Where the job *was* outlined by administrative policies, the policies were very vague. In addition, the study clearly demonstrated that while the child care worker has maximum exposure to the child, he has minimal authority in making decisions. Hromodka states that "the only areas in which all child care workers in all institutions were free to make decisions was that of determination and assignment of housekeeping chores to children" (14, p. 12).

---

* The same conflicts and demands are inherent in other "total institutions" where there are rehabilitative objectives. See, for example, efforts by Jones (15) and Wilmer (32) to solve similar problems of "custody versus treatment" in psychiatric hospitals, and the efforts in California prisons (9, 16).

Second, child care has been defined as surrogate parenthood rather than as a treatment process. Jerome Goldsmith writes:

Elaborate settings with professional personnel were established for work with sick youngsters only to leave them in the care of so-called "naturals" during a major part of their day. In this manner we joined with the rest of society by stating that anyone can be an effective parent to children. Waking them up, putting them to bed, feeding them, guiding and talking with them, playing with them, settling their disputes requires no special skill, merely common sense. This zone of care was open to all. It escaped therapeutic interest for years [11, p. 1].

Third, there has been adoption of psychotherapeutic concepts and practices in the child care institutional setting, but it has been a relatively recent phenomenon. And principles applicable in more traditional office treatment settings were superimposed on the institutional setting.

The modern history of residential treatment began with a sharp distinction between the professional psychotherapeutic and the nonprofessional management functions. Much of the child care literature sought to "translate" psychotherapeutic concepts for the nonprofessional and to impart to him a greater basic understanding of human dynamics while generating greater self-awareness (7, 12). But the general aim was to give recognition and support to the dedication of the nonprofessional and to extend his tolerance of children's behavior and his understanding of their needs, rather than to include him as an essential member of the psychotherapeutic treatment team.

From this frame of reference flowed many generalized prescriptions relating to routines, nurturing, informal education, recreation, and discipline (2, 4, 21). Many "common sense" guidelines were written with the purpose of modifying staff attitudes and achieving a more rational and sensitive handling of children, which would result in improving their living conditions (3, 7). Manipulative techniques and gambits for controlling difficult children and critical situations were also offered (27).

For the most part, however, the custody-treatment separation remained. The favored residential treatment model combined a structured benevolent and benign living environment with a strong but separate clinical therapy department. One exception was the simple, undifferentiated institutional system proposed by Jules Henry (13).

Some of the recent literature on child care deals with investigations into the daily living environment of the child. Increasingly we have come to realize that what happens in the living situation and the ways in which children live together have a great impact on the agency's capacity to do its job of treating the individual child.

Wheeler, Ohlin and Lawrence, Polsky, and others have shown that inmate peer cultures in institutional settings frequently hinder and undermine agency goals (23, 25, 29, 31). Polsky and others have demonstrated that where child care staff are isolated from professional staff and are given only custodial responsibilities they accommodate to and actually reinforce the delinquent peer group culture in order to maintain control and order (8, 22, 25, 26). Vinter and Janowitz have pointed out that new treatment practices instituted by professionals are of little value if clients continued to experience custodially-oriented conditions (30).

As a result of the above findings there have been increasing attempts to bridge the gap between the clinical and the custodial services of the institution. Efforts have been made to use social group workers and other specialists to bring direct treatment closer to the group living situation (1, 18, 20). Henry Maier, for one, has proposed that child care be recognized as a valid social work method because its activities depend upon the use of diagnosis. He states that ". . . this is the very process that lifts it into the realm of professional activities and differentiates it from parenting and other forms of lay child-caring" (19, p. 12).

The movement toward professionalization of the child care job has been growing throughout the country. There has been a corresponding demand for school and in-service training programs to develop child care curricula that draw upon the wealth of knowledge and experience of our present child care practitioners (6). Eva Burmeister has written of child care work as it is experienced by child care workers (5). In general, however, there is very little in the child care literature that illustrates the integration between daily living tasks and treatment tasks on the operational level.

THE SETTING

The Hawthorne Cedar Knolls School, located approximately 30 miles from New York City, is a division of the Jewish Board of Guardians. It is a residential treatment center that serves emotionally disturbed children who for one reason or another need to be removed from the community to be treated effectively. These children can be placed in the School on the recommendation of private physicians, hospitals, the Department of Welfare, schools, social agencies, or the courts.

The behavior patterns of children who come to Hawthorne cover a wide range. Some are hostile, aggressive, or destructive; others are withdrawn or bizarre. They fall into all three of the broad diagnostic categories of neurosis, character disorder, and psychosis.

Hawthorne has a capacity for approximately two hundred children—both boys and girls. The boys range in age from nine to eighteen; girls are between thirteen and eighteen. The children who are accepted are in the normal range of intelligence, and they are able to live in an open group situation. Children who attack staff members, set fires, are suicidal, or who persistently run away cannot be treated at Hawthorne, since it is an open setting with no gates, fences, or locked isolation rooms.

Over a period of 60 years the School has been progressively transformed from a training school for children designated as delinquents to a pioneering residential treatment center. The institution has been moving away from merely punishing the "bad" child and toward helping him understand why he acts the way he does, attempting to help him find better ways of handling his problems. Much of this has been brought about through the one-to-one relationship between the individual therapist and the child. More recently attempts have been made to shift the treatment process to the cottage—the basic living environment of the children.

The specific client population described in this paper is the senior boys—fifteen through eighteen years old—who until very recently lived in cottages in groups of from fifteen to eighteen. Several of the illustrations in this paper have been drawn from the author's 3½ years experience as a child care worker in a cottage.

THE SKILLS OF CHILD CARE

The concept of child care as a treatment profession implies that staff tasks should relate to the children's therapeutic and developmental tasks—that is, their attempts individually and in groups to negotiate and come to terms with the various parts of their environment in ways that work for them. Helping requires *skill*, which I define as ability, proficiency, or expertness in performing the specific tasks * or operations that are described below.

Establishing a Contract with the Children. This involves a variety of transactions by which the worker and the children arrive at an understanding of *what* they are doing together,

* The formulation of the major child care tasks was developed from our work with our consultant on the planning of a manual for child care practice.

and *how* they will work together. It means clarifying the functions of the agency, the group, the individual, and the worker; searching for the common objectives of their work; establishing a culture of work; delineating the types of problems they will work on together; and clarifying the stake of each and the expectations each has for the other. It includes helping the children come to terms with *who* the worker is—that is, the worker should make himself predictable to the children in certain ways so that they do not have to continually test him to find out who he is or what he will do. It requires facing reality limitations and requirements imposed by the nature of the setting.

In the following illustration a student social worker applies himself to the task of helping a youngster come to terms with who he (the worker) is. The skill involved is the worker's ability to focus on something that needs to be talked about directly and honestly:

When I went into the cottage I reminded the boys in my cleanup group that we would be starting work at 3:30. I saw Marty going down the stairs to the basement. I called to him and reminded him of our job. He answered, "Not me. I have stuff of my own to do. I'm not working today." He continued down the stairs and I did not follow him or answer. I was afraid of not being able to handle a confrontation.

Around 3:30 I called the boys out to work. I went down to the basement where Marty was working on his sculpturing and talking to Phil, another staff member. I told Phil that I had come for one of my workers. He left and Marty said, "You'd better not have very much for me to do because I'm only working a couple of minutes." Suddenly, and I wish I knew why now and not at other times, I felt my own anger welling up, not in a way that would cause it to burst out in a catastrophe, but in a way that I felt I had to express it and whatever came out would feel right. I said, "Marty, this is really starting to get me angry. Every week I'm even afraid to mention the work to you. We both know that we have a job assigned. My part is to have you guys work. I told you that if you don't like your part, or if you think that it's unfair, I'll try to help you do something about it; but it's your problem, and I'm not going to let you push it off onto me and make it my problem." He looked at me curiously but said nothing. I said, still angry, "It's getting to be a real pain in the neck running after you every week, worried that you will refuse to do what I say. If you want to do something about it, okay, but I'm not going to accept any more crap that just means that you're trying to get out of it the easy way." He said, "I guess you're right. What do we have to work on?" I asked, "That's all?" He said, "Well, I think you're right," and he went up the stairs to get his coat.

If the worker is to be helpful, he must, in the context of the work, be able to share his feelings with the children. In this way he helps them come to terms with him as a real human being, and he presents a model of the way they can work with one another. One task in establishing a contract is to help the children come to terms with the *differences* between them and the worker in feelings, opinions, functions, responsibilities, and tasks, without engaging in a battle of wills.

In the following incident the task was to help the children come to terms with the worker. The skill involved was that of defining limits and asserting one's rights and feelings in the context of the work:

I was taking three boys on a shopping trip in my car. The radio was tuned to a station that was playing classical music. One of the boys changed the station to one that played popular music and I promptly switched it back to the former station. He then announced, "Let's take a vote what we should listen to." I said, "No, I don't come into your room and turn off your music or tell you what to listen to. Right now you're in my car and I want to listen to this music." The matter was settled. The boys groaned and poked fun at my tastes but did not question the fact that I, too, had my rights.

Helping the Children Work on the Internal Structure of the Cottage. This means helping the children deal with all the daily tasks of living together, and with the ways in which they are living together; focusing on the ways in which they affect and need to use each other; and working on group problems, such as scapegoating, stealing, and the theme of "Am I my brother's keeper?" It involves helping them deal with obstacles that prevent them from achieving their aims or that impede the group's productivity; helping the group handle its deviants; intervening in the informal structure; helping the children to help each other; and helping them to plan and to carry out activities.

Although the worker's function is different from that of the children, he is an integral member of the group. He, too, has a stake in the internal structure of the cottage; his actions also have an impact on the ways in which the group will live together, and the cottage's internal structure will affect his ability to do his job. This means that the *worker* must also come to terms with the differences between him and the children, and he must help them to express their differences. He must reach for negative feelings, demonstrating by personal example that "while we don't have to agree with each other, we do have to find ways of living together." In the following excerpt the worker's task was to help the members work on their task of making a decision that would affect the group as a whole. The skills used were the worker's abilities to express his own feelings and to help others to express theirs and disagree with him:

The cottage had always had a baseball team and had engaged in vigorous competition against other cottages. Because of the number of players needed, the rule had been that everyone was required to participate under the direction of the team captain. I had taken it for granted that this year we would have a team again, and I prepared to have nominations for a team captain at the cottage meeting. I introduced the subject of the baseball team and one of the boys responded by asking whether we had to have one because he felt that many boys, himself included, were not interested in it. I responded by saying that I had never thought about it before and had always assumed that a cottage team was an accepted fact. I said that personally I would like very much to have a cottage team, but I could think of no reason why we had to have one, and I could live with a decision not to have one if that was what they wished. I then asked the others how they felt about it. The debate that ensued was very heated; I was surprised that so many boys had strong feelings against having a team and that I had been completely unaware of it.

It is easier for the worker to listen to good feelings than to reach for negative ones. At the same time, if he does not reach for them, especially when things seem to be going his way, trouble may emerge later and create even greater problems.

In the following example the group appeared to have reached consensus; the worker used his skills to reach *beyond* the consensus for the negatives that were lurking there. The task was to help the children work on the cottage's internal structure and to make a specific decision:

I had called a cottage meeting in order to find out how the boys felt about admitting into the cottage a boy who was having difficulty in his own cottage and whom the unit administrator wanted to transfer for his own welfare. The impression I got as I listened to the boys talk about the youngster in question was that he might be disrespectful toward staff and present problems for them but that they themselves did not feel threatened by him. The boys were pretty well agreed that he should be given a chance in the cottage, although he might be somewhat immature and disrespectful to staff. As one boy said, "I feel he should come to the cottage and let the counselors struggle with him." Nobody seemed upset at the prospect that he would come to the cottage, but I continued to ask whether there were any reasons why he should *not* come to the cottage.

Barry said, "I think a little inconvenience on our part is worth it if we can help the guy, but I don't like to see the cottage used as a dumping ground for guys who can't make it anywhere else." Immediately, several boys responded with, "Yeah, how come we get all the trash?" Suddenly, we were talking about something else—the fact that the boys had strong feelings about how they were viewed by the rest of the campus as the cottage that had all the "sickies" that couldn't make it in any other cottage.

Helping the Group Negotiate its Relationships with Other Systems. The living unit—the cottage—functions as only one of many systems within the larger system of the institution-as-a-whole. The living unit both affects and is affected by other subsystems in the institutional system, such as other living units, recreational programs, administrative policies and procedures, and food and maintenance services. The children are members of the overall institutional community at the same time as they interact together as members of their cottage community. The worker's task is to help the group come to terms with other systems within the institution and to contribute to the institution's ability to accomplish its goals of treatment—which are also the children's ultimate goals.

In the example that follows the worker's main task was to help the group cope with an external system—the administration; the skill demonstrated was his ability to help them express their feelings and, in the process, to help them do something about these feelings. While working on this problem, however, the worker also had to continue to help the group come to terms with the way they were using him and each other; and he had to define limits, avoid a battle of wills, express his own feelings and concerns, and make a demand for work:

A high-ranking administrator had addressed all of the children in the institution and announced that a more restrictive clothing policy would take effect immediately in order to curb their use of clothing that carried the connotation of a delinquent "style"—tight pants, black shirts, garrison belts, boots, etc.

When the boys returned to the cottage they were furious and most of them proceeded to search frantically through their wardrobes for every article of clothing the administrator had banned. Those boys who owned none of the prohibited clothing improvised to look as deviant as they could. I walked into the room where they were assembling and asked them what they were doing. They answered with real group spirit that they were going to rebel and were planning to march to the administrator's office *en masse*. I said that it was okay with me, but if they followed through with their plan they should also be prepared to live with the consequences, since the administrator would be sure to view their action as a direct challenge to his authority. My statement knocked the wind out of their sails; they re-evaluated their plan and took off the clothing.

About a half hour later I called the boys together for a cottage meeting. I began by saying that they all knew that I had no strong feelings about clothing styles but that they also knew I had a responsibility as a staff member to enforce the rules of the institution. I had felt uncomfortable previously because they had almost forced me into a choice of either sanctioning or suppressing their "rebellion," and I was unwilling to do either because I wouldn't encourage an action that could only result in them hurting themselves; and I wouldn't allow myself to get caught in a battle of wills with them. I said I knew they were angry but that more important to me than the clothing policy were the ways in which we were living together—what we were feeling and doing to each other and how we were working to deal with our circumstances.

In the discussion that followed the boys expressed a great deal of anger toward the administrator, but they also acknowledged that what they had planned wouldn't have accomplished anything for them and, in fact, would have created more problems. Some of the boys took the attitude that "we don't like it but we'll just have to live with it; there's nothing we can do about it." I asked them if they felt the situation was hopeless. They debated whether it was and emerged with a decision to send a delegation of three boys to meet with the administrator the next day to express some of the group's feelings and to request that he meet with the entire cottage.

Helping Individual Children to Negotiate their Environment. The worker must help the children as they make decisions and take actions in their attempts to resolve the complex reality problems of their individual situations. This includes helping children work on problems related to school, family, peers, other staff members, girls, and rules and regulations.

One of the most difficult problems confronted by all child care workers, and one that obstructs the helping process, is what can be termed the "battle of wills," that is, when the worker and the child are at odds with each other and each is struggling to get his own way. The assumption here is that if staff and children engage in a battle of wills, they both lose. The skill involved is the worker's ability to avoid such a battle and to change the nature of the encounter before resistance and anger are mobilized, making the situation worse. There is a distinction between defining limits and engaging in a battle of wills. Defining limits implies that the worker will do what he feels he has to do and that the child should do what he feels he has to do; the battle of wills implies an attempt on the part of the worker or the child to dominate the other, that is, to assert superiority or exercise control.

In the next example the worker's task was to help the child come to terms with a restriction that had been placed on him and to deal with another staff member. The skill involved was that of defining the limit while avoiding the battle:

Ted had been restricted from coed recreation by one of the recreation counselors. When I drove up he was loudly protesting and intimidating the counselor, who was half his size. I remained in my car and watched the interaction from a short distance. Ted saw me, waved, smiled, called out a greeting, which I returned, and then resumed his tirade at the counselor. I continued to watch them. After a few final insults Ted stormed away from the coun·selor and approached me.

"I'm not going to take this crap."

"Okay."

"If you think I'm going back to the cottage, you're crazy."

"Okay."

"What are you going to do if I don't go back?"

"I don't know. I haven't thought about it. I guess I can always come up with something if it's necessary."

"Yeah. I'll bet you can."

I smiled, waved, and said, "So long. I'll see you later," and drove off. Shortly thereafter Ted apologized to the recreation counselor and took his punishment. Back at the cottage he said to me, "Man, trying to get through you is like trying to walk through a brick wall."

Children may attempt to transfer responsibility to the worker for finding solutions to their problems, or they may try to make their problems the worker's problems. In the following incident the worker used his skill to define limits and succeeded in avoiding the battle of wills. The task was to help the child come to terms with rules and regulations:

Bob approached me and asked if he needed a shave for the religious services that were to take place that evening. I looked at him and said that I thought he could use one. He said, "I don't feel like taking a shave. Why do I have to take one? I just shaved the day before yesterday." I said, "Wait a second. Let's start all over." Bob said, "Okay. Dave, do I need to shave for tonight," I said, "I think you need one, but you have to make your own decision." He responded, "In that case, I guess I'll take one; but I still don't feel like shaving." I smiled and said, "That's okay. You don't have to feel like shaving in order to shave."

ISSUES FOR FURTHER EXAMINATION

I have attempted to demonstrate how professional skills and discipline can be applied to child care tasks. The record material presented indicates only a very small measure of the repertoire of helping skills that the worker must develop and utilize in order to be effective in helping children in group living situations. We must define and detail more precisely the kinds of tasks to be undertaken and the kinds of skills the professional child care worker needs in order to help his youngsters in a systematic and disciplined way. We must identify the details of daily living that make up and become part of the entire residential treatment process. We must also identify the major problem areas of children in group living situations, the tasks that confront them at the different stages of their careers in the institution, the significance of their daily interactions with each other and with staff.

There is genuine resistance to the idea that the child care function should be professionalized. Some of the resistance is couched in terms of our lack of knowledge about the specific tasks of these workers, or the lack of vocational training of such people in the light of the complexity of the proposed new role and function. While all of this is true, there is an apparent core of resistance that suggests a continued unwillingness to share the coveted treatment responsibility and decision-making power with the child care staff.

While we want better practice among child care workers, this demands greater skill on their part, and improved systems of education and supervision to help them do their jobs. There are feelings that in the light of the manpower, financial, and training problems it will be too hard to accomplish, that the division of labor with other disciplines would have to undergo too drastic a change, that there would have to be new channels of communication and systems of accountability. Are agencies prepared to develop child care workers to become effective treatment personnel? Are we willing to consider a redefinition of the roles of residential "clinical" staff in the light of a superior child care effort? Are we willing to perceive residential treatment as a modality where the healing is *centered* in the living group and those working with it? Is it easier to live with a child care situation that is dysfunctional to the treatment objectives of the organization than to take the necessary but painful steps toward professionalization?

It is valid to question whether we can ever really achieve the level of institutional child care to which we aspire. On the other hand, are we satisfied with what now exists? If we are to provide true *residential* treatment we must exploit to a much greater extent the deep potential of the group living situation.

REFERENCES

1. Netta Berman, "The Group Worker in a Children's Institution," in Suzanne Schulze (ed.), *Creative Group Living in a Children's Institution* (New York: Association Press, 1951), pp. 117–28.

2. Alton M. Broten, *Houseparents in Children's Institutions: A Discussion Guide* (Chapel Hill, N.C.: University of North Carolina Press, 1962).

3. Eva Burmeister, *Forty-Five in the Family* (New York: Columbia University Press, 1949).

4. Eva Burmeister, *The Professional Houseparent* (New York: Columbia University Press, 1960).

5. Eva Burmeister, *Tough Times and Tender Moments in Child Care Work* (New York: Columbia University Press, 1967).

6. Child Welfare League of America, *Training Courses for Cottage Parents in Children's Institutions* (New York: The League, 1960).

7. Child Welfare League of America, *Training for Child Care Staff* (New York: The League, 1963).

8. Richard A. Cloward, "Social Control in the Prison," in *Theoretical Studies in Social Organizations of the Prison* (New York: Social Science Research Council, 1960), pp. 20–48.

9. Joseph Eaton, *Stone Walls Do Not a Prison Make* (Springfield, Ill.: Charles C. Thomas, 1962).

10. Erving Goffman, *Asylums* (Garden City, N.Y.: Doubleday, 1961).

11. Jerome M. Goldsmith, "A New Concept of the Child Care Function," paper presented at the American Orthopsychiatric Conference, Los Angeles, Calif., (March 21, 1962), mimeographed.

12. Hyman Grossbard, *Cottage Parents: What They Have to Be,*

Know, and Do (New York: Child Welfare League of America, 1960).

13. Jules Henry, "The Culture of Interpersonal Relations in a Therapeutic Institution for Emotionally Disturbed Children," *American Journal of Orthopsychiatry*, Vol. 27, No. 4 (October 1957), pp. 725–34.

14. Van G. Hromodka, "Child Care Worker on the Road to Professionalization," paper presented at the General Staff Meeting of the Hawthorne Cedar Knolls School (April 7, 1967), mimeographed.

15. Maxwell Jones, *The Therapeutic Community* (New York: Basic Books, 1953).

16. Gene G. Kassebaum, David A. Ward, and Daniel M. Wilner, *Group Treatment by Correctional Personnel* (Sacramento, Calif.: California Department of Corrections, 1963), monograph No. 3.

17. Gisela Konopka, "What Houseparents Should Know," *Children*, Vol. 3, No. 2 (March–April 1956), pp. 49–54.

18. Gisela Konopka, *Group Work in the Institution* (New York: Whiteside and William Morrow, 1957).

19. Henry W. Maier, "Child Care as a Method of Social Work," in *Training for Child Care Staff* (New York: Child Welfare League of America, 1963), pp. 62–81.

20. Henry W. Maier (ed.), *Group Work as Part of Residental Treatment* (New York: National Association of Social Workers, 1965).

21. Morris Fritz Mayer, *A Guide for Child Care Workers* (New York: Child Welfare League of America, 1958).

22. Lloyd E. Ohlin, "The Reduction of Role Conflict in Institutional Staff," *Children*, Vol. 5, No. 2 (March–April 1958), pp. 65–69.

23. Lloyd E. Ohlin and William C. Lawrence, "Social Interaction Among Clients as a Treatment Problem," *Social Work*, Vol. 4, No. 2 (April 1959), pp. 3–13.

24. Talcott Parsons and Robert F. Bales, *Family* (Glencoe, Ill.: The Free Press, 1955).

25. Howard W. Polsky, *Cottage Six* (New York: Russell Sage Foundation, 1962).

26. Howard W. Polsky, Irving Karp, and Irwin Berman, "The Triple Bind: Toward a Unified Theory of Individual and Social Deviancy," *Journal of Human Relations,* Vol. 11, No. 1 (Fall 1962), pp. 68–87.

27. Fritz Redl and David Wineman, *The Aggressive Child* (Glencoe, Ill.: The Free Press, 1952).

28. William Schwartz, "The Social Worker in the Group," *The Social Welfare Forum, 1961* (New York: Columbia University Press, 1961), pp. 146–77.

29. Gresham M. Sykes, "Corruption of Authority and Rehabilitation," *Social Forces,* Vol. 34, No. 3 (March 1956), pp. 257–62.

30. Robert D. Vinter and Morris Janowitz, "Effective Institutions for Juvenile Delinquents: A Research Statement," *Social Service Review,* Vol. 33, No. 2 (June 1959), pp. 119–30.

31. Stanton Wheeler, "Socialization in Correctional Communities," *American Sociological Review,* Vol. 26, No. 5 (October 1961), pp. 697–712.

32. Harry Wilmer, *Social Psychiatry in Action* (Springfield, Ill.: Charles C. Thomas, 1958).

Group Work in a
Maximum Security Prison

GERALD J. FORTHUN *and*
RONALD E. NUEHRING

AS LONG AS man has been social enough to recognize the danger of criminally deviant individuals within society there has been some form of temporary or permanent imprisonment or isolation from others. Although capital punishment still exists, mankind has progressed toward a more humanitarian approach to social deviance; and many offenders are considered capable, if given the opportunity, of assuming responsible positions within the free community. The responsibility for carrying out the rehabilitation of offenders has fallen primarily upon our prisons, reformatories, juvenile institutions, and probation and parole agents.

THE OFFENDER'S PROBLEM

It must be recognized that great differences of opinion exist about the basic nature of the "problems" of the offender. The differing views of the general public, district attorneys, judges, police officers, social workers, prison officials, and inmates about the latter's situation must all be considered if a realistic treatment approach is to be found.

At one extreme there are those who feel that an offender's main problems are deficiency of conscience, dishonesty, lack of concern for others, unwillingness to sacrifice, and general incorrigibility. They would favor imprisonment of the offender in a highly disciplinary setting to "teach him a lesson" and "teach him how to act responsibly."

At the other extreme are those (prominently the inmates themselves) who see the offender's problems in terms of his misfortune at being apprehended and convicted of a crime in a basically dishonest society, and in terms of his plight of being in prison. The paramount problem faced by the inmate with this point of view is how he can get out of the institution as quickly as possible. This kind of inmate sees his difficulty primarily as a result of his membership in a certain social class or racial group, and it is quite common to hear such statements as "If had more money I could have beaten this rap." Many offenders feel that their main difficulty is that so many people in society are unfair and phony.

Somewhere in between are those who define the offender's problems as both social and psychological. They see his difficulties as stemming from poor impulse control, social and vocational disadvantages, feelings of inferiority and emotional isolation, social rejection, and lack of trust in others. To them the appropriate treatment would include vocational training, education in academic as well as social areas, and experience in honest, straightforward discussion with peers and staff members about important personal issues, such as self-understanding, self-confidence, and the assessment of one's own social realities.

In discussing client problems one should not overlook the agency or institution itself as a source of many problems, particularly as these are perceived by the inmates themselves. For security reasons a prison tends to be a rather repressive setting in which many rules are stringently enforced. The forced conformity, the close physical proximity of other inmates, and the resulting conflicts and frustrations often produce great anger and hostility. Yet few prisons provide ample opportunity for inmates to release these feelings of anger in a constructive and acceptable manner.*

The fact that many inmates distrust people in authority, and that people in authority often do not trust the inmates, creates serious problems for both groups. It is not unusual for an inmate to state in a group meeting that his most pressing problem is how to get a guard "off his back." For other inmates the most pressing problem is how to make life as tolerable as possible within the prison walls.

As in other settings, the concept of client problems in a prison is very complex and relative to one's own position within the system. In treatment, therefore, it is important that the different attitudes toward client problems be discussed and understood and that both the clients and the group worker see their setting in a realistic way, striving to change it where desirable and possible and to work within those aspects of it that they cannot change.

Perhaps one of the most important adjustments of the group worker in a maximum security institution is to resist the lure of overidentification with either the inmates or the authoritarian setting. He must not close his eyes to the personally and/ or socially destructive behavior patterns of many of the inmates; neither can he pretend that all institutional policies and practices are necessary and effective. The worker must develop his own practice philosophy—one that allows him to work with both the inmates and the rest of the prison staff. He must identify with the needs of the inmates, but also with those of the larger societal system of which they are part. The skill and effectiveness with which he confronts both the inmates and the system that surrounds them will be determined by the specific ways in which he implements this "in-between" identification.

* For a description of the characteristics of "total institutions" see Goffman (8).

While group workers in a prison setting have access to the regularly cited literature regarding group work in general, little is available that relates specifically to group work in the prison setting. One reason for this is the relatively recent introduction of group work into this particular work situation.

McCorkle's assessment of the status of group therapy in United States correctional institutions in 1953 is one of the few broad-scale attempts to gather information about the use of group approaches in a correctional setting. Of 312 institutions contacted only 109 replied; and of these, only 39 were using "group therapy." Four out of five having group work programs used the lecture-discussion approach (12, p. 80). Hopefully these figures have changed somewhat during the last decade and a half.

One of the few works on the practical application of group techniques in prison settings is the guide to group counseling developed by Norman Fenton (6). It was intended primarily as an outline for developing programs involving lay persons, such as the custodial staff, in the group counseling process in order to change the attitudes of staff as well as inmates. Nevertheless, it contains much useful information for the professional. Kassebaum, Ward, and Wilner (11) and Eaton (5) have written about the results in California of the program developed by Fenton.

For a general description of prison life and its sociological aspects Gresham Sykes' book, *The Society of Captives* (14), is an excellent source. Articles concerning criminal behavior by Halleck (9) have appeared in various journals. In addition, Cressey (4), Clemmer (2), Cloward (3), Ohlin (3), and others have written extensively on the subject. Johnson, Savitz, and Wolfgang (10) have put together an excellent collection of readings on corrections that includes many of the classic articles on the subject.

In summary, there is some literature dealing with group work techniques in correctional rehabilitation, and more specifically in juvenile, young adult, and sex-offender institutions (for example, McCorkle, Elias, and Bixby (13), and the journals *Crime and Delinquency* and *Federal Probation*), but little has been written on the dynamics of group treatment in maximum security prisons.

THE SETTING

Wisconsin State Prison at Waupun is a maximum security prison built during the 1850s. Its 20-foot walls enclose 23 acres of land, a population of just under a thousand inmates, and approximately 350 employees. In contrast to other correctional settings, inmates in a maximum security prison tend to be older, to have longer and more serious criminal records, and, consequently, to be less receptive to group therapy or other rehabilitative efforts. This is true for the inmates at Waupun.

The treatment program within the institution includes educational, employment, religious, recreational, and social and clinical services. The program is conducted, however, within a highly structured custodial environment. Psychiatric services were begun at the prison in 1924. With the beginning of field services, in the late 1920s and early 1930s, the first parole officers operated out of the prison. The actual social service department as it exists today had its beginnings some 20 years ago. It now numbers ten full-time social workers, including a student field instructor with responsibility for four part-time graduate students, and a social service supervisor.

Clinical services were first developed as a separate entity in the form of a residential treatment program for sex deviates. The program was the result of legislation that made psychiatric examinations mandatory for certain sexual offenses prior to sentencing and required treatment for the offender afterward. Several psychologists, clinical social workers and part-time psychiatric consultants have responsibility for providing treatment for inmates in the sex-deviate program, as well as for those inmates in the regular prison population who also require their special services.

Group work activities were intiated in the prison in 1951 as an adjunct to disciplinary control. It soon became apparent that such services helped to reduce tension among the inmates and decrease incidents of misconduct by allowing the prisoners to express their anger through talking rather than acting-out. The group work program has since been enlarged in scope and in size; in 1968 the program involved about 350 inmates who participated in group work sessions.

The growth and apparent success of the program may be attibuted partly to the flexible parole system operating in Wisconsin. The fact that most offenders are eligible for parole after 1 year (except those convicted of first- or second-degree murder, and some types of narcotic offenses) generally gives the men incentive to participate "voluntarily" in group sessions.

PRACTICE OBJECTIVES

In a general sense the task of the group worker in a maximum security prison is to help the prisoner meet some of the problems of life within the institution, and perhaps to ready him to return to his community with some modified perspectives regarding his coping behavior. Although the group work ideal in this setting might be to produce a "well-adjusted," productive member of society, a more realistic objective would stress more limited changes in the offender; that is, it would be directed toward helping him learn to exert more control over his deviant tendencies. The challenge to group work in this setting is to bring a number of offenders together in one room to try to effect some examination of their immediate behavior. The setting within which this takes place is artificial and oppressive, and this increases the difficulty of the task.

There seem to be five important client goals in a maximum security institution. The first is to replace acting-out behavior with talking out, that is, for the client to have the experience of verbally expressing his angry feelings instead of resorting to acts of physical violence. The gain to him is that he less frequently will become the object of disciplinary action by the custodial staff. The second is to practice relating to other people and to acquire social skills, so that the client might become more effective in his social interactions. The third is to learn to deal with the reality of the present here-and-now situation, whether in prison or as a member of free society; this might involve learning new ways of perceiving given situations and different ways of reacting to them. The fourth is to learn more about the connections among one's feelings, one's talk, and one's overt behavior. And the fifth is to accept more responsibility for one's behavior, in spite of the limitations in opportunities for self-determination in a maximum security institution.

These expectations become particularly relevant in a prison, because they mobilize certain specific resistances that inmates typically employ to help them avoid the need to look at themselves. For example, inmates frequently claim that so many things are unfair in the institution that they have been victimized—the implication is that only the institution needs changing, not the inmates. They frequently claim that they cannot change because they are helpless pawns, that everything within the institution is so structured that they do not have the opportunity to practice making their own decisions. It is not surprising that one of the most important tasks of group work in correctional settings is to help the inmates face some of their resistances to whole-hearted involvement in the self-examination process. The next section will be concerned, therefore, with a discussion of some of the forms of resistance most often seen and the various techniques we have used in trying to meet these situations.

INMATE RESISTANCES AND
PRACTICE TASKS

"*The World is Unfair.*" In view of the oppressive nature of most prison settings it is common for a group meeting to develop into a "gripe" session. In fact, as mentioned previously, group work was first initiated at this institution as a method for allowing some of the inmates to vent their anger in more acceptable ways than by fighting or engaging in other disruptive behavior. In this sense, it could be said that a complaint session is a healthy and perhaps necessary reaction to prison life. Frequently, however, the griping becomes an end in itself, and as a consequence little is accomplished other than emotional release. Eric Berne conceptualizes this as a pastime, which he calls "Ain't it Awful" (1, p. 110).

In many cases griping is an effective method by which the inmate avoids facing some of his own problems and limitations. It certainly produces much more anxiety for the inmate to begin looking at his personal problems than to complain about prison food, his monotonous job, or other factors outside of himself. The inmate may be joined by other group members in an unspoken alliance in which no one asks embarrassing or confronting questions of another group member.

One technique that workers have used to meet this kind of resistance is a direct confrontation; they give their own interpretation of what the men in the group are actually doing. Although this method often mobilizes the group's defenses against the worker, it is effective in bringing about, at least temporarily, a shifting of attention toward the group itself.

The following example is taken from a group meeting of convicted sexual offenders. The last several meetings had consisted primarily of complaints about the way the institution was being run, the inequities of the law, and similar injustices:

WORKER: I'd rather have you argue a little bit than keep on the way you have been.

MR. O: In other words, you'd like to see your members in a session of that nature like many weeks ago.

WORKER: Yes. I'd rather see that, than have you sit and bitch about the institution.

MR. B: Do we always have to disagree?

WORKER: You don't have to disagree. I'm saying explore. Explore places where you agree and places where you disagree. You spent 6 months agreeing that you hate the place. I agree that you hate the place. What the hell, there are some things that I don't like about this place either. I can agree that some things should be changed, but that doesn't get us anywhere, you see. Everyone sits around and agrees that it's terrible. It's like talking about the weather. Gee, it's lousy today, and everyone *agrees* it's a lousy day. So what?

MR. H: That ain't going to change the weather, huh?

WORKER: No, that's not going to change the weather. That's not going to change *this* place either.

MR. O: If you ate any of that steak this noon, you'd probably have something to beef about.

MR. H: Say, I want to know, like you said we don't disagree, but we don't know how to approach this thing to really get started, you know?

MR. L: Speak for yourself.

MR. H: All right, I'll speak for myself.

WORKER: Good point, Mr. H.

MR. N: We had a nice discussion going last week, and we got to talking again about the joint * and that this was all brought up before several times. But nothing had happened, so why keep bringing it up?

WORKER: Why didn't you say that?

MR. N: What?

WORKER: Just what you said. Why didn't you break in and say that?

MR. N: Because—ah—I didn't know how the other guys in here felt. You showed me how you felt when I brought up about that conduct report I had a couple of weeks

---

* Prison

ago, so I learned to let it go, you know. I don't want to hear any more about it, you know, about the joint; because I know how it is and why bring it up in the group? We're here to help ourselves and bring out our problems. Like you say, we try to avoid that.

In this case, the worker's direct intervention was effective in reducing the amount of griping done in subsequent meetings. The approach worked here because some of the group members were also getting tired of group meetings being merely gripe sessions; they wanted to accomplish something more constructive.

The worker is actually doing several things here to meet the group's resistance. In a sense, he is attempting to promote some dissonance within the group. He is trying to point out some of their own anxiety, a procedure that is a necessary prerequisite to movement. He is also rewarding those members who show an inclination to involve the group in more productive exchanges.

"Let's Talk About Something—and Somebody—Else." The idea behind this form of resistance is to talk about less related issues and someone else's problems rather than one's own. When group meetings are beginning to become less productive because the members are avoiding personal issues, it may be helpful to review the group's goals and the members' responsibility to keep the sessions focused on relevant topics, that is, to re-examine the group's "contract."

We have found it helpful to tape record these discussions of group purpose and to replay the tape at the beginning of the following session. The playback seems to have an impact; individual members, after hearing themselves discuss their purposes, will often become more solidly committed to making the group meetings more productive. The process of recording and replaying the group's discussion of the purposes of group work was used in this case when the sessions were lagging.

After hearing themselves on the tape the group reacted as follows:

MR. W: Did you notice how Mr. K. said he didn't understand a thing I said? Then five minutes later he came back and said word for word what I said.

MR. B: First of all, Mr. W., the man said, "What is group therapy?" What you said was not even related. You talked about two people in the street * in Chicago or Milwaukee.

MR. W: I was under the impression he was asking what group group therapy *should* be.

MR. B: He didn't say that. He said, "What *is* group therapy?" What does group therapy mean to you?

MR. W: To each one it should mean a different thing.

MR. E: What does it mean to you? Basically, what does this group mean to you? Time to get out of the shop, or what?

MR. W: I think it's soul-searching.

MR. B: What does *that* mean?

MR. W: What makes you what you are, and where are you going to go from there.

MR. E: No, no, not how it relates to all of us. How does it relate to you? I want to know what *you* think of this.

MR. W: Well, ah, that question you asked me, it isn't specific enough.

MR. B: Don't evade the question. He said, "What does it mean to you?"

MR. W: I can't answer that.

MR. J: What do you think group therapy is? What does this group mean to you?

MR. W: I think this group is, ah. . . .

MR. B: You're in a bind.

MR. W: I'm in a bind.

MR. B: You don't know.

MR. W: I don't know. Can anyone help me out?

* In the "outside world."

MR. E: No. Nobody's going to help you out.

MR. W: Maybe no one else knows either.

WORKER: It sounds like some of the guys are saying that you have
            a hard time talking about *you.*

MR. W: No, no. I've talked about myself so often, I'd like to
            give someone else a chance.

MR. J: When and where? Where did you talk about it so
            often?

MR. W: In here.
            (*Short silence.*)

MR. J: Where have I been? I haven't heard you very much.

MR. M: Well, maybe you were in a different group, Mr. W. I
            don't know—I haven't heard you either.

In this example the worker's specific intervention was to
add structure to the group meeting by reviewing the purpose
of the meetings, and more specifically, by recording and replaying the group's discussion of this issue. What the worker
has done, in effect, is to encourage the group members to take
an active part in meeting the resistances of its individuals.
Many of the members solidly confront the resistive member
in an attempt to get him to talk about himself.

"I Can't Change Because They Won't Let Me." One of the
real treatment limitations of a maximum security prison is that
behavioral requirements are so structured that inmates actually
have few opportunities for demonstrating autonomously responsible behavior—and consequently *change*—in themselves.
Although a relative minority of the total inmate population at
this institution is held under "close" custody—a classification
necessitating maximum supervision—the security considerations of operating a maximum security institution necessitate
strict regulation of the activities of the total inmate population. Only a few inmates are allowed relatively unrestricted
movement within the institution, and even in these cases it is
limited to those activities required by their jobs in the institution.

As they adapt to the day-to-day life of the prison, certain inmates are more than happy to relinquish themselves to the authority of the correctional treatment staff. In justification of their own passivity they fix on the fact that prisons tend to foster dependency. This type of inmate, when confronted with his weak-willed dependency in a treatment situation, will often respond with something to the effect that "you're the college graduate expert—you tell me!" Or he will say, in so many words, "What happens to me really depends on those other people. I don't have any responsibility for making decisions for myself." In this way inmates are able to resist the idea that they may have to change something about themselves.

A further consideration, of course, is the fact that it is not "socially acceptable" within inmate circles to deviate from *subcultural norms*, that is, the "inmate culture." Acceptance by fellow inmates necessitates passive refusal to change the manner in which the individual inmate relates to his correctional environment. Both facets of the above are clearly seen in the following discussion:

MR. C: You tell us . . . uh, me . . . to be . . . what did you just say—yah, assertive. Take the responsibility for the way I act. Fat chance. I'm a con, I know it, the screws * know it, and that's the way it's gonna be.

WORKER: Only if you want it to be.

MR. C: What do you mean?

MR. N: He means you may be a con, but you don't have to act that way. You know, you can be considerate. . . .

MR. C: To a screw? Not in here. I'd be labeled a rat before you you know it.

WORKER: By whom?

MR. C: You know who.

WORKER: Are the other inmates in here more important than getting out and not coming back?

* Guards

MR. C: They're the only friends I've got. Anyway, what dif-
          ference is it gonna make how I talk to the screws. Far
          as they're concerned I'm still a con and always will be.

The worker has attempted to introduce an area within
which the inmate can exercise responsibility; that is, the manner in which he relates to staff and peers. The worker has also
attempted to clarify for this individual the determinants of
his behavior. The worker's main concern is to draw the group's
attention to this point. On the one hand, the inmate indicates
there are few ways he can demonstrate change in himself,
with or without the desire to do so. On the other hand, he
points out that to disregard the authority differential, that is,
to treat the staff with consideration, would be unacceptable to
fellow inmates and staff alike. This may be true, but recognizing the source of pressures and the concommitant challenge
may stimulate the inmate who desires to move in new ways.

*"I Can't Change Until I'm on the Streets Again, Faced with
Real-Life Problems."* A corollary to the "I Can't Change Because They Won't Let Me" form of resistance is one in which
inmates resist changing by claiming they have accomplished
as much as they can while in the institution. In group work,
one approach to this resistance is to focus very definitely on
the immediate day-to-day problems confronting persons within
the institution. One important area, for example, is how well
an individual is able to relate to others around him and
whether he has been able to change this in any way since
joining the group. The individual can also examine whether
he has become more assertive in his work, or if he has been
able to take positive steps toward improving himself through
education, recreation, hobbies, and other pursuits.

The worker in the following excerpt is trying to deal with
this form of resistance by encouraging the group to focus
explicitly on the individual's behavior within the institution:

WORKER: I realize you are kind of limited in the things you can do here, but perhaps you men in the group could give Mr. W. some suggestions on how he could practice being more assertive while here in the institution.

MR. B: (To Mr. W) I think you should try to mix with other people more. It looks to me like you are always wanting to be by yourself. It looks like you are afraid people are going to take advantage of you or something.

MR. M: I think he should pick out a guy that's hard for him to talk to and make a point of going up to him every so often.

MR. W: Well, it's simply just because I'm not interested in sports or any of that stuff that all the people here talk about. I just love lectures and concerts and . . . .

MR. M: For Chrissake, get back in here. You're in prison. You know they don't have any of that stuff in here. When I first came in here, I didn't like basketball either, and I told myself that I really wasn't interested in it. But later I decided to try it, because I wanted to do *something*. So I did, and I kinda goofed up at first, but I began to like it, and now I really enjoy it.

MR. W: Well, I like swimming and if. . . .

MR. M: W., will you get back here with us? You're in prison. Can't you get that through your head?

MR. B: I think you are just trying to avoid mixing with people.

WORKER: Is there any kind of activity, Mr. W., that you might want to try during this next week? You can try it and see how you do and then we will talk about it again at our next meeting.

MR. W: Well, maybe I could try shuffle-board, or something like that, but I'm really not interested in anything they have here.

In this example, the worker is trying to make the member's goals more concrete and immediate. The group helps to keep the discussion reality-oriented. It might be noted also that small goals are obviously more easily reached and that the

positive reinforcement of success is very beneficial to one who
has not experienced much success in any of his previous under-
takings. This particular inmate subsequently was somewhat
successful in reaching his limited goal and he was later rewarded by the group.

*"I Broke the Law Because of My Traumatic Childhood Ex-
perience!"* A special kind of resistance is encountered with
some clients who have had considerable exposure to formal
treatment programs and who resist changing their behavior by
using psychological theory to justify this lack of change.[*] They
tend to believe that individual or group psychotherapy is a
process in which they simply discuss their past lives and attempt to isolate the various childhood experiences that have
had undesirable influences upon the development of their
personalities.

Such clients appear to hold two basic assumptions concerning treatment: first, that once a person has found the "cause"
of his objectionable behavior by delving into past childhood
conflicts this behavior will somehow disappear with very little
effort or discomfort on his part; and second, that *unless* the
client finds the "key" or cause of this behavior back in his
infancy or childhood he cannot change his behavior. This
form of resistance can be carried even further by the client
who claims that he cannot change his present behavior because he cannot remember his childhood conflicts. He thus
makes it the staff's responsibility to identify and bring out his
painful childhood experiences through the use of hypnotism,
drugs, and other aids to psychotherapy, even though the setting may preclude the use of such aids.

In attempting to work through this form of resistance, the
group worker challenged the theory that understanding early
childhood conflicts is *all* that is necessary for changing present

---

[*] This is similar to Berne's formulation of the game of "Wooden Leg,"
that is, "What do you expect of a man with a wooden leg (or such a
poor childhood)?" (1, p. 152).

behavior; in fact, he questioned whether it is even a necessary prerequisite (7). The following excerpt from a group meeting illustrates the client's resistance and the steps taken by the worker to deal with it. One member of the group had earlier complained that he was not getting anything out of group treatment. He went on to talk about his past treatment in other institutions and his feeling that he had made much more progress through hypnosis. It later became apparent that what he experienced as "progress" was a psychotherapist being interested in him and giving him a great deal of attention, rather than any observable behavioral changes on his part:

MR. B: I think hypnotism would be more helpful than group therapy, because a man who's trained with hypnosis, ah, can get right through to find out the real you. There's a lot of things that you ain't gonna remember because your mind has buried it so far back that it might take you a hundred years of therapy to really bring it out—to see it, to notice and to be able to bisect it and see what the hell it is.

MR. O: Yah, but there ain't enough psychiatrists to take care of the people the way it is, let alone try to use hypnosis with everyone.

MR. W: You make it like your mind is so complicated that you could never understand it.

MR. B: I think everybody's mind is complicated—the most complicated thing you can find—and we're just scratching the surface. We shouldn't really expect too much anyway. I think there are a lot of things that I could remember about if I wanted to, but they are buried so damn far and it's so doggone threatening to me that I don't even scratch the surface as far as getting to them.

WORKER: I guess what you have been saying today is that the only way that you will be able to change is if you can bring all these memories back, to know everything or to know a lot of things about your past life. And once you have reached this point where you understand the

reasons for your problems, then all of your present behavior is going to change and you won't have any further problems.

MR. B: I'm not saying the behavior is going to change immediately—no, but the more you know about your
childhood, the better off you are. What I am saying is
that I just can't remember some things that have happened that I just don't want to remember. . . . Don't
you think it would be a good idea to get these dang
things out—to have a look at them?

WORKER: Sometimes, yes, but realistically we can't expect to
understand ourselves completely or to know everything
that has happened in our childhood.

MR. B: No, I'm not saying that from therapy you are going
to know everything about yourself, but you should learn
some things about yourself which can be important.

WORKER: I'm not denying this at all. I guess what's happening
to me now is that I'm getting angry. Let me explain
why. Because it sounds to me like you are blocking the
whole idea of being able to change because you can't
find these keys in your childhood, whatever they might
be, that have given you some trouble or conflict. You
are putting a block in there and, in effect, you are
saying, "I can never change until I find out all these
things about myself from my childhood." And then it
seems as if you are going further by saying, "Well, I'm
not receiving the right kind of treatment, such as hypnotism or drugs or what not." What I'm saying then,
at least the way it looks to me, is that you are blocking
out the possibility that you might be able to change
your behavior.

MR. B: I'm not blocking everybody's view of it. I'm just blocking
my own view.

From this point the group moved into a lively discussion
about whether one has to understand his earlier life conflicts
or know the cause of his objectionable behavior in order to
change that behavior. Then one group member described how

he had been able to make some changes in his present life even though he did not understand a lot of things about himself. The following resulted:

MR. B: Maybe I'm just raising a big bitch session—I'm just so goddam mad with that psychiatrist—just rejected what I talked about without even analyzing it. That bugged me. I just believe there's somethin' out there. I suppose I'm a little bit like the guy who's lookin' for the wonder-drug cure for cancer.

MR. O: Well, that's natural. I'd like to go over to the State Hospital and get shock treatment and have all this past shame and stuff knocked out of me, too. But it's impossible to do, because they're not gonna let you. Let's put it that way . . . I mean, everybody would want hypnotism or shock treatment sure, but why do *you* want this, Mr. B? Is it because you think you would get more help that way or is it just because it is easier?

MR. B: I really think I can get more help that way, not just because it's easier. I've seen these changes take place in other people because. . . .

MR. O: Well, then, we've got it down then that you honestly believe it would be easier?

MR. B: Well, let's put it this way . . . when you come right down to it, it would be easier, yah.

MR. O: Now comes the fact, or can you accept the fact that you're just not gonna get it?

MR. B: I guess I'll have to, even though I don't like it.

MR. O: Yah, see this is what I'm gettin' at; here's where the upset comes in. . . . Once you get to the point where you accept the fact that you're not gonna get the damn stuff, you got control over something, see? A minor thing, maybe it's a big thing—who knows? But you get control over one thing; then you can go on to the next thing.

In this instance the worker tried to clarify what he felt was the main issue under discussion and to confront what appeared to be a resistance to change. At that point the worker became more frustrated by the continued resistance and began to show anger. He acknowledged his anger and explained his feelings. As it turned out, this show of honesty seemed to have a beneficial influence on the group members, and they subsequently became increasingly open with their own feelings and motivations.

SOME FINAL COMMENTS

The social worker who practices in a correctional institution must be aware of his values, attitudes, and identifications as they are related to both the administration and his clientele. This is particularly significant in a maximum security institution, where considerations of custody and security are ever present. While these factors are restrictive, avoidance of them constitutes one stimulus for change. Denial by the inmate client of any personal problems must of necessity fly in the face of the realities of imprisonment. At the same time, inmate identification of "treatment" with "mental illness" may preclude participation by inmates who prefer the rewards of the inmate subculture to the painful process of self- and social-analysis often required for re-entry into society and release to the "streets" (9, p. 410). The group worker who is aware of the dynamics of this three-way relationship between the client, the inmate subculture, and the administration, can adopt a treatment position somewhere in between—a too close identification with any one of these positions can severely hamper, or even eliminate a work-oriented communication with the inmates. Sincerity or honesty in personal views is a prerequisite in forming working relationships with inmate client groups; they are usually hypersensitive to insincerity or hypocrisy.

The resistances listed above—avoidance of "problem areas," failure to recognize reality, resistance to personal involvement, and resistance to painful self-analysis—arise out of individual personalities and the subcultural determinants of the prison setting. The opposing positions usually adopted by the inmate population and the prison administration make the small peer group an extremely important vehicle for addressing the objective of inmate identification with societal values. Constructively directed criticism or reward by the peer group is much more effective than the same behavior on the part of the worker, who is essentially an outsider.

One must keep in mind that the goals of the correctional worker seldom include basic personality change; they are more likely to focus on more limited objectives. The worker may be able to help his clients recognize new behavioral responses to the situations commonly encountered in the prison setting. As an extension of this approach, a program is being developed at Wisconsin State Prison to "teach" appropriate responses to "real-life" experiences for those inmates, many of limited intellectual capacity, who appear to have gained little from traditional discussion approaches. Tape recordings, movies, teaching machines, and role-playing could provide simulation of real-life situations and allow offenders to experience modifications in their social behavior. More specifically, learning to actually express one's feelings, as in handling anger in a group setting, is assumed to be preferable to mere discussion of the need for behavioral modification. It is our belief that such an approach is one of the ways in which we can make our group programs more effective for a greater number of offenders.

REFERENCES

1. Eric Berne, *Games People Play* (New York: Grove Press, 1964).
2. Donald Clemmer, *The Prison Community* (Boston: Christopher Pub. House, 1940).
3. Richard A. Cloward, *et al.*, *Theoretical Studies in Social Or-*

ganization of the Prison (New York: Social Science Research Council, 1960).

4. Donald R. Cressey (ed.), *The Prison* (New York: Holt, Rinehart & Winston, 1961).

5. Joseph W. Eaton, *Stone Walls Do Not a Prison Make* (Springfield, Ill.: Charles C. Thomas, 1962).

6. Norman Fenton, *An Introduction to Group Counseling* (Washington, D.C.: The American Correctional Association, 1957).

7. William Glasser, *Reality Therapy* (New York: Harper & Row, 1965).

8. Erving Goffman, *Asylums* (Garden City, N.Y.: Anchor Books, 1961).

9. Seymour L. Halleck, "The Criminal's Problem with Psychiatry," *Psychiatry: Journal for the Study of Interpersonal Processes*, Vol. 23, No. 4 (November 1960), pp. 409–12.

10. Norman Johnson, Leonard Savitz, and Marvin E. Wolfgang (ed.), *The Sociology of Punishment and Correction*, 2nd Edition (New York: Wiley, 1970).

11. Gene G. Kassebaum, David A. Ward, and Daniel M. Wilner, *Group Treatment by Correctional Personnel* (Sacramento, Calif.: California Department of Corrections, 1963), monograph No. 3.

12. Lloyd W. McCorkle, "The Present Status of Group Therapy in United States Corectional Institutions," *International Journal of Group Psychotherapy*, Vol. 3, No. 1 January 1953), pp. 79–87.

13. Lloyd W. McCorkle, Albert Elias, and F. Lovell Bixby, *The Highfields Story* (New York: Henry Holt, 1958).

14. Gresham Sykes, *The Society of Captives* (Princeton, N.J.: Princeton University Press, 1958).

"Program" in Group Work: Another Look

LAWRENCE SHULMAN

CONCERN about the validity of "program" has been a recurrent theme in the development of group work. Group activities that deviated from the "talking" or "discussion" model of interaction, central to social work with individuals, have often been viewed with some degree of skepticism by the profession as a whole. Most group workers can recall their student days and the sometimes sarcastic, often envious, comments of their colleagues who had observed them as they engaged in folk dancing and finger painting in their "program" class. While it might appear that the appropriateness of such activities is no longer in question, a survey of social work educators revealed that there were ". . . expressions of sensitivity (from faculty, agency staff, and students) about emphasis on activities in social group work education" (8, p. 50).

The difficulty can be traced, in part, to an earlier stage of professional development and to the original formulation of "program" as a separate and unique category of group-member interaction. Our continued efforts to rationalize the inclusion of this "separate" entity into our practice has reflected an inability to free ourselves from early misconceptions. Trapped by our first steps, we have proceeded to create new and equally unreal dichotomies in an attempt to shore up the old ones. For example, we have concerned ourselves with distinctions between activity and discussion, process and program, and task and growth, when our efforts should have been directed toward identifying the different ways people in groups use each other for mutual aid and the role of the worker in assisting them to do so.

In this chapter I shall try to point out how conditions earlier in our development affected formulations in our practice theory. Some of the ways in which people use each other will also be examined in a beginning effort to develop clarifying categories, and the role of the worker will be discussed. In the process of exploring these themes some of the assumptions underlying earlier developments in group work practice theory will be challenged.

SOME BACKGROUND

Our early historical roots are firmly implanted in settlement houses and national service organizations. Grace Coyle suggested that:

The very nature of the functions to be performed set the problem that the developing body of practitioners had to solve. Their first problem centered around the questions as to what people wanted to do for recreation or what they wanted to learn in their spare time. It was out of these first questions that there developed the extensive experience with program activities [2, p. 39].

The task of these early practitioners was not a simple one; as Gisela Konopka points out, "for many years group work and recreation/informal education were erroneously considered synonymous" (7, p. 4). From the beginning these practitioners were faced with the dual tasks of distinguishing themselves from recreation and education professionals—who appeared to be engaged in similar activities—and finding their connection with the social work profession. Part of their problem, as they apparently perceived it, stemmed from the difficulty in integrating a predominantly "doing" or activity-oriented group work profession into a mostly talking-oriented social work profession. The magnitude of the task was great when one considers that much of what we now know about communications, learning, psychoanalysis, and group dynamics was not yet available to them.

Poised between the recreation worker who refused to disclaim kinship and the social worker who could not see a connection between what he did and the group worker's "fun and games," it became necessary to develop a position to resolve the conflict. Unfortunately, the earlier thinking was postulated upon the existence of a dichotomy between "talking" and "doing." These earlier events led to some of the dilemmas that still haunt us today.

Attempts to resolve the dichotomy began when a causal relationship was suggested between program and individual growth. While it was true that a party, a trip, or a crafts activity was important to group members for the simple enjoyment it provided, stress was placed upon the additional dividend of its impact upon the individual's learning and growth. Part of group work's uniqueness as a profession, it was suggested, was related to our knowledge and use of these connections.

Subsequently, Coyle argued that our concern with process as well as program and our understanding of relationship meant that we would enhance the value of program (3, p. 9). In this way the social worker's use of program might still outwardly resemble that of the recreation worker, but our concerns with the relationship among members and the ways in which program affected them would distinguish us as professional social workers. We would use our knowledge of the relationship between program and individual growth to influence the process among members, and the group worker was thus obliged to diagnose the needs of his group members. A premium was placed upon the worker's ability to prescribe activities designed to meet those needs.

While the "doing" of program was accepted as different

from "talking," the worker's use of program to influence
growth and change would at one time separate him from
recreation and at the same time unite him, in terms of goals,
knowledge, and values, with casework. The issue of a method
and skill held in common with the professional recreation
worker would be obscured by vague terms, such as "enhance"
and "enable." While the group member might *think* he was
simply involved in a recreational program, in actuality he was
being indirectly and secretly influenced by the worker. Program, at first a source of embarrassment, was thus transformed
into a potent "tool" of the worker.

A MIXED TRANSACTIONAL MODEL

To take the next step, the word "program" itself must be
recognized as an unproductive construct. Based upon the
notion of a dichotomy between doing and talking, it ignores
the fact that relationships among people can best be described
with a *mixed transactional model.* In the complex processes
of human interaction people express feelings, ideas, support,
interest, and concern—an entire range of human reactions—
through a variety of mediums. The concept of a mixed transactional model implies that all of these mediums—words, facial
and body expressions, touch, shared experiences of various
kinds, and other forms of communication (often used simultaneously)—be included when considering the means by
which transactions are negotiated and consummated. We
should not fragment human interactions by forcing them into
such categories as "talking" and "doing" but should focus instead on the common denominators among transactions, defined here as *exchanges in which people give to and take
from each other.* As group workers we are concerned with
helping people who are pursuing common purposes to carry
out mutually productive transactions.

From this point of view one does not need to ascribe social

work purposes to specific forms of activity, but rather to identify how group members use a particular *medium of exchange* to meet their common needs. If we accept and respect the notion of a mixed transactional model of human interaction then we need go no further in our attempts to justify activities except in terms of their utility to our clients, and their acceptability to them.

This frees us from the meaningless hierarchical struggle in which "talking" becomes a preferred form of interaction and represents the professional goal of the worker. The question is simply a functional one: Which medium of exchange will the members choose in attempting to meet their common needs?

SOME FUNCTIONS OF SHARED ACTIVITY

Negative reactions to some of the media commonly used by group members may be related, in part, to grandiose claims in support of their use. Surely people and their developmental processes are more complex than is implied by claims that specific activities will improve self-image, support ego, or create spontaneous, creative individuals. We stand on much firmer ground if we describe, instead, the specific and immediate functions of various mediums as they are played out by group members who make use of them for their own purposes. Let us look at some examples of their functions— some obvious and some more subtle.

Human Contact. A central function of shared activity is to provide people with the opportunity for contact with each other. The first evidence of this need for human stimulus comes from observation of the effects of stimulus deprivation on the young child. Cut off from human contact, he quickly shows marked developmental retardation and in extreme cases may even die. Thomas Szasz points out that modern psychoanalytic thinking is very much interested in physical object-seeking mechanisms, such as touch and caressing, through which man seeks to make contact with others. He continues by suggesting the same object-seeking function for verbal language. He points out that there is a

. . . general intellectual tendency to assume that the important thing in verbal communication is the (logical) content of the message. Thus we look for all sorts of meanings in language, and rightly so. This very meaningfulness, however, distracts attention from the non-specific object-seeking function of language [11, p. 145].

Eric Berne discusses the concept of "stroking"; he talks of the need of adults to get verbal-social equivalents of the physical stroking contact considered indispensable for the total well-being of the infant (1, p. 15). If we accept the notion that there is a basic need for human contact, then people are faced with the necessity for developing ways of achieving this. Berne describes this process as one in which individuals must "structure their time" when together (1, p. 16). A shared experience, which may offer individuals other specific rewards, is one way in which group members may structure their time together so that they may meet their human-contact needs.

This function was put into words by a member of a Senior Citizen group in the following record excerpt. The worker (new to the already established group) had just described her function; she then began to work with the group toward reestablishing its central tasks:

"Now that you have some idea of why I'm here, what do you want from the group?" Without a second thought, Mrs. Lamb threw up her hands, laughed, and said "Pleasure." Mrs. Dan, who had moved her seat closer to me said, "Respect and understanding." The entire group laughed, and I felt as though some barrier had been broken. The group seemed to feel this also. . . .

Mrs. Fair began talking about war and poverty, and she began using her hands. She continued by saying that so much is happening in the world. . . . "If we, in our little group can have . . . human feeling, this means so much." She talked a while longer and ended with the words "human feeling." Mrs. Base broke the mood by saying, "Don't make me cry."

Data-Gathering. As members work on their common tasks they may need access to data that are not immediately available. While a great deal of relevant data are contributed by group members and the worker, certain tasks may demand specific information requiring a degree of expertise in a subject. Welfare clients interested in work training, for example, might invite an employment counselor to answer their questions. Senior citizens might arrange a meeting with a social security administrator to clarify their rights. Teen-agers preparing to enter the work field might arrange a series of trips to business or industrial complexes. In each case the activity itself promotes the purpose of the group. The function of such activities can be described as *data-gathering.*

In the following excerpt a worker helps a group of welfare mothers in their initial meeting identify how they wish to use the group experience offered by the agency. Their first impulse is to seek information. It is interesting to note that much of what they want to know had already been shared with them in other contexts. As they pursue data-gathering in the group, however, they do so actively, investing a good deal of energy and reaching out to help each other understand:

I said we're at the point where we are going to begin to look at what we're going to talk about. I nodded toward the group and asked, "What do you think?" Immediate reaction: Mrs. C. started talking about food stamps and it being the most important thing right now "because it's new and a lot of people don't understand it." Miss C. backed that up as did Miss D. and Miss B. There were nods of agreement. I waited. Miss C. said that she wanted to talk about this thing called "Work Experience" that you people have down at the Welfare Department. Miss B. nodded to that, saying that she knew of an in-work experience that is "working out real good" and that she knew people who have had terrible times and she wants to know what it's all about. After some discussion about Work Experience Miss B. started talking about job training—"like on-the-job training, you know?" Her questions related to what happens to the AFDC check should a person be accepted for job training. . . .

Rehearsal. Another important use of activity by members is for the development of skills in preparation for specific life tasks. Group members who are faced with the immediate demands of a situation or are preparing to take on new developmental roles may structure a practice situation in which they can experiment in relative safety. An example of the first might be the use of role-playing by school children as a way of preparing to meet with a teacher to discuss classroom problems. An example of the second would be a teen-age group that plans a party to create an opportunity for members to practice the social skills necessary for the courtship phase of life. The following record excerpt illustrates the "rehearsal" nature of the social activities of mildly retarded adolescents in a residential institution:

About 15 minutes before the party ended Henry (who was twenty-one years old) walked up to me with a broad grin on his face. He asked me if I remembered his telling me that he did not have a girl friend. I said I did. He replied, still grinning, ". . . well I have one now." I told him that I thought that this was great. A few moments later he brought over the girl who had come without a date and introduced her to me. On the way back to the cottage Henry lagged behind. He asked if he was allowed to kiss the girl goodnight. I said he was if he wanted to. He said good and walked off. As we were returning to the cottage he approached me hesitantly with a very serious expression. He said that he had not kissed the girl goodnight because he was embarrassed. I told him that I had been embarrassed on my first date. He added that it was his first date and that he would try next time. I said that I was glad that he had a good time. He said he did have a good time. Just before he entered the cottage he said that he hoped the group would have another party . . . soon. The group did have one. Henry tried a kiss, and succeeded.

Deviational Allowance. A more subtle function is related to the idea that as people interact with each other there is a flow of affect between them that can result in a good feeling about the activity and those who share in it. People who enjoy things together are also involved in demonstrating their similarity to each other.

This can result in the accumulation of what Edwin Hollander describes as "idiosyncrasy" credits. These are ". . . positively disposed impressions of a person held by others . . ." (4, p. 39). When members of a group have built up enough of these credits through essentially conforming behavior they are able to deviate from the group's norms with some safety. Hollander uses this idea in connection with leadership behavior, but it can be applied to deviations by group members who might, for instance, raise concerns and problems in sensitive areas, or who risk expressing ideas and feelings that might otherwise be taboo. Activity, then, may be used by group members to structure their time together as they build a reservoir of good feeling and mutual esteem, which in turn allows for individual deviation. Thus, shared activity could be seen as having a latent *deviational allowance* function.

In the following record excerpt teen-age boys are able to raise their concerns about sex after weeks of trips and social activities. The worker's earlier attempts to respond to their cues in this taboo area had been rejected even though the original contract described the group purposes as including talk about these concerns. We might hypothesize that the interaction of the first few weeks allowed a member to build up credits that he could then utilize in discussing a concern that violated the norm of the group:

The boys could not settle down to discussing the trip. There was a good deal of kidding around and bravado. John responded to

Fred's cracks with a mock challenge, quickly leading to a mock wrestling match. As John held Fred in a wrestling hold the others began to kid him about "making love" to Fred. They continued with comments which alluded to homosexual and heterosexual relations. The two broke up. This was followed by a round of comments, in falsetto voices, accompanied by effeminate movements. There was a pause.

I said that although there was much that was funny in their kidding around I still wondered if this whole business of sex didn't make some problems for them. John asked what I meant. The others were quiet and attentive. I asked if there weren't times when they felt concerned about sex, a little confused about rights and wrongs, and not sure about what to do when they were with girls. Lou said he knew what to do. The others laughed. John said he talked a good game but when it came right down to it, he was always a little scared when he made it. He looked around the room; no one laughed. Ted and Bob nodded in agreement. With this, the door had been opened and the questions began to fly.

Entry. Group members may also use specific activities as a way into discussions on sensitive and taboo areas that are difficult to talk about. These activities may set the stage for members to use indirect communications, such as hinting, as a way of getting at strongly felt concerns. Members may be unaware of this function, and the subtle communications sometimes emerge only with the help of a skilled worker. An example would be the spontaneous play-acting of young children as they create roles and situations that often reveal their concerns of the moment. The function of the medium, in this case, is to help reveal as yet unexpressed concerns of group members, to provide them an *entry* into difficult areas of discussion.

The healing powers inherent in the group come into play when members can share their painful feelings, find others "in the same boat," and begin to mobilize their strengths. Such is the case in the next excerpt, where a worker helps a group of adult foreign nationals, living in the United States, to surface a common concern.

As they discussed their last meeting—a trip to a Black Power rally—the worker listened carefully. She was aware that their interest in the problems of an American minority might be a way of *entering* the sensitive area of their own status. She moved to free the group members by reaching for their concerns:

Edward broke in with a description of some Philadelphia slums he had seen that week. He continued by saying that he never thought such things existed in America. I asked if they had any other disillusionments. Martin mentioned the superior attitude of the U.S. in regard to other countries. "But this you know before coming here surely," Edward said. Everyone laughed. Several members apologized to me until Carol pointed out that I was laughing too. "Many Americans think all of us Latins are Indians," Carol said. "They think we have feathers and drums," she continued. "That's nothing," Martin said, "Some think we climb trees and eat bananas." Everyone laughed. I asked if they thought any of the people they had contact with in the U.S. had changed their feelings through knowing them. . . . Carol said that at least some people now know she doesn't wear feathers.

With the group free to discuss this area, a member moved right to the core of the problem by sharing his painful feelings. The worker supported the members by communicating her understanding of their difficulty. She then helped them begin to work on the central question of what they could do about the feelings they had:

Quentin said that they know that Latins like to joke, but to continue seriously, he felt the plight of the immigrant would always be one of proving himself. He then described how he had been a wealthy pharmacist in Cuba till Castro came. He had to begin in Miami as a dishwasher. It had taken him 4 years to work up to his present lab technician position, but he still couldn't be a pharmacist because U.S. requirements were different. He continued, "You cannot imagine how much I suffered, how much we all do when we are not recognized for what we feel we are." Quentin had captivated the group with his comments. Edward said that Carol told us earlier that sometimes she feels homesick. I said that it must be very difficult for all of them.

I asked Carol what she did when she felt sad. She said it was as Quentin had put it, that strange people had to prove themselves to the others. I pointed out that this must take a good deal of patience. Fred added, "And courage as well." "For different races it is even more difficult," Ted pointed out. "We have less hope." Carol said that when she was sad, she tried to ignore it and keep going until something good happened to make her forget.

THE FUNCTION OF THE WORKER

A central issue facing the group and the worker is the division of labor; that is, the functions to be performed must be partialized and distributed in a way that best guarantees that the work will get done. Thus, group members may carry certain functions and the worker may carry others.

What are the functions to be distributed? Two suggested earlier were the identification of the client's needs and the selection of forms of activity to accomplish this. These are the familiar concepts of "diagnosing" client needs and "prescribing" treatment. In the formulations of group work theory according to the earlier steps in our theoretical development, these functions are assigned to the worker, either to be carried by him alone or shared by him with the group members. It is the validity of this functional assignment that I wish to question.

As the interaction between worker and group members is examined, it becomes clear that this is part of a larger question, a question that involves the very nature of the helping process. With this in mind, let us pursue our inquiry along two lines of concern, each of which has a bearing upon the issue of the division of labor. The first is the nature of the relationship between the client group and the agency setting; the second, some propositions about how people learn.

The Agency-Group Relationship. The actions of the worker and the members of his groups are affected by the setting within which their work takes place. The concern of the agency must be reflected in the work of the group, otherwise the agency has no reason for sponsoring it. The agency function, therefore, provides one boundary within which the group members and the worker carry out their respective functions. This principle does not sanction the worker, on behalf of the agency, to *use* the group for the agency's purposes.

Misunderstanding on this point has led workers to secretly influence group members, while claiming to be working as a resource for them on their own tasks. While claiming "agency sanction" and knowledge of the client's "real needs," some workers will disregard group members' rights and manipulate their movements. They rationalize their actions by claiming that members can reject their efforts, thus preserving their right to self-determination.

This misses the fact that group members often sense when they are being manipulated, and they may then become distracted from their real tasks, spending their energy instead on defending themselves against a worker who cannot be completely trusted. They may "go along" with the worker— creating an illusion of real effort—while actually withholding themselves from meaningful involvement. Resentment at being manipulated may be indirectly communicated by behavior that the worker may interpret as a testing of his authority. Through all of this, of course, the worker is providing a role model in which a significant adult attempts to use others, through indirect means, toward his own ends.

My own view of the agency-group relationship is ably described by Abe Vinik, when he says:

The group is not a tool. There is integrity to its own existence. It has a right to its own purposes and may expect help from the worker in seeking to realize its own purposes and work out its own problems. . . . The group is not the worker's or the agency's but the members' [12, p. 103].

From this stance, instead of directing one's efforts toward developing ideas or programs that would move group members on the basis of agency interests, one attempts, as William Schwartz suggests, to "search out the common ground" between the purposes of the group members and those of the agency (10, p. 17). It is at the points of convergence that the worker is able to serve as an honest resource for group members and at the same time may represent the agency's purposes and functions. The fact that it may be difficult to perceive the connection between the purposes of the group member and the agency does not give the worker license to ignore this central task. The more obscure the connection, the greater the demand for worker skill. If there is no common ground between the group and the agency interests, then the group is working with the wrong agency. The importance of working on the group members' own purposes is emphasized as we consider how people learn.

Learning. The dynamic force in the helping process comes from people searching for ways of negotiating the demands of their environments to meet their own needs. The parent of a retarded youngster seeks support and specific help from other parents on how to deal with his child. The teen-ager moving toward adulthood is concerned about the many new expectations of him and seeks to share this concern while learning how to meet the expectations. The lonely senior citizen must learn how to make significant connections with his peer group to replace the intimacy lost with the death of a loved one. It is on the basis of our understanding about how people learn that we must decide upon what the worker will do in the group. Let us examine three related propositions in this area.

First, the individual must be fully involved in the learning process. He is not a passive recipient of external stimuli, and thus he will not make connections with ideas or information unless he confronts them actively. This view of man, proposed by William James and elaborated by John Dewey, suggests that: "The organism is not simply receiving impressions and then answering them. The organism is doing something; it is actively seeking and selecting certain stimuli" (9, p. 43).

Translating this proposition into the group work situation suggests that members will see, hear, and remember selectively. A member may be "involved" in the work of the group and yet not be learning from it at all. He will, in fact, accept only the information to which he finds some connection. For example, a worker attempting to "teach" group members how to share by limiting the number of paint brushes available may find them concluding that the agency is too cheap to give them enough brushes.

Second, an individual will seek from the many stimuli in his environment those that he finds relevant to some immediate, personal task. He will not learn a concept that the worker may feel will be of some future use to him, no matter how attractively the worker presents it, unless there is some sense of current urgency to activate the individual's impulse to seek out the learning. John Holt describes this process of an individual ordering his own learning as follows:

A child learns, at any moment, not by using the procedure that seems best to us, but the one that seems best to *him;* by fitting into his structure of ideas and relationships, his mental model of reality, not the piece we think comes next, but the one he thinks comes next [5, p. 126].

Herbert Kohl, writing about his experiences as a new teacher in a Harlem school, supports this point. He describes his thoughts during the lunch break on his first day of attempting to structure his students' learning according to the school's curriculum: "There was an hour to summon energy and prepare for the afternoon, yet it seemed futile. What good are plans, clever new methods and materials, when the children didn't—wouldn't—care or listen?" (6, p. 5).

Finally, a group member's need to work on a task is felt *partially* and *temporarily*—it is not permanently fixed. His need emerges at certain points and disappears at others. Tasks with which the member may identify one week may be irrelevant to him the next week.

The worker who attempts to determine in advance the needs that the group should work on undertakes an impossible task. At best he can use his knowledge to prepare himself to hear the members' direct and indirect communications at the moments they occur; he can then lend his skill to *their* efforts to identify what is of greatest importance to them. But it is only the members who can, ultimately, identify their group needs.

These arguments raise doubts about a division of labor that assigns to the worker the task of "prescribing" for group needs. It is the *members,* not the worker, who can best determine their needs of the moment. It is the *members,* not the worker, who must decide how these needs will be met. Efforts by the worker to assume those responsibilities, even on a shared basis, result in confusion, resentment, anger, and lessened productivity in the group. In addition, the worker's ability to carry out those functions that *are* clearly his will be seriously hampered because of the lack of clarity about his function.

If there is real doubt about such a division of labor, then what is the function of the worker? If it is the member's task to determine what needs are to be met and how this will be done, what tasks are left to the worker?

A MODEL FOR ACTION

Schwartz has suggested a functional assignment for the worker that leaves the task of determining their immediate needs and ways to meet them to the members themselves. It is embodied in his "mediating model," in which he posits a relationship between the individual and his environment that is essentially symbiotic, ". . . each needing the other for its own life and growth, and each reaching out to the other with all of the strength it can command at a given moment" (10, p. 14). The functional assignment for the social worker is thus to ". . . mediate the process through which the individual and his society reach out for each other through a mutual need for self-fulfillment" (10, p. 14).

In the small group—a special case of the individual-societal encounter—the symbiotic theory leads us to assume a potential for mutual aid. That is, as members of the group engage in the pursuit of mutually agreed-upon purposes, they will be able to assist each other. This process is a complex one, often frustrated by obstacles that obscure the group members' essential interest in each other and in their mutually desired goals. It is the emergence of these difficulties that creates the need for the worker.

We are not describing a passive role; the worker is busy working on the tasks that are appropriately his. He recognizes the problems his group members will have in using each other, including the difficulties involved in "talking real" to each other, the internal struggles for status, the recurring efforts to move away from the work when the going gets rough, and the difficulty in dealing with the worker—a representative of external authority. The worker will listen carefully to pick up the subtle messages and clues from the members that reveal the presence of these obstacles, and he will openly point them out. In this way he becomes a catalyst for the group members, helping them to deal with obstacles that frustrate their mutual efforts. He must then support them as they struggle to free themselves to return to productive work. It is, however, *their* struggle; the worker should not take over the struggle as his own.

A complex set of worker tasks has been described; it is almost impossible to perform them if the division of labor between members and the worker is not clear and if the tasks that are truly those of the members are assumed to be shared by the worker.

There is another task that must, of necessity, be performed by the group rather than by the worker—the selection of the media by which the group does its work. From the wide range of mediums available for group members to use in achieving their purposes, some groups might use one medium more than others. The selection by the members of one form or another should depend upon the tasks faced. It is a functional part of the members' work. The worker would serve as a resource for the members as *they* decided how and when to use different mediums.

Ideas the worker may have as a result of his experience or training should be made available to group members on the same basis as any other information. The function of the group, as it is *jointly* perceived by the group members and the agency, acts as a general guide to the worker in his selection of what data to offer. Ideas would be presented when relevant to the immediate task of the group, and when such information is otherwise unavailable to the group. The members should be as free to evaluate the worker's input as they would anyone else's contribution and to accept it or reject it as they see fit. The worker should strive to encourage an atmosphere in which members are free to openly reject his offerings when these are perceived as not being relevant to the task at hand.

SUMMARY

The notion of "program" as a distinct entity emerged from our early theoretical misconceptions of the nature of human interaction. A mixed transactional model can be used to describe group work—work in which there is no dichotomy between "talking" and "doing," with group members using a wide range of mediums of exchange, that is, activities, in pursuit of their common purposes. Among the functions of the various mediums are object-contacting, data-gathering, rehearsal, deviational allowance, and entry.

The helping process can be viewed from two perspectives—the nature of the relationship between group members and the agency, and the nature of the learning process. In each case there are questions about the efficacy of a division of labor that gives the worker responsibility for assessing group member needs and "prescribing" to meet them. A model of practice is proposed that leaves to the group members the tasks of determining their needs of the moment (within the boundaries set by the agency function) and the mediums for dealing with them. The worker's function is described as "mediation," that is, to attempt to act as a catalyst and a resource to the members as they use each other to work on their common tasks. Information about possible group activities—mediums of exchange—is one form of informational input that a worker can openly make available when it is relevant to the group's current tasks. Members can then treat such contributions as they would their own, acting on them only when they believe them to be useful.

This is an exciting time for the profession. References in the literature to practice models are a sign of the dynamic changes taking place, where ideas that have served us in the past are being tested and retested in practice. We must continue to evaluate critically our notions about our work in order to lay bare the essential principles and means of our craft.

REFERENCES

1. Eric Berne, *Games People Play* (New York: Grove Press, 1964).
2. Grace Coyle, *Group Work with American Youth* (New York: Harper and Brothers, 1948).
3. Grace Coyle, "Group Work as a Method in Recreation," in

Harleigh Trecker (ed.), *Group Work: Foundations and Frontiers* (New York: Whiteside, 1955), pp. 91–108.

4. Edwin P. Hollander, "Emergent Leadership and Social Influence," in Luigi Petrullo and Bernard M. Bass (eds.), *Leadership and Interpersonal Behavior* (New York: Holt, Rinehart & Winston, 1961), pp. 30–47.

5. John Holt, *How Children Fail* (New York: Dell, 1964).

6. Herbert Kohl, *36 Children* (New York: The New Amer. Lib., 1967).

7. Gisela Konopka, *Social Group Work: A Helping Process* (Englewood Cliffs, N.J.: Prentice-Hall, 1963).

8. Marjorie Murphy, *The Social Group Work Method in Social Work Education* (New York: The Council on Social Work Education, 1959).

9. Paul Pfuetze, *Self, Society, Existence* (New York: Harper and Brothers, 1961).

10. William Schwartz, "The Social Worker in the Group," *New Perspectives on Services to Groups: Theory, Organization, Practice* (New York: National Association of Social Workers, 1961), pp. 7–29.

11. Thomas S. Szasz, *The Myth of Mental Illness* (New York: Harper & Row, 1964).

12. Abe Vinik, "Role of the Group Service Agency," *Social Work*, Vol. 9, No. 3 (July 1964), pp. 98–105.

The "Record of Service":

Describing Social Work Practice

GOODWIN P. GARFIELD *and*
CAROL R. IRIZARRY

THERE ARE VERY FEW written accounts of the events of practice in neighborhood centers and other group-serving agencies. This problem has persisted despite the deeply ingrained conviction that professionals *should* write records, that the profession has a responsibility for transmitting its experience, and that it cannot in fact be taken seriously as a profession until it institutionalizes devices for doing so.*

Those who have tried to describe their own practice in writing and those who have struggled to develop systems for recording can speak readily to the question of why recording is so difficult. It is time consuming; the service is complex, and it is hard to know what to include and what to leave out; the rewards do not seem commensurate with the time and effort expended; the direct work with clients is done largely by untrained practitioners; and more. These considerations are real enough. But there is, perhaps, a more cogent explanation, that is, that records are not written simply because they are not

* The Record of Service was designed in consultation with William Schwartz and was developed for use in the United Neighborhood Houses Pre-Teen Delinquency Project.

used. The fact that recording is not generally demanded by the agency comes close to the crux of the matter, for recording is an instrument of accountability, requiring that the agency and its workers make themselves accountable to each other and to the community for the work they are responsible for doing. In order to have a viable system of written accountability an agency must know what its service should be, it must provide clear directives to its workers, and it must require them to report systematically on their efforts to carry them out. Such a system implies that the records will be read and used in practical ways—for supervision, orientation, and in-service training, for maintaining a running account of the agency's service, and for interpretation to the Board and to the general community. From this perspective, recording difficulties arise mainly from agency difficulties in clarifying the nature of its function and service.

The recording device that will be described in this paper is one agency's response to the problems outlined above (5). The Record of Service emerged from real questions about the nature of services in a project to help delinquency-prone youngsters and their families. We had questions about what the project was supposed to do, what it should hold its workers accountable for, and what the work should look like in action, and this forced us into a deeper consideration of the theoretical basis for community service in general and group work in particular. Our efforts to integrate the recording of service with the definition of the service program itself, provided a live example for us of the important thesis that writing records is not a formalistic problem alone but a pragmatic one closely tied to our basic understanding of what we were doing in the community—the *raison d'être* of the work itself. To put this another way, there are no "recording problems"—only problems of understanding and describing the practice of social work.

SOME CRITERIA FOR A RECORDING SYSTEM

If a recording system is to reflect the agency's effort to keep track of the specific ways in which it serves its community, there are a number of considerations to be borne in mind (4, 6, 8). First, the records must show not only the *quantity of work*—number of interviews, attendance, number of meetings, and the like—but its *quality* as well.* Quality control requires that the material reveal the technical problems of service and the level of skill brought to bear in the service actually rendered. Furthermore, the records must show not only the "process" of work; they must also *summarize* from time to time, bringing the tasks and problems undertaken by the agency into focus and defining the agency's service in specific terms. It should also be noted that "process" recording, contrary to common opinion, is not meant to record everything that happens—an aspiration that could inhibit any kind of writing. It means simply that one selects from the total process those events that show the work in action and highlight the technical problems and subtleties involved in serving the client. When these details are later included in a summarized account, they help in taking stock of what the work has done for the client *lately*.

Finally, the record must reflect a theory of the work. Since recording is of necessity a selective process, it is essential that the selecting be done—as it always is, consciously or unconsciously—according to one's own ways of generalizing about the work. Without a theory or set of generalizations about practice one does not have a clearcut basis for deciding what is relevant or noteworthy and should be recorded, and what is not.

* For a discussion of some of the considerations involved in assessing agency effectiveness on the basis of such output variables as quantity and quality of services, see Stein, Hougham, and Zalba (9).

All of this adds up to a concept of accountability that calls upon the agency to show the *what,* the *how,* and the *why* of what it does. It must know what needs doing, it must do it well, and it must record what it has done so that others will know and understand.

The Record of Service is a device designed to fulfill the summarizing and focusing requirements described above. For it to be used properly, therefore, it must exist within a structure that collects both statistical and process data.

The process material collected in the project was in the form of a diary or "log" in which each worker wrote accounts of the events that transpired in his work with individual clients and with groups. The Record of Service was then used from time to time to summarize specific services provided by the project in the various areas of its work. It was, for us, an *existential* document, taking its form from the specific tasks of the clients and the actual services that the workers tried to perform. It forced the workers to concentrate on what they did and how they did it rather than on what they knew, or felt, or hoped to accomplish. While the document did report and describe the worker's knowledge, convictions, and aspirations —and it was assumed that these qualities were indeed indispensable to action—its essential function was to provide a clear description and analysis of the practice itself. The Record was the worker's—hence the agency's—effort to answer the question: What did you do in this specific area of service over a specified period of time? What were your helping strategies, and how did you try to convert your knowledge and sensitivity into the acts of skill necessary to carry out your agency's service?

Both the *Individual* and the *Group* Records of Service contained certain assumptions about the tasks faced by clients as they tried to use the service of the agency. The *Record of Ser-*

vice: Individual was developed on the premise that each client deals with a network of interlocking systems of demand and opportunity—the school, the welfare department, the peer group, the family, and others—and that the challenge to each individual is to make his impact on these systems, to make them work for him, and to extract from them the satisfactions they are supposed to provide. We assumed that these systems, particularly in ghetto and slum areas, have become so overwhelmingly difficult to negotiate that help is often needed to manage one's world, system by system. This does not mean that clients must conform to the structure of these systems as they are, accepting their terms and fitting in like cogs in a machine. On the contrary, to make an impact means that one must retain his dignity and exercise some control as he goes about the process of dealing with these complicated systems. Since the client's tasks arise from his interaction with these various systems, the worker, as he described his activities, focused not only on how he helped the client negotiate the systems but also on how he helped the systems deal with the people they were there to serve. In the facesheet information of the *Record of Service: Individual* the worker was required to identify the specific system around which the present account—which was only a part of the total work with the client —was woven.

The *Record of Service: Group* was developed from the assumption that the group-as-a-whole—the peer collective—has certain specific tasks to pursue as it moves to establish its group identity and do the work for which it was formed. It is not necessary to adhere to any particular theory of group development to agree that certain group tasks develop in group life and that certain kinds of help will be required in the process of pursuing these collective tasks.* In our own work, we

---

* There are many theoretical points of view from which one can categorize group tasks. See, for example, Altman and Terauds (1), Bales (2), Bion (3), and Homans (7).

took the position that there are four major tasks with which our groups needed help, and these then provided the framework around which the recording took place. The first was *group formation,* which included problems created in the process of beginning—membership requirements, contract consensus, perception of the worker, organization for work, and relationship to the agency. The second was *group structure,* involving problems of status distribution, role development, lines of production, internal communication, planning, decision-making, and modes of action. The third was the development of the group's *relationship to its environment* and concerned the problems that arose from the group's interaction with the agency, other systems, and other groups in their community. And fourth was *satisfying members* that the group was properly meeting their needs and offering them a sense of fulfillment and a "good time." The facesheet of the *Record of Service: Group* required the worker to specify *which* group task he was helping with at that particular time.

The form for the Record of Service begins with a brief heading that includes the name of the client—individual or group—age and sex, and the period of time for which the service on a particular problem is being summarized. For the individual client the worker designates the *system* within which the problem arose. For the group client he designates the *task* within which the problem emerged. In each instance he must identify the *problem* in specific, action terms, defined in such a way as to lend itself to description of the ways in which the worker and client addressed the problems together.

Having indicated what the record will be about, the worker then divides his account into four parts: (a) how the problem came to his attention; (b) a summary of work, with record excerpts reproduced to illustrate the work; (c) a current assessment, indicating where the problem stands now, at the moment of writing; and (d) specific next steps contemplated by the worker. The following, in brief, is an elaboration of the instructions implicit in each of these sections.

How the Problem Came to the Worker's Attention. The worker indicates how and when the client's difficulties first became established as a focus for work. Operating on the assumption that work is a collaborative process between client and helper, the worker tries to show how a particular problem first became a matter of mutual concern, how the problem was initially felt and perceived by the client, and how the client appeared to be dealing with it when it was first noticed by the worker.

Summary of Work. The worker then summarizes and characterizes his efforts to help the client with the problem in question. This account is illustrated, wherever possible, by excerpts from his Log, selected to highlight the nature and quality of the work required in various encounters. The essence of this recording task is to show the work in action, emphasizing the particular skills it took to address himself to the problems at hand.

Assessment. The worker indicates where the problem now stands. What steps has the client been able to take so far? What has he achieved? What difficulties still need attention? What strengths and problems does the client show, *in this regard,* as he moves from this point?

Specific Next Steps. Finally, and based on his assessment of where the client stands now with this specific problem, the worker describes what he plans to do next in the immediate future. The emphasis here is on specific strategies and immediate moves as well as on the "tuning-in" required to get ready for these moves.

ILLUSTRATIONS

Two records of service are presented here, to give some sense of this device and its possibilities. Other workers may show different ways of handling the instrument, varying their recording in length, detail, and intensity of analysis.

These were developed early in our experience, and they are not offered as "ideal" prototypes of the device. For example, our work with systems-representatives would be more in evidence today. Nevertheless, they are close enough to what we were after to illustrate both the problems and the potentials of this device.

RECORD OF SERVICE: INDIVIDUAL

Period Covered: *6/28/63 to 7/1/64*

Name: *Tata Vilar* Age: *12* Group: *Wanderers* Worker: *C.R.*
System: *School* Sex: *Female* Problem: *Tata's fear of failure in school; her need for some outside help in learning.*

How Problem Came to My Attention

6/28/63: Three of the girls were discussing another club member having been left back. Tata said it had happened to her once and that she had felt like crying when the teacher announced it to the class. She added that she "would give anything to be smart."

A retired teacher from the area used to help the girls with reading. Tata was always expressing her dislike of this teacher, Barbara, and was terribly suspicious of my even stopping to speak with her. On one occasion when I crossed the street to join the girls after speaking briefly with Barbara, Tata screamed at me, "Are you going to make us do reading?"

Summary of Work

I responded to Tata that she still didn't know me too well but that she would get to know that I tried not to make people do things they didn't want to do.

I made a special effort not to ask Tata to read signs or instructions or to add difficult amounts of money on trips. Rather, I treated her dislike of school and intellectual activity as ordinary and a thing that many people felt. During the three summer months school was seldom mentioned, and Tata and I had no further discussions about it.

In September they all started back to school and I casually mentioned that I would help anyone who wanted with homework after club. Tata immediately responded that we wouldn't catch her sitting around doing homework. I said that I wasn't trying to talk anyone into doing it, but that some people might just want help and that she might want to change her mind someday herself.

Another girl in the group began bringing her homework and for about a week she was the only one who did so.

9/23/63: The girls didn't arrive at the Center until about 4:00. Tata and Judy said they had to stay in after school because their work hadn't been finished, and the others had waited for them. I said they probably felt pretty mad and asked if they wanted to play the new basketball game they had worked out. This met with immediate approval. It involved a lot of running around, screaming, shouting and knocking over chairs. They played steadily for 45 minutes, then stopped for kool-aid and cookies.

After we had finished eating, Tata said she had brought her homework, and I remarked that it must have been hard for her to do so after such a bad day in school. She didn't answer, but started opening her book. I hugged her, saying that maybe if I helped her do her homework, she wouldn't have so much trouble with the teacher.

This was how I began helping with actual academic material, and as I started I realized very soon that Tata could not answer social studies questions because she couldn't even read them. This influenced all aspects of her work and seemed to make her feel completely helpless and powerless in the face of her overwhelming task.

As we worked together she spoke continuously of the trouble kids got into when their work wasn't finished and how teachers always thought she was stupid. She appeared to be worrying about this more than about her work; in a matter of days I abandoned my idea to help her "learn" and concentrated on helping her finish. This evolved into a new way of our working together: I did most of the intellectual work, looking up answers and dictating them, while Tata wrote them down. In arithmetic I would do most of the questions, stopping to ask her an easy multiplication that I was sure she would know. Since several of the girls were in the same class, they sometimes copied each other's homework, and Tata would take great delight in sharing "her" answers with her friends. She began to bring her books to the club every day and was seldom retained after school because her work wasn't finished.

11/10/63: Tata was in a particularly angry mood and refused to do any homework. She just kept knocking over chairs in the room, refusing to talk to me about what was bothering her. One of the other girls from the same class mentioned the social studies project they were having, saying everyone was worried because it was so hard. I offered to help them both make something for the project. Rosa accepted; Tata still refused to be involved. We began making a box of the country they were studying, with a typical background, trees, and figures. Tata became furious that I would help her friend and not her and was thus drawn into the activity.

The next noon-time both girls came rushing to the Center, saying the teacher had given them each an "A" and had put their boxes on display for the entire class. For weeks Tata spoke with great excitement over her project and the attention that it had received.

After this experience Tata seemed to feel that I was infallible in relation to her school work, and that success in school involved only having me help her with homework. She never missed a night of bringing her books to the Center and became extremely angry and upset if for some reason we had to leave without homework time. Her tolerance for dealing with subject matter she didn't understand was still minimal, but she began to ask a few questions here and there that related to understanding.

One night, when I was particularly tired, she kept running out of the room to play, leaving me with her homework. I kept trying to engage her in helping, but she kept leaving. Finally I closed the books and walked out for a drink. Tata came rushing over and asked if I had finished. I responded, "I have no intention of sitting in there doing your homework while you play around. I like to play too, you know, and you're smart enough to be helping me."

I expected that she would react as she often had to confrontation, by starting to curse and leaving the Center. But sensing, I think, the honesty of my frustration and concern, she went into the room and started working without saying a word.

After this I became more reluctant to do work *for* Tata, often even leaving her with some problems while I helped someone else. She seemed able to take this and more often began bringing me work to check rather than complete. But there were still days when she seemed completely overwhelmed by school and its pressures, and to support her progress I would do all or most of her homework. It became quite a joke with the girls that their teacher had said he would not accept any more work in Carol's handwriting. Tata was at least required to recopy.

Toward the end of the year Tata's change of attitude was reflected many times in her comments while we worked.

One afternoon as we started some arithmetic questions I began automatically what seemed to be the most difficult addition. Then I heard a voice shouting in my ear, "Hey, don't do those, I can do it myself. What do you think I am, stupid?"

The new anger in her voice implied that I underestimated her ability to handle the problems.

Assessment

The theory I followed in helping this girl academically is common: people learn by moving from what they know and can do comfortably to more difficult and threatening material. The theory applied specifically to this twelve-year-old, in that I found I had to begin by practically doing Tata's homework, due to her concern that it be finished for the next day. This involved dealing with my feelings about whether this was honest and whether it was helping her "learn."

During the course of the year, however, it became very obvious to me that a tremendous amount of learning had gone on around our experience together. The immediate gratification provided by the simple completion of her homework provided an impetus to seek other rewards. Status in the classroom and recognition before her peers was of crucial importance to Tata, who previously had spent long hours in school receiving from teachers only negative comments that added to the frustration of her not understanding.

Reports from the school obtained in the fall of '63 spoke of this child as "slow, frequently truant, 2.8 reading level, and in need of remedial reading instruction." In May I visited her present teacher as he was preparing end-of-the-year evaluations. He spoke of Tata as shy, but bright, indicating great advances in her reading, social studies, and arithmetic since last September. Significantly, although she is loud and demonstrative of angry emotions in the Center and with me, he spoke of her as "well-behaved and fairly quiet" in school.

Tata's family moved recently, and her mother spoke with me about making special arrangements for her to continue at her present school. She said she could hardly believe she was waking up the same girl in the morning this year, as compared to last year. She reported that Tata hated to go to school before and had avoided it whenever possible, but that now nothing would keep her home; even when she was really needed for something, she made a fuss about staying.

Another important factor must be mentioned in looking at her life this year: Tata's teacher is a fairly young male and seems like a flexible person. She likes him a great deal and I think was even more rewarded by his pleasure in her progress.

Specific Next Steps

School is now out for the summer—a summer that includes Tata moving to a new house and neighborhood, my leaving the agency, and her anticipation of junior high school. Meanwhile, Tata expresses pleasure at her new home, indifference to my departure, and happiness at moving on to this new junior high. I think she is very frightened and that having now tasted the flavor of recognition and success she fears it will not be repeated but rather that she will return to her former frustrations and status. To prove herself right, she may again in the fall express intense dislike of school and academic work, and shun any part of it. I think that this type of regression is to be expected.

Since Tata will continue at the Center, I am currently taking every opportunity to recognize her achievements of the past year and the other staff have joined me in this. I am also watching for opportunities to help her express her fear of next year and possible difficulties that may arise.

In a month the worker who is replacing me will start work and begin contact with Tata, which allows for a month before school reopens. September and junior high bring a new world for Tata, and I think she will ask in one way or another for help in operating within it.

RECORD OF SERVICE: GROUP

Group: *The Wanderers*

Group Task: *Structure*

Period Covered: *Jan. '64 to Jun. '64*
Ages: *10–13*   Sex: *Female*
No. *11*   Worker: *CR.*
Problem: *Helping to create an atmosphere in which the worker and the group members can "level" with each other on important feelings and attitudes about each other.*

How the Problem Came to My Attention

One afternoon as the Center was closing I was having the usual difficulty getting the girls to leave. Noemi kept insisting there was more time as she continued a game of tag. In exasperation I told her it was late, already past 6:30. She disappeared, returning in a few minutes with Tata, whose watch, she pointed out, indicated the time was only 6:15. She demanded to know why I had told them it was after 6:30. The thought occurred to me to dismiss the issue by saying I had just been guessing, but instead I replied that I had told them it was after 6:30 in order to hurry them up, because I was tired and wanted to leave. She had started to protest violently but stopped at my explanation and stared at me half-smiling. Without a word she ran to the other girls and I overheard her telling them the story, adding that she thought they should go because I was tired. Everyone left without further hesitation or comment.

The event had a happy ending for me, but it began a more serious questioning on my part of when I was honest with the girls about my own feelings and responses and what effect it had on them. The image that kept returning to me was of Noemi's smile, for it had registered her recognition of something real. It was unusual, too, because her expected response would have been to argue at great length.

I was also led to this same questioning by my early relationship with Tata, a very bright girl who managed to find out quickly any little thing that bothered me and mockingly make a public event out of it. With great patience I waited for this period of "testing" to pass, thinking I was doing my utmost to reach her. I encouraged her to talk about her negative feelings for me, but she refused to talk directly to me at all until one day about 2 months after the club had started.

On a subway train three girls were standing between the cars and I insisted that they sit down or not be allowed on the trip planned for the next day. Two of them sat down immediately; one remained standing defiantly—Tata. As we left the station I explained to the girls that I was very sorry Tata would not be able to come the next day because she didn't sit down, etc. The girls were upset and argued with me; Tata insisted she would come anyway, while I insisted to myself that the reason for my action was that they were testing me and that if I gave in and changed my mind I would never maintain group discipline.

Then Tata blurted out, "You're punishing me because you don't like me!" The accusation was so direct and well-aimed that I was unable to respond at the moment. It was only the next day that I felt ready to reply to her and I told her that I guessed I hadn't been very honest with her since sometimes I really didn't like her. I said that I wanted to like her but that she was always making me so mad. She didn't say anything but listened carefully. Up to this point whenever I had tried to talk with her she would either plug her ears and scream or run away.

Tata continued to be cautious and suspicious toward me, but the force of her ridicule and defiance gradually diminished. At the same time, my own feelings began to change toward her, and bit by bit we started on the long road to a relationship of trust. For both of us I feel sure this was made possible by my attempt to deal honestly with feelings that I had been denying but that she had all along been interpreting correctly.

From these and other instances I realized the discrepancy between encouraging the girls to be honest and at the same time not responding to them honestly myself. The necessity for their being honest with me in order for me to understand and help them was obvious from the beginning, but only gradually did the need for an equivalent honesty in my response become known. I could no longer escape the problem by saying it wasn't professional for the simple, pragmatic reason that I became increasingly aware of how accurately the girls knew many of my real feelings, fears, and motivations as we spent more and more time together.

Summary of Work

I tried to show that honesty regarding feelings was not only acceptable and desirable but also essential to the group working together.

1/23/64: . . . Cathy, Tata, Noemi, and Rosa were extremely angry with me one afternoon in the Center. Cathy and Tata in particular had expressed violent feelings of hostility toward me.

Margarita, the President, walked in on the middle of the session and became very upset at the other girls. She shouted at Tata and Cathy, "You know you should respect Carol!" Turning to me she insisted I make them do so. I replied that I was more interested in what they were feeling, even if the feelings were hard to talk about. Cathy screamed, "Don't think we respect our teachers just because we're polite to them. I don't like *any* grown-up people."

From Cathy's remark I was able to connect their anger with the fact that I was an adult for whom they were beginning to have affection. But it was a long time before they began to feel that "we get mad at each other" meant that not only were they able to express anger toward me but that I could and did have the same feelings toward them.

For example, on various club excursions one of the girls kept climbing over the side of the subway platform, threatening to stand on the tracks. Finally, one day I grabbed her by the arm, pulled her back to the platform and in great anger told her not to do that again. It wasn't until much later, in a discussion about the previous summer, that she did an imitation of my actions, revealing that I had communicated to her a great concern for her safety.

But the expression of anger was the easiest and most acceptable way to be honest. A deeper and more threatening area to function in with honesty was in the differentiations I made among the girls. It became increasingly evident to me that I had different feelings about the girls and different ways of relating to them. The issue was brought up by the girls themselves.

> *3/17/64:* . . . Carmen, Rosa, and Noemi were in the Center doing homework with the volunteers while Tata and Cathy helped unload some books for the Center.
>
> It was late when they finished, and the Center was closing. Everyone was packing up their things, but Cathy said she hadn't done her homework. I said I was sorry but it was too late now as it was time to go home. She started to cry, insisting that she couldn't go to school the next day without her homework done. The other girls seemed as surprised as I was, since Cathy had never cried before in the group. Judy asked why I didn't stay a few extra minutes with Cathy, and Tata said one of the volunteers could take them home. I said I would do this, even though it wasn't fair to them, if they really could go with a volunteer. Tata said of course they could, and they left.

Their reactions, however, were not always so congenial. On the contrary, more often conflict was created and they became very upset over any so-called unfairness.

> *4/14/64:* . . . One day Carmen, a girl who seldom came to the club, dropped into the Center and I gave her a picture of the girls that had been taken at Christmas.
>
> That afternoon Noemi, Lydia, Tata, and Judy arrived, furious

at the club, demanding to know if Carmen had paid 5 cents for her picture as they had. I said that I had given her an extra. Judy, who lived next door to Carmen, had seen the picture and said that it wasn't fair for me to have *given* Carmen one when they had all paid 5 cents.

I replied that I was sorry, that I had just forgotten, and they were right: it wasn't fair. Judy insisted that I take the picture back from Carmen. The other girls shouted that I should do this because it wasn't fair, etc. I refused to take it back since I had given it to Carmen. Tata insisted I should do so or give them all back their money. She added, "You are supposed to treat us all the same, aren't you? Well, it isn't fair for her to have a free picture."

I answered her that I knew it wasn't fair but that it seemed to me life wasn't always fair and that I hadn't heard anyone getting all upset when I lent a girl 5 cents or 10 cents to get into the pool—something that had never happened with Carmen because she never came.

Noemi said that was different, and I replied that I thought the difference was because *they* were in the pool. Tata said she was mad and would go to tell John (supervisor). I told them I was sorry they were so mad, but that it didn't seem possible to me to treat them all the same. Judy said she'd never known anyone as funny as me.

This was the first time I had made a real attempt to be honest regarding the whole matter of fairness and equality. As it continued to come up in different ways, with different dimensions showing, I became more able to respond directly, and it also seemed to become less traumatic for the girls.

6/12/64: . . . We drove in the bus to the pool to see if it was open yet, and finding that it wasn't we sat in the park. Cathy and Tata had money and bought drinks. I bought one for our bus driver and myself, and seeing Lydia and Judy without anything, got them one also.

Tata immediately started saying that this wasn't fair and that I couldn't get something for them and not for her. I replied that it might not be fair but that this didn't seem so important to me as the fact that Lydia and Judy were thirsty and I had some money. She still looked mad and I said that she knew I didn't give everyone exactly the same thing. Cathy told her not to get too excited about it, and I agreed that this suggestion was a good one.

What remains still unsolved is the whole matter of my different feelings toward individual group members. It is amazing how acutely aware the girls are of each other's relationship with me.

6/25/64: . . . When the girls were eating cookies I said I was wondering if they had decided anything yet about Noemi. (She had recently been expelled from the club.)

Judy replied she was out of the club "period." Cathy shouted, "Noemi, Noemi, all you care about is Noemi!"

I said, yes, I did care but that I hadn't interfered with them when they did what they wanted.

Tata jumped up. "I didn't see you getting so excited about Lisa when she was kicked out last winter." Judy added, "That's right, you didn't say a thing."

I answered that I hadn't known Lisa very well or very long and that I had seen Noemi a lot in the last year and I missed her. There was silence at this remark; their faces showed what looked like surprise. I added that maybe more important than my feelings was my thought that no one was too happy at her being out, whereas no one had really wanted Lisa from the beginning.

Carmen said she was happy Noemi was gone, and Cathy asked why I didn't think they all were. I said that I had noticed she had been the only one to do much talking when they had actually kicked Noemi out and that no one else had said much at all. Cathy insisted everyone had wanted it and I replied that that could be, or maybe they were afraid to say anything. Cathy replied the whole bunch of "crackers" could say what they wanted.

Noemi was shortly readmitted to the club on a day when Cathy was absent, and nothing else was said about the matter.

The next time we were at the pool, however, Noemi, who was the weakest swimmer, began her usual demand for me to spend all my time helping her. When several of the other girls called from the deeper water, Noemi feigned she was choking to keep me back. I helped her to the edge and said, "You know, Noemi, I *can* stay with you, but I think sometimes the others get jealous and then want to take you out of the club."

She knew exactly what I meant and what an important issue was involved for her. For the first time that I can remember she let me go and replied, "Why don't you play with them; Judy can help me here." Even more unusual was that she stayed with Judy without incessantly yelling for me to return.

What made so much sense to Noemi was not the logical reasons for having to share me with the others but that I had hit directly upon a matter that was crucial to her—staying in the club. The tremendous importance of this helped her to act differently.

The task of reaching past a constantly hostile behavior pattern is a most difficult one, requiring, as I found, frequent re-evaluation and use of new ideas.

After almost a year of meeting with the group I knew that the girls' relationship with me had importance and meaning for them. I tried using my own feelings as a way of confronting them with the reactions their behavior could evoke in others. I knew that they cared how I felt and that only now, after a year, they might not be too threatened by such a confrontation.

I had been away for 2 days. On my return I was greeted with angry demands for a watermelon. When I didn't buy one, they insisted that I didn't like them.

6/10/64: . . . I said that I thought after a year they should know whether I liked them or not and that it didn't have to depend on my buying them a watermelon. Cathy said I was cheap.

I asked them how they thought I felt. There was general surprise. Judy asked what I meant. I said that I came back after being sick for 2 days and the only thing anyone could say was did I buy them a watermelon. I added that I felt as if they were asking me to buy them that to *prove* I still loved them and when I didn't want to prove it that way, they got mad.

Cathy said *she* wasn't mad! Judy asked how I was feeling now and put her arm around me. Tata said I looked okay now. I smiled and said they didn't have to overdo things; that I didn't blame them for feeling upset when I was away but that sometimes I wondered what they felt for me too.

Cathy then began to tell me what had happened to upset them while I was away.

Assessment

On the question of honesty perhaps more than on any other, I have changed in my thinking and approach. The girls were involved in this, not only because they also changed but because their reactions and demands created the impetus for me to look at things in a new way.

Two points have become extremely important in my understanding of honesty. The first is that being honest does *not* mean a compulsive need to tell all I am feeling or thinking! It is, rather, my responding to the girls as a real person and in a way that lets them know I am aware of the real world in which we both live. This world is not (for them or for me) one in which people are fair, or are treated alike, or are responded to in the same manner, or where the good are rewarded and the bad even caught, let alone punished.

And I am convinced that part of the group's "acting-out" behavior is an expression of the anger they feel toward adults and authority figures who keep pretending and/or insisting that the world is different from what the girls already know it to be by experience. They inevitably become impatient with any of the trite ways of being superficially honest as expressed in such clichés as, "I like you but not what you're doing," or "It's not important how *I* feel, it's how *you* are feeling that counts!"

For example, in the subway episode mentioned early in this record when Tata had accused me of punishing her because I didn't like her, I experienced a sudden *pang of recognition*. What was it? Was it a part of what was going on in the group? Was it something that the girls were already aware of but I was still hiding beneath professional rationalizations? For only with great effort and loss of self-esteem could I admit to myself that not only did I not like Tata but I had a pretty good idea *before* I gave the command that she, and only she, would defy me.

This brings me to my second point of concern, the conflict I felt initially between being honest and being professional. Somehow I had the feeling that it wasn't professional to be too honest with the girls because it might not be good for them. The most pragmatic of reasons made me look at the professional function in a different way. In so many cases the girls seemed to know what I was thinking and feeling, whether I *wanted* them to know or not. They were extremely sensitive and with great accuracy recognized my preferences, likes, dislikes, and what things made me comfortable or uncomfortable.

The real test they were putting me to was whether I would cover up these real feelings with a thousand rationalizations as did most adults they had known, or whether I could come closer to acknowledging something we both knew to exist. How in the world could I ask them to be honest with me—to examine what was really going on in the group—if I could not in some significant way acknowledge and deal with things we both knew I was feeling? Thus, my professional focus shifted to helping them deal with real feelings, emotions, and situations by deciding *when* and *how* to share my feelings.

Certainly conflict arose, but the conflict was related to reality, and this they would likely be struggling with long after I left. Not everything that went on in the group was "fair," and not everything that went on between each individual girl and myself was "fair," especially if "fair" meant treating them all exactly the same. They were smart enough to know that it is impossible to treat eleven girls exactly alike or to feel exactly the same toward them, especially as we grew closer and spent more time together. And they also were smart enough to see that a different kind of fairness existed—that I, too, was struggling to understand myself as well as them, and to not let my feelings interfere with what they were doing. It was an indication of deep trust and understanding on their part when I could say that I didn't think it was a good idea to do something and they decided to do it anyway.

I think part of the fear of responding honestly is similar to the fear of letting group members express socially unacceptable behavior. In the same way that I have often heard the comment that they might beat someone to death, I have also heard that it would be destructive for them to know the worker's real feelings. I think the picture conjured up is one of an "honest" worker turning to a girl she dislikes and saying, "I can't stand you!" Of course this is not what I mean, but I don't think anyone would normally interpret honesty this way.

What I mean, rather, is the expression within a growing relationship with these young individuals of a consistent effort not to avoid real feelings, emotions, or situations. In this context it would be perfectly honest for a worker to reply that she didn't want to discuss her personal sex life even though she knew they must wonder about it, because she didn't feel like talking about it with them. This approach may make them angry, but it is based on the reality of the type of relationship where the girls often discuss personal problems and the worker seldom does. Furthermore, I think it is drawing a thin, arbitrary line to say that it wouldn't be helpful to know the worker's private life (it may in fact be *very* helpful!), or to say that only *their* questions and feelings are important, not the worker's own.

Another comment frequently heard is that there would be too much competition among the girls to gain the worker's attention or affection if they weren't all treated alike. There is no question in my mind that this goes on in any case *and* that the girls know what pleases and upsets their worker and how she responds to individual members. Because their relationship with her can be unique—one that helps them examine their own behavior and responses—it offers an opportunity to bring into the open what is really going on and being felt.

This way of helping may be a unique experience for the worker as well. Instead of worrying about being fair she can help the youngsters deal with their lack of fairness—she can point out their competitions and their subtle manipulation of each other. She may not stop them from expelling a group member whom they believe to be the worker's favorite, but she can be honest about why she believes the event took place. And inasmuch as her emotions and feelings are present or felt in any situation pertaining to the girls, some manner of acknowledging and sharing becomes of great significance to the group.

Specific Next Steps

It is difficult to say where being honest, in the sense I am suggesting, can lead. So far the girls have responded by opening further to different ways of sharing themselves, particularly with me. This has encouraged me to keep examining the question of dealing honestly with feelings and situations between us.

One aspect of this question that has only been scratched is that of different feelings for individual members. I anticipate that the girls are going to bring this up again, especially as I encourage them not to fear expressing anything they are feeling. I am not, however, completely decided on how to answer or deal with a direct, honest question, such as, who is my favorite girl, or who is it I really don't like. I think this will come eventually and somehow must be dealt with in the context of honesty

Since the girls have also shown great reluctance to talk about my leaving or any sad feelings they may have about it, I have started expressing my feelings about missing them, etc. My hope is that this will help open the door for discussion of this event and the unhappiness I think they are feeling. The important matter, I believe, is to keep the question of honesty in mind and, guided by the reactions of the girls, to keep looking for ways to use rather than avoid real feelings.

USES OF THE RECORD

As described earlier, the Record of Service is designed to report the actual help given by a worker on particular, stated client problems over a specified period of time. Although it is primarily an accountability device, it can be used for other purposes as well. Any conscientiously produced agency document provides data that can be valuable in analyzing the service of an agency and interpreting it to its community. The Record of Service should make it possible, for example, to identify in detail the various systems in which the agency does most of its work, thus helping that agency determine where it is investing most of its service. It would also be possible to develop inventories of the kinds of client problems in which the agency is most actively involved; this would allow the explication of latent agency objectives and the identification of the particular client tasks it tends to accept or reject.

Furthermore, it provides focused examples of the processes by which help is given, clarifying the skills and the problems of practice, situation by situation. In our own experience, for example, it became quite clear that our workers were most effective with individuals and far less so with groups. In addition, they could use their skills more readily with primary clients than they could with systems representatives—teachers, welfare workers, and others.

The Record of Service has also been of considerable value in interpreting the Project's way of working to its Board and to the local community. It has helped pierce some of the mystery that cloaks the practice of social work, revealing to others the excitement of the service drama. It can do this for the layman as well as for the professional, since there is nothing in the practitioner's art that lies beyond the *understanding* of the informed layman. What distinguishes the professional from the layman is not the ability to recognize the skill and artistry involved in a good piece of practice, but the capacity —and the responsibility—to carry it out.

Finally, the Record of Service, even in its present preliminary and exploratory form, has considerable value in that it draws attention to the detailed problems of social work practice. It thus leads us closer to the heart of the matter—our ability to serve people skillfully and to describe the experience to others. One worker said, as he struggled with the instrument: "It feels like a glaring spotlight has been turned on me." It is time we all agreed to turn that light on ourselves, so that we might more clearly see what we are doing.

REFERENCES

1. Irwin Altman and Anita Terauds, *Major Variables of the Small Group Field* (Arlington, Va.: Human Sciences Research, November 1960).
2. Robert F. Bales, *Interaction Process Analysis* (Cambridge, Mass.: Addison-Wesley, 1950).
3. W. R. Bion, *Experiences in Groups* (New York: Basic Books, 1961).
4. John Frings, Ruth Kratovil, and Bernice Polemis, *An Assessment of Social Case Recording* (New York: Family Service Association of America, 1958).
5. Goodwin P. Garfield and Saul Goldzweig, *Social Work with Preadolescents and their Families: A Report on United Neighborhood Houses Pre-Teen Delinquency Prevention Project* (New York: United Neighborhood Houses of New York, 1967).
6. Gordon Hamilton, *Principles of Social Case Recording* (New York: Columbia University Press, 1946).
7. George C. Homans, *The Human Group* (New York: Harcourt, Brace, 1950).
8. Anne W. Lindsay, *Group Work Recording* (New York: Woman's Press, 1952).
9. Herman D. Stein, George H. Hougham, and Serapio Zalba, Assessing Social Agency Effectiveness—A Goals Model," *Welfare in Review*, Vol. 6, No. 2 (March–April 1968), pp. 13–18.

Index

Abramson, Arthur S., cited, 98

Acting-out: on welfare check day, 40; in public school, 50; of paraplegics, 100; *see also* Testing

Action, v, 15; and social work skill, 5, 6, 75, 94; phases of work in, 13; of community versus SROs, 26; neighborhood, a base for, 73; themes of social, 160, 161; and traditional agency problems, 164, 165

Activities, 221, 223, 224; illegal, in SRO, 28, 29, 36; interventive, 48; background of, in services, 74; lack of participation in, by poor, 84, 85; worker outreach in, 91; "character building," 93; shared, 118, 225-32; and group process, 148; selection of media for, 238; described, 245; *see also* Program

Addicts, *see* Drug addicts

Adolescents, vii; in gang group, 8; under stress, 14; and move to adulthood, 234; *see also* Foster care

Adoption, 122; and parent groups, 8; emerging themes of, 14

Advocacy, role of, 94

Affect: flow of, 8; as an investment, 12; in hospital setting, 112, 119; *see also* Feelings

Aged, the, 14, 98; as city's rejects, 25; as senior citizens, 234

Agency, v, vi, 76; traditional, 5; and group purpose, 8; service of, 8, 10, 18, 19, 50, 91-92; structure of, 10, 21, 91, 92, 93, 179; demand for work by, 11; tyranny of, 14; and move to group services, 18-24; Department of Welfare, SRO, 26; and role of "detached" worker, 27; and public school, 50, 52, 53; "character-building" efforts of, 74; distrust of, 77; commitments of, 90; risks of, 90, 91; and mediation, 94; and foster care, 139; service by, to antipoverty programs, 162-74 *passim;* and client symbiosis, 178; and child care, 179; and group relationship, 233-34; recording by, system of accountability, 242, 243; *see also specific types of agency, e.g.,* Public; Private; Hospital; Welfare

Alcoholics, 39, 40, 122; as urban

Authors indexed are only those referred to by name in the text. For a complete list of authors see the References section at the end of each chapter.

Foster care (*Continued*)
ral, 138; *see also* Record Excerpts
Frame of reference: as purpose and common tasks, 7; contract as, 8, 15, 16; function as, 48, 49; for mediation, 108; for antipoverty programs, 162, 163; psychotherapeutic, 183
Freudian influences, 158, 159
Function, vii; traditional, of social work, 5; conception of, 6; emergence of, for worker, 9, 10; mediation as, 10, 11, 80, 86, 108; supervision of, 21-22; limited, of ghetto children, 45; need for statement of, in public school, 47, 48, 49; conception of, 59; requirement of generalist, 91; of worker, 94; theory of, in hospital, 103, 119; clarification of, 152; in antipoverty program, 162-64; in child care, 189; of shared activity, 225; in program, 232-36, 237; *see also* Mediation

Gang, the, 76, 86, 163; as adolescent group, 8; socialization of, as model for SRO practice, 27
Gans, Herbert, cited, 74, 75
Generalization: as skill, 17, 21; of intervention effects, 40; in recording, 243
Generic enterprise, 6
Generic worker, 31; need for, in social work definition, 5; on-site method of, 43
Ghetto, 30, 41; education in, 45; service needs of, 157; problem-solving difficulties in, 169; feelings of helplessness in, 171
Goals, 27; and parallel process needs, 10; formulation of, versus "tuning-in" process, 14; movement toward, in group, 21; of intervention in SRO, 31; of

worker-tenant, 32, 37, 39, 42; status, 77; value of limited, 84; in hospital, 102; of symbiotic relationship, 178; in child care, 187; in prison, 204, 205, 213, 214
Goffman, Erving, cited, 201n
Goldsmith, Jerome M., quoted, 183
Group, the, v-viii, 150, 245; in social work practice, 3-24 *passim;* as client, defined, 7; purpose of, 7, 8, 123, 128; worker in, 9-13; work in, 13-18; emerging themes of, 14; services for, 18-24; regulatory powers of, 20; as viable, 31; as "near group," 42; formation of, 119; differentiation in, 122; as referral vehicle, 138; counselling in, 203; and agency relationship, 233-34; major tasks of, 246; *see also specific types of group, e.g.,* Small group
Group culture, 8; and ways of working, 9; role of group leader in, 148
Group dynamics, 103, 223; work as, 8; "all-in-the-same-boat," 11-12; language of, 21; race consciousness as, 130; in trade union, 150; *see also* Group process
Group experience, 4; nature of, 7; social tasks in, 8; phases of work in, 13; opening stage of, 15; transitions and endings in, 17-18, 66; skills in, 21; casework supervision in, 22; role-play in, 61; in collective action, 84
Group formation, 246; *see also* Beginnings
Group living situation, 177, 178, 179, 181, 184, 196
Group process, 8, 9, 19, 20, 237; and worker-client tasks, 10; and worker, 17; ways of working in,

RECORD EXCERPTS